Examination of the links between science and literary history is providing valuable new insight for scholars across a range of disciplines. In *Wordsworth and the Geologists* John Wyatt explores the hitherto unexamined relationship between a major Romantic poet and a group of scientists in the formative years of a new discipline, geology. Wordsworth's later poems display extensive knowledge of contemporary geology and a preoccupation with many of the philosophical issues concerned with the developing science of geology. Letters and diaries of a group of leading geologists reveal that they knew, and discussed their subject with, Wordsworth. Wyatt shows how the implications of such discussions challenge the simplistic version of 'two cultures', the Romantic–literary against the scientific–materialistic, and reminds us of the variety of interrelating discourses current between 1807 (the year of the foundation of the Geological Society of London) and 1850 (the year of Wordsworth's death).

CAMBRIDGE STUDIES IN ROMANTICISM

This series aims to foster the best new work in one of the most challenging fields within English literary studies. From the early 1780s to the early 1830s a formidable array of talented men and women took to literary composition, not just in poetry, which some of them famously transformed, but in many modes of writing. The expansion of publishing created new opportunities for writers, and the political stakes of what they wrote were raised again and again by what Wordsworth called those 'great national events' that were 'almost daily taking place': the French Revolution, the Napoleonic and American wars, urbanization, industrialization, religious revival, an expanded empire abroad and the reform movement at home. This was an enormous ambition, even when it pretended otherwise. The relations between science, philosophy, religion and literature were reworked in texts such as *Frankenstein* and *Biographia Literaria*; gender relations in *A Vindication of the Rights of Woman* and *Don Juan*; journalism by Cobbett and Hazlitt; poetic form, content and style by the Lake School and the Cockney School. Outside Shakespeare studies, probably no body of writing has produced such a wealth of response or done so much to shape the responses of modern criticism. This indeed is the period that saw the emergence of those notions of 'literature' and of literary history, especially national literary history, on which modern scholarship in English has been founded.

The categories produced by Romanticism have also been challenged by recent historicist arguments. The task of the series is to engage both with a challenging corpus of Romantic writings and with the changing field of criticism they have helped to shape. As with other literary series published by Cambridge, this one will represent the work of both younger and more established scholars, on either side of the Atlantic and elsewhere.

For a complete list of titles published see end of book

CAMBRIDGE STUDIES IN ROMANTICISM 16

WORDSWORTH AND THE GEOLOGISTS

William Westall's etchings of the limestone features of the neighbourhood of Ingleton,
Yorkshire, drawn in 1818, include closely observed geological features, such as this
cavern with its faulting, its typically eroded limestone rocks and the cascade of water,
no doubt feeding an underground stream. The couple gingerly peering into the depths
were not unusual in their interest in these phenomena. Wordsworth knew Westall, who
lived near Keswick, and wrote three sonnets on limestone caves and cliffs after looking
at the collection of etchings, one of which is the picture above. William Westall
married the youngest sister of the geologist, Adam Sedgwick, who became a close
friend of William Wordsworth.

WORDSWORTH AND THE GEOLOGISTS

JOHN WYATT

CAMBRIDGE
UNIVERSITY PRESS

Published by the Press Syndicate of the University of Cambridge
The Pitt Building, Trumpington Street, Cambridge CB2 1RP
40 West 20th Street, New York, NY 10011–4211, USA
10 Stamford Road, Oakleigh, Melbourne 3166, Australia

© Cambridge University Press 1995

First published 1995

Printed in Great Britain at the University Press, Cambridge

A catalogue record for this book is available from the British Library

Library of Congress cataloguing in publication data
Wyatt, John.
Wordsworth and the geologists : a correlation of influences / John Wyatt.
p.   cm. – (Cambridge Studies in Romanticism)
Includes bibliographical references and index.
ISBN 0 521 47259 8 (hardback)
1. Wordsworth, William, 1770–1850 – Knowledge – Earth sciences.
2. Literature and science – England – History – 19th century.
3. Earth sciences – England – History – 19th century.
4. Geology – England – History – 19th century.
5. Influence (Literary, artistic, etc.)
6. Earth sciences in literature.
7. Geology in literature.
8. Romanticism – England.
I. Title.   II. Series.
PR5892.G42W93   1996
621.'.7–dc20   95 149 CIP

ISBN 0 521 47259 8 hardback

To Susan and Sally who collected minerals and fossils with joy

Contents

Illustrations

Acknowledgements

A search for the origins of this book would be like a geological exploration. Below the surface are strata of experience which have only become significant as I dug deeper and deeper into an enquiry that aimed to explain a literary and scientific landscape of over one hundred and fifty years ago. As an undergraduate, supervised by that remarkable teacher and devoted Wordsworthian, Hugh Sykes Davies, I stored in my memory for much later consideration his exclamation of surprise on re-reading *The Excursion*: 'Do you know, it's a poem with considerable qualities!' The poems of the older Wordsworth remained a quarry to investigate for many years. It was the stimulus of two members of the English section at the Chichester (West Sussex) Institute of Higher Education, the Head of section, Dr Paul Foster and the Reader of English, Dr Margaret Grainger, which gave me the confidence to engage with a theme of literature and natural history. This inter-disciplinary study was one to which they both contributed distinguished scholarship (and Paul still contributes, for, sadly, Margaret died in 1992).

My colleagues awakened a lightly slumbering interest in geology and landscape, which also began as an undergraduate at Cambridge, but in pursuit of a different Tripos. I was fortunate when I began to enquire into the relationship between literature and geology to find a doctorate supervisor in Professor James Sambrook of the University of Southampton whose own mind ranged with keen enquiry into the people who made literature and science. In addition he was a first-rate teacher, so that I found my way firmly but happily to areas of work and standards of presentation which were unknown to a reasonably busy 'education manager', to use a current piece of jargon. My daily struggle with language was eased by the generous time given by Paul Foster and Dr John Vickers, who suggested improvements. Their efforts brought rewards to the text, the errors in it remain my own.

Specific thanks must also be given to a number of librarians who readily directed me to their collections. They were at: the University College London, particularly useful for the rich seam of George Greenough's papers; St John's College Library, Cambridge; the Wren Library, Trinity College, Cambridge; the University Library of Cambridge; and the Library of the Geological Society. The librarians at the Chichester Institute of Higher Education which I am privileged to lead have been invaluable and untiring in their support. I am also grateful to the Institute's Governors and Academic Board Research Committee for their support and interest.

Any enquiry in an inter-disciplinary area depends upon dialogue and discussions, none more so than a study in Romanticism. Perhaps in the endless quest for that most slippery definition of what Romanticism is, we should be satisfied with: 'it is about people talking'. I am very grateful to so many people sharing their ideas with me and engaging with my endless questions about how scientists and writers behave. There are too many to mention here, but if I group them as my colleagues in the Institute, fellow Trustees of the Higher Education Foundation, fellow Council members of the Society for Research in Higher Education, and anonymous referees and identifiable editors of the Cambridge University Press, I shall have covered most of the ground.

Finally, I thank with considerable warmth the practical production of the manuscript by Mrs Debbie Bates of the Institute and the management of my time by my personal assistant, Mrs Isabel Cherrett, both of whom took a keen interest in my work.

Abbreviations

WORDSWORTH MAIN TEXTS

WP (followed by volume number):	*The Poetical Works of William Wordsworth* eds. de Selincourt, E. and Darbishire, H. Five volumes I: 1963, II: 1944, III: 1954, IV: 1970, V: 1972. Oxford: Oxford University Press.
Prose:	*The Prose Works of William Wordsworth* 1974, eds. Owen, W. J. B. and Smyser, J. W. Three volumes. Oxford: Oxford University Press.
WL (followed by volume number):	*The Letters of William and Dorothy Wordsworth*, ed. Hill, A. G. Eight volumes: 1967, 1969, 1970, 1978, 1979 (volume IV 1821–1828 originally numbered erroneously as III). Oxford: Oxford University Press.
Prelude:	William Wordsworth, *The Prelude, 1799, 1805, 1850* 1979 eds. Wordsworth, J., Abrams, M. H., Gill, S. New York and London: Norton, W. W.
Cornell texts:	referred to by editor's name: all Ithaca, Cornell University Press: Darlington, B. ed. 1977 *Home at Grasmere.* Butler, J. ed. 1979 *The Ruined Cottage and the Pedlar.* Curtis, J. ed. 1983 *Poems in Two Volumes, 1800–1807.* Ketcham, C. J. ed. 1989 *Shorter Poems 1807–1820.*
DWJ:	*Journals of Dorothy Wordsworth* 1941 ed. de Selincourt, E. London, Macmillan.

GEOLOGISTS' TEXTS

GBG, CUL,   Cambridge University Library or University
or UCL: College London. Collections of G. B. Green-
     ough's papers (followed by box number or note-
     book number). The Cambridge University
     Library collection of Greenough papers has been
     moved recently to University College London.

GBGGS: Geological Society, London, G. B. Greenough
     collection.

DCLAS or   Dove Cottage Library, Adam Sedgwick corre-
CULAS: spondence; Cambridge University Library, Sedg-
     wick collection (Hughes, T. M. bequest) (follow-
     ed by box or letter number).

DCLW: Dove Cottage Library, Whewell correspondence.

TCAS or TCW: Trinity College Wren Library Cambridge, Sedg-
     wick or Whewell collection.

Douglas: Whewell's biographer: Douglas, S. 1881 *The Life
     and Selections from the Correspondence of William
     Whewell.*

Todhunter: Whewell's scientific biographer: Todhunter, 1,
     1876 *William Whewell. An Account of his Writings.*

CHAPTER I

Introduction

Thirty-four years separate the travels of two literary figures of the end
of the eighteenth, and the beginning of the nineteenth, centuries. These
travellers across Europe looked at geology in markedly different ways.
The first was Goethe travelling to Italy in 1786:

I spent the whole of this beautiful day in the open air. The moment I get near
mountains, I become interested again in rocks and minerals. I seem to be an
Antaeus who always feels new strength whenever he is brought into contact
with his mother earth...On the way there, after leaving behind some
sandstone hills, I came upon whole boulders of muscovite mica, sticking up
out of the ground. The hill where spa is found is not far from a brick kiln and
a stream formed by the conjunction of a number of brooks. At first I thought
it was alluvial clay which had probably been washed down from the
mountains by rain, but, on closer inspection, I found that its solid rock was a
finely laminated schist, alternating with bands of gypsum.[1]

The second traveller was Dorothy Wordsworth in 1820 travelling with
her brother, William, his wife, Mary, and other close friends over what
was for them virtually sacred territory, the pass over the Alps that her
brother had traversed as a young man. Mary and Dorothy were
approached by a boy and a girl selling minerals: 'We had no dealings
together in that line; but William dispatched them to bring us milk
from their hut'.[2]

The surface message of these two pictures of travellers in Europe is
that there is a distinction between a poet who respected geology and a
near-contemporary poet and his family who appeared to reject any
contact with this science. The contrast is superficial confirmation of a
commonly held theory of the separation between science and forms of
Romanticism. The line of that argument would be that the Romanticism displayed by the Wordsworths was markedly different from the
'Naturphilosophie' of Goethe's contemporaries, that the Wordsworths
clearly found the universe of stones and minerals uninspiring, and that

I

on a visit to the grand setting of the Alps the last thing they wished to do was to 'pry and pore' over the minor components of the huge panorama before them. Further evidence could be produced from poems and letters to confirm this point of view. In a letter of 1827 from Dorothy to Mary Laing, for instance, the poet's sister somewhat condescendingly declines to assist in finding rock specimens for her friend's new hobby: 'I am so ignorant of all that lies beneath the surface of this earth of ours that I think there is little chance of my bringing home anything that the geologist would care about. Whenever I find a very pretty stone I shall think of you and pick it up.'[3] Mary Laing must have persisted, because a year later Dorothy wrote that she was glad that Mary had 'so many rational and agreeable amusements', but she herself was 'neither mineralogist nor geologist'.[4]

Mary Wordsworth was similarly modest, or perhaps accurate, about her interests in geology. Writing to John Kenyon in August 1827, she tells that a neighbouring cottage has been rented by two maiden ladies, 'who are admirers of scenery and understand the ologies (in the latter we do not participate, the sciences do not flourish at Idle Mount)'.[5] Mary Wordsworth used a family joke for the name, Rydal Mount, but are we to assume that she was serious about the lack of interest in the 'ologies' and, in particular, geology? The traditional answer to this question is to find confirmation of a lack of sympathy with geologists in Wordsworth's statement written in 1813 in book III of *The Excursion*, where the Solitary condemns

> He who with pocket-hammer smites the edge
> Of luckless rock or prominent stone, disguised
> In weather – stains or crusted o'er by Nature
> With her first growths, detaching by the stroke
> A chip or splinter – to resolve his doubts;[6]

The simple view that the Wordsworths had no interest in geology is, however, contradicted by another incident from Dorothy's Journal of 1820. Shortly after the rejection of the children's offer of minerals, she records a signal of interest. She and Mary Wordsworth actually purchased two crystals: 'the only treasure we have brought home from the Alps'.[7] This minor inconsistency of behaviour will serve as an emblem for one argument of this book, which is that the poet most clearly identified with the first flowering of English Romanticism, who eventually occupied in the eyes of a large section of the public the stature of a moral as well as a literary leader, was closer to the popular and morally respectable scientific pursuit of his times than later generations have chosen to admit.

There are many reasons why a general impression has persisted that Wordsworth and geology occupied separate and even antagonistic worlds. The common source for this impression has been the judgement by generations of historians of literature that English Romantic writers exalted the inner life, distinguishing its richness from what they judged to be the mechanical theories of mind and perception held by materialist philosophers of the eighteenth century and by utilitarian psychologists of the nineteenth century. Some modern critics have continued to endorse the distinction between an inner life and the outer material realms, linking imaginative literature with the first and science with the second. As late as 1984, Nicholas Maxwell represented this analysis in his study of scientific ideas, *From Knowledge to Wisdom*:

It never occurred to the 'philosophers' of the Enlightenment to divorce passionate concern for the inner life of man from passionate involvement with the imaginative and critical exploration of the natural world being undertaken by natural science. Romanticism created this divorce. Rousseau, Blake, Wordsworth, Keats, Tolstoy, Kafka, D. H. Lawrence and a multitude of other novelists, poets, dramatists and artists passionately pursued person-to-person understanding – exploration of the experiential world – in a way that was divorced from, if not actually hostile to, science.[8]

Even if we avoid taking up the sweeping historical simplification of this range of writers, we must weigh with care the value of the clause, 'Romanticism created this divorce.' The simple view that Romanticism can be summarized as one single movement, or that it was uniformly opposed to science, has been untenable for a long time. Seminal studies by Lovejoy and by Piper[9] were followed by detailed work on individual literary figures and the interaction between their writing and the work of contemporary scientists. Gliserman's analysis (1975) of Tennyson, Levere's work (1981 and 1990) on Coleridge and science, or Gillian Beer's subtle study, *Darwin's Plots* (1983), about the interrelationship of ideas found in Charles Darwin's writing with incidents in novels of George Eliot and Thomas Hardy, have established clear roads for anyone tracing the complexities of the relationship between literature and science in the nineteenth century. I hope by this work to add something more to correct the perception of a polarity between literature and science.

Any modern study that attempts to understand Romanticism in its relationship to science, must be indebted to those who remind us that both 'Romanticism' and 'science' are themselves modern constructs, largely built by those who wrote in the years after the very active decades of cultural innovation between 1770 and 1850 (the period of Wordsworth's life). As Butler (1981) so succinctly states: 'Romanticism, in the full rich sense in which we know it, is a posthumous movement; something different was experienced at the time.'[10] The situation is doubly complex, not only do we inherit definitions of Romanticism by its successors, we have access to deeper strata of evidence: Romanticism's own statements about the way the world was changing and the role that poets and natural historians were playing in changing it. An example of the layered difficulties of understanding is provided by the problem of either accepting or interpreting from our historical position the historicism of a past age. Certainly, as Eichner (1982) has elaborated, the early nineteenth-century scientific temper was as strongly historicist as that of leading sections of literary and artistic culture. McGann (1983) warns us of the creation of a Romantic Ideology by an uncritical absorption of the age's own definitions, and de Man (1993) gives us an image of generations (rather than one generation) in theoretical conflict: 'From its inception, the history of romanticism has been one of battles, polemics, and misunderstandings: personal misunderstandings between the poets themselves; between the poets, the critics, and the public; between the successive generations.'[11] Discouraging though this may be for a modern interpreter seeking crisp definitions, there is, in the early nineteenth century, unexplored material which provides encouragement to search with more rigour for the evidence of relationships between those who made science and those who made poetry.

Even in the period after Wordsworth's death there were observers who attempted a reconciliation of Wordsworth and science. Although Leslie Stephen's 'Wordsworth hates science' stands at one extreme, at the other, as early as 1854, R. Spence Watson (1889) argued in a talk to the Wordsworth Society that the poet was not confronting science, but over-specialization. The two most dedicated Wordsworthians of the second half of the century, Canon Rawnsley and Herbert Rix, Assistant Secretary to the Royal Society, contributed to Knight's major edition of Wordsworth's poems a set of footnotes with detailed evidence of the poet's attention to natural history and to topographical detail. Wordsworth's interest in, and even passion for, Newton has, of course, never been doubted and continues to attract scholarly enquiry.[12]

The evidence of Coleridge's and Wordsworth's close connection with radical politics, which was also the world of radical science, has also provided further support for a reconciliation between poetry and scientific interest. Roger Sharrock's article of 1962 on the origins of the enlarged 'Preface' to *Lyrical Ballads* of 1802 led the way in this field. Coleridge's notes of Humphry Davy's Royal Institution lectures on chemistry in 1802 enabled Sharrock to begin a reconstruction of a network of poets who had aspirations to engage in science and a network of scientists who aspired to be poets.[13] It may well be that an unexpected outcome of these studies on the early poetry of Wordsworth has been to neglect the later years of the poet's life, or more likely to confirm that the later poems are problematic. So, political and social criticism of Wordsworth has tended to see his poems written after 1807, not only in the way early twentieth-century critics saw them, as a falling off of lyrical vision, but also as recantations of radicalism and a defensive compensation for loss of political liberalism.[14] Critics of our own generation, like Shelley in his, have taken an opportunity to give the conservative Wordsworth a stern dressing down for abandoning the opportunities that were opened to him by his early radical friends and by their enlarged, liberated vision. I shall argue later that a close analysis of Wordsworth's middle and later years gives no support to the notion that he retreated from the scientific community. On the contrary, the work of these years demonstrated a connection with a new and different subgroup of that community.

Before moving to the details of Wordsworth's association with geologists and what this association meant for him and for them, it is worth considering further why it is difficult to trace the interest shown by literary figures of the early nineteenth century in scientific activity. One immediate difficulty is the word 'Science' itself. In the period of Wordsworth's life, the term continued to mean what it had largely conveyed in previous centuries (an organized body of knowledge); and yet simultaneously it gained the special, more limited range of meaning it has in our day. An example of the semantic trap waiting to catch the unwary observer can be found in a remark by Wordsworth to Crabb Robinson in 1837 on visiting the archeological sites at Nimes: 'I am unable through ignorance to enjoy these sights...I have no science and can refer nothing to principle.'[15] Here Wordsworth does not mean he lacks knowledge of the techniques of archeological investigation; rather he claims an inability to exercise an orderly investigation based on principles. Less technically, the Wordsworth's family idiolect could use 'scientific' to mean 'orderly' or 'systematic'. Dorothy Wordsworth refers to Derwent Coleridge and his quality of mind thus: 'He is very clever. I should wish him to be put in the way of some profession in which scientific knowledge would be useful; for his mind takes that turn. His is uncommonly acute and accurate.'[16]

Sometimes, as in book II of *The Prelude* of 1805, Wordsworth uses 'Science' to cover a range of studies which we would call 'philosophy' or 'social science':

> Thou, my friend, art one
> More deeply read in thy own thoughts; to thee
> Science appears but what in truth she is,
> Not as our glory and our absolute boast,
> But as a succedaneum, and a prop
> To our infirmity.[17]

Wordsworth was not unique in applying 'science' to a wide range of intellectual activities. His contemporaries, whom we would now call scientists, frequently referred to themselves as philosophers or natural philosophers. A significant date in the history of the word 'scientist' occurred long after the establishment of many organizations for the study of the sciences. It was in 1832 that the newly created British Association for the Advancement of Science discussed the appropriateness of the term. No less a figure than Coleridge addressed the assembly on the subject and solemnly warned the Association members against their continued use of the word 'philosophy' for their burgeoning activities and techniques.[18] Two of the geologists considered in the following chapters were still at odds with the term 'scientist', as late as 1840. William Whewell mused on the right term for a growing profession in *The Philosophy of the Inductive Sciences* thus: 'We need very much a name to describe the cultivator of science in general. I should incline to call him a *scientist*, thus we might say that as an Artist is a Musician, Painter or Poet, a Scientist is a Mathematician, Physicist or Naturalist.' Adam Sedgwick, the geologist, wrote in the margins of his copy: 'better die of this want than bestialise our tongue by such barbarisms'.[19] In this pithy comment there is a message for succeeding historians: our assumption of two separate worlds of science and philosophy was far from commonly accepted. Whatever Coleridge in his most dogmatic mood may have determined, men who dealt with material things saw themselves as part of a unified high culture.

The *locus classicus* for the study of the differentiation between science and the humanities is Wordsworth's own manifesto on the responsibility of the poet in the 1802 revised 'Preface' to the second edition of *Lyrical Ballads*. The famous argument about the difference between the Poet and the 'Man of Science' has been taken to be the schismatic moment for the two cultures. It deserves closer consideration. There are two important distinctions in the central section of the 'Preface'. The first is in a footnote to the debate on the distinction between poetry and prose, where Wordsworth notes that the true distinction should be between 'Poetry and Matter of Fact, or Science'.[20] Once again, 'Science' in this antithetical statement has a wider reference than the specific knowledge field of natural history. It is to do with 'fact' in opposition to affairs of poetic or imaginative activity. The second distinction between poetry and science in the 'Preface' is more important for my argument at this point. It arises from the section on the appropriateness of language for depicting 'real passion' which, Wordsworth says, is a valid subject not only for poets but also for other men whatever their specialized roles. A distinction which has been well and truly aired in twentieth-century debates is the separation of 'the two cultures'; but which culture is Wordsworth discussing in 1802? A quotation from the same 'Preface' reveals that Wordsworth is not separating a literary from what we now call a scientific culture: 'Poetry is the image of man and nature, the obstacles which stand in the way of the fidelity of the Biographer and Historian, and of their consequent utility, are incalculably greater than those, which are to be encountered by the Poet who comprehends the dignity of his art.'[21] Wordsworth's intention is to identify the Poet as a figure distinct from, yet inextricably also in membership of a social category, 'Man in general'. Because of his concentration and narrowness, the (non-Poet) specialist can possess neither 'fidelity', nor 'utility', and, most important, he is separated from 'the image' of reality. Wordsworth, Davy, and Coleridge were fully aware that the recording of reality by numerical formulae, by creating new words, or by maps and diagrams was a major preoccupation of the scientific community of the early nineteenth century. As an emerging group the 'Men of Science' were evolving a new language, but were still not clear about their difference from 'men of letters'. Wordsworth's analysis of such distinctions in the revised 'Preface' was inspired by one Man of Science's attempt at a definition of science as a legitimate activity of a well-established cultural society. We shall see further tussles with such definitions in the chapters that follow.

This study intends to consider one branch of scientific activity, geology, in order to illustrate in closer detail the intricacies of the connection between literature and science in the first half of the nineteenth century. Because Wordsworth has been considered for too long as one of the originators, if not the originator, of an anti-scientific faction, I have concentrated on the evidence to the contrary in his writing, with particular attention to the second half of his creative life, from 1810 onwards. The work of Wordsworth's later years has recently received respectful attention. For simple convenience, I refer to the period as the middle and later years of the poet's life.[22] A number of reasons come together to endorse that special period as one of interest. In the first place, although these years are traditionally regarded as providing evidence of the declining powers of the poet after his remarkable decade of creative endeavour from 1798 to 1807, as far as his contemporaries were concerned, the poetry of Wordsworth from *The Excursion* (1813) onwards was truly significant. There are hidden, unexpected pleasures in the later poems, but it was not for rare gleams of lost glory that Wordsworth's contemporaries either loved or disliked them. There is no doubt of the importance of the later poems in helping to confirm ways of thought amongst a younger generation of readers, some of whom established the major institutions for the study of science in England. Prominent amongst these enthusiastic readers were members of the Geological Society of London who were also Fellows of Trinity College, Cambridge. The interconnection of these geologists, all of whom achieved their maturity as scholars after 1810, is one of the themes of this book. Adam Sedgwick (1785–1873) and William Whewell (1794–1866) are the two chief characters under consideration in the pages that follow.

In the period 1810 to 1850, there were many other eminent geologists who respected Wordsworth. Some, like William Buckland, Reader in Geology at the University of Oxford, met the poet in the Lake District and possibly in Oxford and London, although the evidence of their meeting is slight.[23] A major figure of a younger generation, Charles Lyell, read Wordsworth and quoted him, but there is little information about whether they actually met. Both Buckland and Lyell, as giants in their territory, are considered in the following pages, but without the close attention given to Adam Sedgwick and William Whewell with whom Wordsworth had a continuous and warm friendship.

One major figure who is considered in some detail alongside the two Trinity men is George Bellas Greenough (1778–1855), the first President of the Geological Society. His voice is introduced as evidence at various points of the argument, not because he was any closer to

Sedgwick and Whewell than to other Council members of the Geological Society, but because, through a reading of his private notebooks, we can see the formation of the mind of an organizer of geology which complements the detailed knowledge we possess from letters, personal records, and scholarly writing by the Cambridge academics. In addition, Greenough's association with Coleridge, chiefly from 1798 to 1805, makes an indirect link with Wordsworth. The significance of Coleridge as an influence on the younger Wordsworth (and Wordsworth's influence on him) is beyond doubt. Greenough therefore steps on stage in the early period of Wordsworth's life. In later acts he figures, as I have said, as a complement to the philosophical and literary interests of his friends in the Geological Society. A similar actor, again most closely associated with Coleridge, though within the milieu of Wordsworth at least until 1815, is Humphry Davy. Davy's interests as a geologist occupy attention in my argument at certain points, because, like many of his contemporaries, his literary and philosophical thinking was far from peripheral to his scientific interests.

Humphry Davy is at first associated with younger Wordsworth's residence in Alfoxden and the early years of residence in the Lake District. Wordsworth's understanding of geology in this early period has received a degree of attention recently. Major studies (for example, Nicolson (1963), Sheats (1973), Kelley (1988), and Bewell (1989)) have paid close attention to the sources of Wordsworth's knowledge of seventeenth- and eighteenth-century geology as it is revealed in poems written before 1807 and in the key prose work, *A Topographical Description of the Country of the Lakes*, first published anonymously in 1810. Although my main attention, for reasons indicated above, is given to Wordsworth's later poetry, it is important to recognize the continuities of the poet's life and the complex but permanent influence of the eighteenth century on his work. Continuity of the same two periods is also a theme of the history of English geology as Laudan (1974), Rudwick (1976), and Porter (1977) have shown. I have therefore summarized in chapter two the main examples of geological understanding in Wordsworth's early writing as well as in works of his later years. The major geological concept for the first decades of the nineteenth century, Catastrophism, will be considered in that section. There are interesting modern studies that illustrate Wordsworth's comprehension of Catastrophism and of the associated hypothesis, Diluvialism, and I have added suggestions of my own. I also put forward the case for a closer consideration of the late eighteenth-century geologist, James Hutton, not as a teacher of a rival school or as a theorist offering alternatives to Catastrophism, but as an instance of the many variants of geological ideas in active circulation during Wordsworth's younger years. It is true that there is considerable diversity in the history of early nineteenth-century geology, just as there is in the history of literature. Often uniformity and coherence have been qualities imported by later generations.

The word 'influence' has already appeared in this introduction and it has to be grappled with in any consideration of the relationship between literature and geology. Modern critical theory, whether from sociology, history, or literary criticism, is justly suspicious of the search for influences. Foucault's strictures are severe:

To ransack history in order to rediscover the play of anticipations or echoes, to go right back to first seeds or to go forwards to the last traces, to reveal in a work its fidelity to tradition or its reducible uniqueness, to raise or lower its stock of originality, to say that Cuvier had more predecessors than one thought; these are harmless enough amusement for historians who refuse to grow up.[24]

Suspicion of a search for 'influences' is not a modern phenomenon. This is from Coleridge on 'influence': 'Hume – and the French imitated him and we the French – and the French us – and so philosophies, fly to and from a series of imitated Imitations – Shadows of shadows of a farthing candle placed between two looking glasses.'[25]

My theoretical position in this study is not to eschew 'influence', but to consider evidence provided by Wordsworth's own accounts of his reading of past authors and of contemporary sources. 'Influence' is a linguistically convenient device for referring to correlations between different discourses. It is clear that Wordsworth was a reader with wide-ranging tastes who had access to many different sources of information in the libraries of friends and in his own book collection. He was a writer who did not hesitate to appropriate themes and sometimes phrases from his predecessors, as both he and modern editors acknowledge. What is not so well understood is that his reading ranged over books and journals which included scientific articles or excerpts, although their titles do not always indicate to our specialist age that they are about science. In chapter three I elaborate on this theme, but do not confine myself to printed material in the pursuit of 'influence'.

Rom Harré (1983) suggests that in seeking correlations between the arts and the sciences, there are three levels of 'shared' phenomena: a common content, commonality of style, and a shared 'metatheory'. In explaining how correlations at any of these levels occur Harré places as much emphasis on 'representations sociales' as on literary contexts: 'There is another all-encompassing and permanent but ever-changing human reality, the endless conversation that binds human beings into a society. I believe that it is the quality and demands of that conversation that is the most potent influence in forming our minds.'[26] It is with this theoretical support that I enter into discussion in chapters three and four on the contexts, written and 'spoken', which helped to form the texts of both Wordsworth and the scientists with whom he came into contact.

To return to the first of Harré's three levels for the formation of correlations between science and art, 'the common content or direct and explicit borrowings', I have to confess from the start that Wordsworth presents few examples of this form of influence: I examine them in chapter two and their possible origins in chapter three. These geological allusions are important to record, but my main purpose is to explore the second and third of Harré's categories, where there is something in common between the way that science and literature are made and where there are instances of shared attention to high-level general concepts, such as 'decay and renewal' or 'universality'. There have been poets who committed their Muse to praising or elaborating scientific theories. The eighteenth century provides notable examples, highly likely to have been well known by Wordsworth. Joseph Addison, for instance, praised in a Latin verse Thomas Burnet's *Telluris Theoria Sacra*.[27] Erasmus Darwin's *The Botanic Garden* includes sections of geological theory, with extensive footnotes on James Hutton's *Theory of the Earth*, also quoting de Luc, an opponent of Huttonian theory. The advertisement to *The Botanic Garden* indicates the purpose of poetry in Darwin's terms: 'the general design of the following sheets is to enlist Imagination under the banner of science and to lead her votaries from the loose analogies, which dress out the image of poetry, to the stricter ones which form the ratiocination of philosophy'.[28] The tradition of using poetry as an elevated vehicle for conveying the achievements of Enlightenment science would have been well known to Wordsworth, but we must remember that it was a tradition which he did not pursue. There are, it is true, brief comments on science in 1805 in *The Prelude*, in 1814 in *The Excursion*, and in poems as late as 'Steamboats, Viaducts and Railways' of 1833, but the burden of Wordsworth's song is not about the march of science which pushed back the frontiers of knowledge. Inevitably therefore the references to geology are allusive. As I hope to illustrate, like all allusions these references are many layered, connected with linguistic devices of metaphor, their meaning mediated by grammatical structures, and they are included in poems which were written with no intention of conveying scientific fact or theory.

If the map of 'influences' is to be constructed, then it must be of use. The instance must lead somewhere, the meaning of the evidence must be related to the poem or sequence of poems. Valuable studies which integrate influence and interpretation have recently been published by Levere (1981 and 1990) on Coleridge, by Bewell (1989) who concentrates on Wordsworth and his inheritance of the Enlightenment's attention to anthropology and the basis of morality, and by Kelley (1988) who constructs a fascinating new study of Wordsworth's aesthetic theory. I shall acknowledge these and other studies in chapters two and three where I shall examine the sources they have traced from the late seventeenth-century theological writers on geology through to the eighteenth-century natural philosophers who developed influential theories to explain not only the origin of the earth but also changes and developments in natural and human history since the earth began.

One further theoretical position I shall try to hold originates from Foucault's thesis in *The Archeology of Knowledge*. I extend beyond his disciplined constraints on methods of study of culture and attempt to draw conclusions which he would not have done. Foucault's work is particularly relevant for this study because he attends to the change of philosophical attention from natural history to the scientific disciplines of botany, biology, and geology taking place as the nineteenth century left behind the practices of the Enlightenment. Foucault advised the student seeking a distinctive 'discursive formation' to look for 'regularities' between what is superficially dispersed and uncoordinated in a culture. In characteristic manner, Foucault applies not one term but a list of appropriate terms for these 'regularities':

Whenever one can describe, between a number of statements, such a system of dispersion, whenever between objects, types of statements, concepts or thematic choices, one can define a regularity (an order, correlation, positions and functioning, transformations) we will say for the sake of convenience, that we are dealing with a discursive formation.[29]

I attempt to identify 'regularities' in the very different spheres of writing by Wordsworth and by a group of geologists. Gillian Beer

(1990) has made good use of Foucault's concept of 'transformation', whereas I have found his term 'correlation' useful for the process of identifying common preoccupations, shared ways of interpreting the world, and consistencies of dialogue. 'Correlation' is also conveniently a technical term in stratigraphy to mean the identification of similarities that exist in lithology or fossil content; thus geographically isolated stratigraphic units or successions may be 'correlated', or equated in terms of 'time'.[30] 'Correlation' has acted as a useful reminder during my own process of writing that there are detailed similarities requiring interpretation, as do fossils and their traces, in Wordsworth's writing and in the work of his geological contemporaries. Where there are larger philosophical or moral issues about which poet and geologist shared views and values then the parallel with geological maps – the 'larger' geological material – comes to mind.

Following the detailed evidence of chapters two and three, the philosophical and moral themes common to Wordsworth and to his geological contemporaries occupy the majority of this book. Chapter four moves firmly into the mature years of Wordsworth's life, from 1820, when I trace a significant friendship network established through Trinity College, Cambridge, where Christopher Wordsworth, the poet's brother, had become Master. The two dominant figures, Adam Sedgwick and William Whewell are introduced initially as part of a social network in which the Wordsworth family was involved. This chapter attempts to operate with a theoretical viewpoint on the nature of science. In common with writers like Barnes (1974), Porter (1977), Rudwick (1976 and 1985), and Secord (1986), I see the history of science in the way that Roy Porter expresses it: 'All sciences are made. They are fabrics constructed by human choice and work.'[31] Science was made in human communities and continues to be made in that way. The point of this chapter is that it was not only science which was made in communities and, furthermore, the community of science and the community of letters were not distinct or separated.

It is my intention to give detailed consideration to one particular community which met and communed in Cambridge, the Lake District, and in wealthy houses in London, in a triangle of intellectual trade.[32] Butler (1981) reminds us that in the period of this study there was 'a community which generated art and provided its public'.[33] The decision to concentrate on a few geologists, like all such decisions, implied a path not taken. A study of other nineteenth-century geologists could be fruitful. Although Buckland, Conybeare, Phillips, and eventually Lyell, Murchison, and de la Beche are names of great significance in the history of geology and although they were contemporary members with Sedgwick and Whewell of the Geological Society, they are commented on here to a lesser extent than their Cambridge associates, chiefly because the Trinity College geologists had a much closer relationship with Wordsworth. I shall comment in chapter four on the distinctiveness of the Trinity College geologists, not only because of their social relationship with Wordsworth, but also because of the variety of intellectual positions taken up by geologists in the 1820s and 1830s. It is as much a mistake to think that all geologists were similar, marching to one theoretical tune, as it is to classify poets of the period as belonging to one 'school' of literature. The intellectual currents were flowing fast and there were contradictions and counter-movements in the Geological Society as in the Reviews and the publishing houses. Chapter four will therefore seek to discover common views and shared values, but it will also acknowledge the divergences, even amongst 'Trinity Men'.

The first President of the Geological Society, George Bellas Greenough is a useful character to introduce in the chapters that follow. On the one hand he illustrates very different characteristics from the Trinity men; on the other hand he also reveals patterns of thought and belief that are in accord with the different tradition of Sedgwick and Whewell. Usually considered to be the prime leader of Baconian stringency in the Geological Society, because of his emphasis on empirical studies rather than on speculation, Greenough in his unpublished notebooks discusses philosophical, theological and moral matters in a manner which is remarkably close to the writing of those who were committed to a different methodology.

Greenough's wide range of interests was not at all unusual; his literary and philosophical interests were typical and mirrored the scope of intellectual absorptions of the two Trinity College men and of many members of the Geological Society. A fundamental point of view of this book is that the geologists of the early nineteenth century continued in the tradition of the eighteenth-century natural historians by working in many fields of study. These were men who classified themselves as philosophers and, in many cases, as theologians as well as geologists. As I shall attempt to illustrate in chapters five to nine, the geologists' concerns were with issues of perception, with the power of the human mind, with the justification of Divine Will, and with all the large human issues with which major poets from Wordsworth to Tennyson engaged. I have explored the themes that Wordsworth and geologists explored in this wide-ranging way in each chapter with correlations observed in each case. These major topics are: order, clarity, and distinctness (chapter five), the idea of universality (chapter six), the tension of observing duration as well as evidence of decay in nature (chapter seven). In chapter eight, I turn to consider the attraction of poetry for the geologists. At this point, a reader should note a reversal of influence, away from Wordsworth's understanding of geology to the geologists' understanding of Wordsworth. In chapter nine, I aim to elaborate on the way in which the geologists solved an inherent problem in their studies. Geology deals with the non-living, with aridity and coldness. Its glimpses of heat and light are volcanic and apocalyptic beyond the human scale, and yet Sedgwick, Whewell, Greenough, and others like them saw their discipline as an essentially human pursuit leading to major advances in human thought and to the encouragement of moral development. In their resolution of this professional tension, Wordsworth played a significant supporting role.

This book challenges in most chapters the unsatisfactory polarity of what has became a commonplace of cultural description, the 'Two Cultures', science and humanities. For many intellectuals in the period covered by this study, geology was a bridge between literature and science. Part of the reason for this conciliatory alignment lies in the common educational background of the scientists and the poets, so I shall frequently comment on intellectual formation. Some sociologists have taken a further step to interpret common origins by asserting that the social class to which poets and scientists belonged explains their shared values and even their progress towards certain types of geological understanding. I hope to create a more rounded picture than one of social determinism. To propose complexity may be an academic quirk, but I believe that the records of those involved in the early years of the Geological Society of London justify an approach, which highlights differences and pays regard to the individuality and variety within the Fellowship and to the changing emphases in geology between 1807, the year of the Society's foundation, and the 1850s, by which time many of its founders had died. The concluding chapter not only touches on these summary themes, it also attempts, in briefly considering the diverse response of writers other than Wordsworth to geology, to identify why Wordsworth appealed to the geologists who are the main focus of the book's attention. The fundamental stance is that Romanticism had many forms and that two ideologies, the ideology of the writers themselves and that of researchers like myself, can too easily create a picture of uniformity and unified doctrine. A glance at the dates of Wordsworth's birth and death should give pause for thought.

The passage of history, from Wordsworth's birth before the American War of Independence to his death eighty years later, included social and technological change on a major scale. In literary history, the range of writing is awe inspiring. In terms of geology, this span of years encompasses a sequence of major shifts: from a predominance of 'cabinet collections' to the making of geological maps and the foundation of museums for rock and fossil specimens; from mineralogy to geology and palaeontology; from purchasing collections accumulated by others to field-work carried out in person. When Wordsworth was a young man, geology was the interest of amateurs and of a few natural philosophers. His middle and later years saw the growth of a nationally-esteemed pursuit supported by increasing numbers of men who began to adopt a 'scientific career'.[34] They in their turn were sustained by institutional structures in London, in the provinces, and in the universities. The chapters that follow attempt to trace some of the issues which were discussed in these turbulent years in the history of a science, and to correlate these issues with a major poet's realization of the nature of the physical world and its relationship to the human mind.

CHAPTER 2

Wordsworth's geology: references and allusions

Allusions and incidental references to science in poems suffer from the fate of any dispersed clues and vestiges of biographical information. At best, they can be intriguingly conjectural and, at worst, historically risky. The pit of anachronism has to be avoided by traversing the thin tightrope of barely verifiable sources. Often a historian of literature will make connections between a poetic reference and a school of scientific theory in a particular period. When that episode in the story of science is being re-written by historians of science, the literary historian's links and suggested influences may be rendered unreliable and unsupported. Allusion-hunting can also be an exhausting collection of evidence which in the end produces trivial, confusing, or inconclusive findings. In the last thirty years, attempts have been made to go beyond the listing of references and allusions to geology in English Romantic poetry. Some writers have progressed to a more interesting stage than identifying geological nomenclature and have made more wide-ranging claims for the interpenetration of science and literature. Widening the discussion to the European Romanticism and science has had a considerable benefit for the understanding of the culture in which English poets and scientists of the early nineteenth century flourished.[1]

Studies of the history of geology and of English literature have been brought together by a number of recent writers who have made large claims for the energy created by their interconnection. Dennis Dean (1968) examined a range of British Romantic writers, including Wordsworth, and concluded that 'literary trends influenced geological theorising; geological trends influenced literature'.[2] Marilyn Gaull (1979) concentrated on Wordsworth's poetry up to and including *The Excursion* to make the point that Wordsworth was fully aware of geological controversies. Cannon (1964 and 1978) turned to the later poems, particularly the *Itinerary Poems of 1833*, in order to find evidence of 'the conversion of Wordsworth', proposing that in his older age he revised his previous views about geology. In the 1970s and 1980s a distinctively different direction has been taken by substantial studies of Wordsworth's geological understanding and its context in politics and aesthetics. I shall take the opportunity in the following paragraphs to indicate the allusions that authors such as Sheats (1973), Bewell (1989), and Kelley (1988) have identified. It is important at the level of theory to note that this group of authors have, in their different ways, gone beyond identifying geological references and placed Wordsworth's geological knowledge in a social and political context. Kelley, for instance, has produced a valuable analysis of the prose works of Wordsworth's later years and related geological allusions to Wordsworth's changing aesthetic and political values. Sheats and Bewell both concentrate on the poet's early years, which I shall want to consider in the following paragraphs as a preparation for my main theme, the poetry of the later years.

Listing a writer's allusions to geology begs immediate questions about the nature of the science itself. It is important to recognize that 'geology' has been for a long time a portmanteau term of convenience for a wide range of scientific activities. Because we are very conscious of the rapidly dividing fields of study in modern science, there is a tendency to assume that early expressions in the evolution of a science were structurally simple and even singular. In 1790, and even in 1820, the term 'geology' was used alongside such phrases as 'natural philosophy' and necessarily covered a range of different pursuits. For some enquirers a form of concentration or early specializations had begun to emerge, but individual geologists did not concentrate exclusively on one aspect of the subject. By the end of the eighteenth century there were discernible special groupings or 'subfields' of geological knowledge which we would now identify by labels some of which were not created until later in the nineteenth century: stratigraphy, palaeontology, mineralogy, lithology, geomorphology, and economic geology. The early years of the period saw a rapid growth of the subject with different emphases in different cultural traditions, from Germany, where mineralogy and stratigraphy dominated, to France, with its reputation for what became known as stratigraphy, geomorphology, and palaeontology. Rupke (1983a) argues that these activities bypassed England until the later years of the second decade, when men like William Buckland absorbed French geology in a way that had been impossible during the long period of the European war. Twenty years earlier, and occurring simultaneously with the rapid growth of historical geology on the Continent, Scottish geologists located in Edinburgh, were notably active as researchers. One Scottish perspective, Huttonism, was for thirty years only partially acceptable to the geologists of London, whereas another rival perspective of Edinburgh geologists, Wernerism, was fully compatible with leading opinion in England. In short, there are two questions to ask in identifying a geological allusion by a poet: 'whose geology are you identifying?' and 'what kind of geology are we talking about?' In order to simplify the last question, I propose to examine Wordsworth's references and allusions under very broad headings which will cover the three subdivisions into which geology was beginning to divide at the start of Wordsworth's life as a poet and for decades to follow: the study of rocks and minerals, the shape of the landscape (geomorphology as we would now call it), and the theory of the changes that have occurred on the surface of the earth. These three broad headings interconnect. 'Theories of the Earth' may determine classification of strata and the minerals in them; explanations of the process that produced the landscape in turn may be based on an overarching theory of the earth.

ALLUSIONS TO ROCK TYPES AND MINERALS

Instances of Wordsworth's knowledge of the names and descriptions of rocks and their constituent minerals are infrequent, except in the prose topographic description of the Lake District (in the following pages called *A Guide*, the most popular 1835 edition being entitled *A Guide to the Lakes*). The context of this popular guidebook encouraged the identification of rock types. In Wordsworth's poetry written after 1810 there are more instances of naming rock types than in poems composed before that date, but, again, the context of the later poems was encouraging – there are more sequences of poems of travel in the later period with opportunities for description of scenery. *A Guide*, with various titles, went through a number of editions. References to mineralogy increased with each new edition particularly from 1823 onwards, culminating in the 1843 edition which included Adam Sedgwick's 'letters' on the geology of the region. Kelley (1988) rightly traces a close connection between *A Guide* and Jonathon Otley's *A Concise Description of the English Lakes*, published in 1823. Correspondence, lists of books in Wordsworth's library and references in autobiographical accounts of visits to the Lake District, such as those of Clement

Carlyon (1836), confirm that Wordsworth knew Otley, walked in the
mountains with him, and possessed a copy of a map drawn by Otley to
accompany his pocket guidebook.

Mineralogical terms used in *A Guide* deserve close attention. In a
section describing the mountains and the formation of scree at Wastdale, Wordsworth writes about the effects of chemical action: 'The iron
is the principle of decomposition in these rocks; and hence, when they
become pulverized, the elementary particles crumbling down, over-
spread in many places the steep and almost precipitous sides of the
mountains with an intermixture of colours, like the compound hues of
a dove's neck.'[3] The beauty of the simile has perhaps blinded readers
to the question of where the poet obtained chemical knowledge. From
a date earlier than Otley's guidebook, there is an almost identical
passage in John Playfair's *Illustrations of the Huttonian Theory of the Earth* of
1802 describing a similar process:

Among the various aeriform fluids which compose our atmosphere, one is
already distinguished as the ground principle of mineral decomposition...By
the action of air and moisture, the metallic particles, particularly the iron,
which enters in such abundance into the composition of almost all fossils
becomes oxydated in such a degree as to lose its tenacity, so that the texture of
the surface is destroyed.[4]

Further indications of the possibility of an earlier source of knowledge
of rock types than Otley's *A Concise Description* is found in one of
Wordsworth's clear lithological identifications of the rock called schist.
As early as the first edition of *A Guide* (1810), Wordsworth writes as
confidently as any mineralogist: 'The mountains are for the most part
composed of the stone, by mineralogists termed schist, which, as you
approach the plain country give way to lime-stone, but schist, being the
substance of the mountains, the predominant colour of the rocky parts
is bluish, or hoary grey – the general tint of the lichens with which the
bare stone is encrusted.'[5] One apparent oddity about Wordsworth's
knowledge of schist rocks is that he appears to be attributing this rock
type to a large area of mountainous country which consists of many
different rock types. In fact, Wordsworth was similar to many contemporary geologists in identifying schist as a general name for a
variety of rocks which were younger than the so-called 'primitive
rocks', but older than rocks which were laid down under 'secondary
flood conditions'. James Hutton, the Scottish natural philosopher,
differentiated types of schist in 1785[6] in just the same way that Otley

did in 1823. A similar classification of schist is recorded by Humphrey Davy in a lecture at the Royal Institution in 1811.[7] George Greenough applied the word 'schist' freely to mountain areas of the Peak District and the Lake District in *A Critical Examination of the First Principles of Geology* in 1819. The use of the term 'schistose' for a broad category of lithology persisted for years. Sedgwick in his Presidential address of 1831 writes about the same landscape as Wordsworth, revealing that the poet is reasonably in line with what was then the orthodox description of this rock type:

Within these limits are found two distinct classes of rock, all the central region being composed of crystalline, unstratified rocks, irregularly associated with great formations of schist, which are subdivided (according to the system first published by Mr Otley of Keswick) into three well-defined groups, while on the outskirts of these older formations is a broken zone of carboniferous limestone and extensive deposits of secondary rocks.[8]

The earliest 'incident' in a poem where Wordsworth identified a mineral is in the *Descriptive Sketches* of 1793: an account of his vacation visit in 1790 from Cambridge to France and the Alps. In a description of the highest pikes, Wordsworth specifies them as 'needle peaks of granite'.[9] There is well researched documentation to help identify the source of this information. Wordsworth himself in the first edition and in the revised edition of 1849 acknowledges his reading of 'M. Raymond's interesting observations annexed to his translation of Coxe's tour in Switzerland'.[10] Theresa Kelley (1988) has examined this source with care and I will draw on her work later in this chapter.

As with 'schist', we should not be misled by the reference to a specific rock, such as granite, nor assume that Wordsworth was making as precise a mineralogical identification as any modern geologist. 'Granite' in the late eighteenth and early nineteenth centuries was, for the non-specialist, a term of convenience for what were deemed to be the oldest most 'primitive' rocks. Their characteristic features were their hardness and their crystalline detail, with no evident layering and no evidence of fossils. A clinching piece of identification of a rock as granite was its occurrence in 'primitive' landscapes. Dorothy Wordsworth gives three examples of this convenient term in her *Journals on a Tour of the Continent of 1820*: 'the white granite of the mountains', 'shut in by the granite and the snowy summit of the Alps', 'Mount Blanc is granite'.[11] Mont Blanc is composed of granite according to William Coxe in the 1789 English edition of *Travels in Switzerland*.[12] 'Granite' is introduced into *A Guide* in 1823 in a different manner. As we have seen, in the two previous editions Wordsworth had described the lithology of the hub or central dome of the Lake District Mountains as composed mainly of schist, with an outer sector of limestone. In 1820 he added 'freestone' to this last sector and 'granite' was identified as the constituent of 'the ridge that divides Eskdale from Wasdale'.[13] Here Wordsworth is being more precise and closer to the mineralogical orthodoxy, almost undoubtedly that of Otley, as Kelley has observed. A mineralogical observation which is reasonably technical is in a poem of 1822, 'Desultory Stanzas' in *Memorials of a Tour on The Continent*, where Monte Rosa is described as a 'granite ridge'. Wordsworth appends a footnote: 'Some say that Monte Rosa takes its name from the belt of rock at its summit – a very unpoetical and scarcely a probable supposition.'[14]

One other small instance of mineralogical knowledge is found in *Itinerary Poems of 1833*, in 'Flowers on Top of Pillars' based on experiences of Staffa. Again, there is a footnote illustrating some background reading in geology: 'Upon the head of the columns which form the front of the cave, rests a body of the decomposed basaltic matter, which was richly decorated with that large bright flower, the ox-eyed daisy.'[15] 'Basaltic columns' had previously been mentioned in the prose excerpt of 1811 or 1812, *An Unpublished Tour*, in a passage offering the reader images of duration opposing the wasting force of the sea. Basalt was frequently specified in contemporary guidebooks, but its origins remained controversial for the first two decades of the nineteenth century.

For the rest, the evidence of a keen mineralogical eye is slight. Limestone is identified at Caldbeck in *An Unpublished Tour*, in a late poem, 'Nuns Well, Brigham', published in 1833, and there is observation of caves in limestone country in the poems of 1818 'Malham Cove' and 'Mr Westall's Views of the Caves', although the inspiration here is from Mr Westall's art rather than directly from geological observation. Wordsworth read the introductory pages in the collection of Westall's 'Views' (Westall, 1818). He would have seen geological and mineralogical terms lightly used. There is even a reference to evidence of extinct animals; one of the sketches contains sketches of bones in the foreground. Wordsworth's poetry, however, does not refer to them. An instance of identifying a rock type occurs in 'Peter Bell', written in 1798 and published in 1819, where there is undoubtedly personal observation of the distinctive scenery associated with chemical erosion and faulting in 'karst' or limestone scenery. Peter's conversion is dramatic and his inner turmoil is mirrored in the strange shapes of the 'scars' or cliffs of the Yorkshire limestone dales:

> The rocks that tower on either side
> Build up a wild fantastic scene;
> Temples like those among the Hindoos,
> And mosques, and spires, and abbey-windows,
> And castles, all with ivy green![16]

An indirect connection with geology is that 'Peter Bell' was quoted by William Whewell in his review of Lyell's *Principles of Geology* in *The British Critic* in 1832.[17]

Wordsworth's lifelong passion for walking along the Lakeland roads, up the mountain paths and across the high fells, inevitably involved the observation of the rocks and stones in river beds, exposed cliffs, and boulders. In the Duddon sonnet sequence of 1820, he notes the blue stones of the mountain river's bed. In the poem 'The Black Stones of Iona' in *The Itinerary Poems* of 1833, Wordsworth cannot resist a correction of accuracy on the colour of the stones: they 'were at that time, as now, in colour grey'.[18] These items of observations are hardly indicative of mineralogical learning, but, corresponding to the poet's eye for the shape of the larger landscape, they confirm that Wordsworth had a sense of detail.

THE SHAPE OF THE LAND

Modern geomorphology displays two interconnecting activities, the descriptive and the analytical. The importance of the descriptive function explains why geomorphology and physical geography are brought together in many school syllabuses. Geomorphology is a descriptive subject but differs from geography. Like the geographer, the geomorphologist seeks out patterns in the landscape, uses cartographic techniques, and analyses the information from maps, aerial and satellite photographs, and field surveys. The geomorphologist works at a level beyond description supported by the power of underlying theories, theories which explain how patterns have arisen, how vestiges of former landscapes can be discovered; that is to say, the geomorphologist's study is historical. Even in the early nineteenth century, well before the specialist subdiscipline was named, the twin processes of description and explanation could be seen at work in the writing of scientific travellers, such as Alexander von Humboldt, in the work of regional geologists, like Brongniart in the Paris Basin, or in technical guidebooks, such as Jonathon Otley's of the Lake District. Wordsworth's own presentation of a region, *A Guide*, from its very first anonymous edition in 1810, also describes and explains.

A Guide has deserved considerable praise for the descriptive quality of its prose. Gill describes it as, 'a gem of Romantic writing'.[19] Perhaps the best approval for it as a practical guide is the fact that it is still published and purchased today in Lake District bookshops. Wordsworth's indebtedness to early guidebook writers has been well explored by modern editors; indeed Wordsworth gives all the necessary acknowledgement of his sources. The difference between the eighteenth-century guides and Wordsworth's is easy to see. Wordsworth's is closer in substance to contemporary practical guidebooks of natural history, such as Otley's, than it is to his acknowledged eighteenth-century predecessors, Thomas West, William Gilpin, and Thomas Gray. A good example of the change from one world-view to another is the section where Gilpin, in 1786, and Wordsworth, in 1810, described the colour of the landscape. Gilpin's description is for those who seek picturesque stations, where painters study their Claude glasses and set up their easels:

The natural colour of the rocks is either grey or red. We have of each kind in England; and both are beautiful; but the grey rock (which is the common species in this scenery) makes the finer contrast with the foliage either of summer or autumn... I call *red* or *grey* the natural *colours*, but more properly they are the *ground* only of a variety of tints. These tints arise from weeds, mosses and lychens of various kinds.[20]

By contrast, Wordsworth's description of the colour of the hills not only identifies lithology and chemical processes, as we noticed in the passage about schistose rocks, it is also about the change in the landscape created by clouds and sunlight. Above all, Wordsworth is conscious of the shapes of the hills and the processes that continue to alter them:

their [the Mountains'] forms are endlessly diversified, sweeping easily or boldly in simple majesty, abrupt and precipitous, or soft and elegant...

The general *surface* of the mountains is turf, rendered rich and green by the moisture of the climate. Sometimes the turf, as in the neighbourhood of Newlands, is little broken, the whole covering being soft and downy pasturage. In other places rocks predominate; the soil is laid bare by torrents and burstings of water from the sides of mountains in heavy rains; and not infrequently their perpendicular sides are seamed by ravines (formed also by rains and torrents) which, meeting in angular points, entrench and scar the surface with numerous figures like the letters W. and Y.[21]

These passages from *A Guide* are the presentations of a sharp observer of natural forms and natural processes. Wordsworth's prose is 'poetic', in the sense of depicting in each scene a sense of mystery and change, but the recording of the landscape is close to the method of the geologist who plots patterns and shapes. Wordsworth's eye is a geologist's eye particularly when it attends to certain favourite features. He often savours the landscape's 'sense of motion' (a phrase from the fragment *The Sublime and the Beautiful*). Again, like the contemporary geologist he is expressing the idea of a transient landscape. Wordsworth makes a further categorization of these shapes:

These lines may either be abrupt and precipitous, by which danger and sudden change is expressed; or they may flow into each other like waves of the sea, and, by involving in such image a feeling of self-propagation infinitely continuous and without cognizable beginning, these lines may thus convey to the Mind sensations not less sublime than those which were excited by their opposites, the abrupt and precipitous.[22]

The embedding of aesthetics and analytical language is typically Wordsworthian, but there is also a similarity with geological writing of the period. The categorization of mountain masses into smooth and continuous or abrupt and angular is a topographical analysis applicable to world-wide contexts. James Hutton made a similar basic distinction in 1795 in a summary paragraph on the earth's mountain patterns.[23] The sense of a landscape 'without cognizable beginning', as Wordsworth puts it, is (perhaps coincidentally) a Huttonian thesis of the unidentifiable origin of the earth and its forms, a topic I shall return to later in this chapter.

Wordsworth's ability to describe characteristics that eventually became the intellectual province of geomorphologists is not confined to skylines or massive, extensive profiles. He is a remarkably accurate recorder of physical features which eventually, but not without contention, became the accepted indicators of continental glaciation. Wordsworth particularly notes the flat bottomed, U-shaped valleys of the Lake District: 'the bottom of these valleys is mostly a spacious and gently declining area, apparently level as the floor of a temple, or the surface of a lake, and broken in many cases, by rocks and hills, which

Figure 1a–d These drawings of Lake District scenes by Joseph Wilkinson were in the collection which Wordsworth's first draft of *A Guide* accompanied. Considerably influenced by the 'picturesque', they are an odd accompaniment to Wordsworth's radical prose views.

Figure 1b

Figure 1c

Figure 1d

rise up like islands from the plains'.[24] The cwms or cirques of glaciation theory figure prominently in Wordsworth's prose and poetry. In *The Excursion*, for instance, the platforms of the high fells on which the dialogues take place between the protagonists of the poem are on the one hand dramatic contexts, locations for drawing apart and exclusion. On the other hand, these episodes include accurate descriptions of the upland 'armchair-like' valleys with a steep back and three side walls, a flat floor, often containing a tarn, and a low moraine on the fourth 'side', typically with a waterfall. These instances of description are doubly loaded as signifiers. Just as in the early poem, 'Nutting', of private, withdrawn experience, there is an imagined stage for emotional and aesthetic withdrawal, so in these descriptions of high mountain scenery there is both a landscape of the mind and a landscape of actuality, a landscape that the geologists were beginning to identify and to explain.

Parallel with description, the geomorphologist attempts an explanation. How did a distinctive shape come to be different from other forms in the landscape? Is the shape related to the mineral content of the rock? A heavily fragmented and eroded limestone 'platform' may be partly explained in this way. Are the strata and the faulting of the rock the reason for a dramatic feature? Massive limestone, granite tors, igneous intrusions, and dykes are examples of this. Alternatively, is the process of change, the history of the landscape, the explanation for the feature? These questions reach right to the heart of theoretical models for the geologist. For many years, and still to some extent today, alternative explanations generated fierce controversy. What did Wordsworth know about competing hypotheses of explanation of landforms? Much of the research into this question has centred on the larger scale questions of the origin or theory of the earth, 'macro' issues such as the separation of the sea and land, the major divisions of mountain and plain, the shape of the continents. I shall reserve this debate to the final section of this chapter and consider immediately explanations proffered for relatively small scale phenomena of the landscape.

One natural phenomenon of the Lake District is fairly straightforward. This is the odd, transitory appearance of Floating Islands. Kelley (1988) has identified Wordsworth's geological source for the references to Floating Islands in *A Guide* as Jonathon Otley's writing in *The Lonsdale Magazine* in 1820 although he had published an account in Manchester in the previous year (Otley, 1819). Wordsworth's comment in *A Guide* is brief, but, as usual, accurately observed: 'It may be worthwhile here to mention (not as an object of beauty, but of curiosity) that there occasionally appears above the surface of Derwent-water, and always in the same place, a considerable tract of spongy ground covered with aquatic plants which is called the Floating, but with more propriety might be named the Buoyant Island.'[25] Yet again there are layers of significance, some geological, some literary in Wordsworth's interest in Floating Islands. The island is also an image of transience, for the phenomenon appears and disappears in mysterious ways. Dorothy Wordsworth's poem on Floating Islands explores this strange natural feature and has itself been the subject of exploration for surface and deep meanings by Susan Wolfson (1988). More complicated historical explanations are necessary for other phenomena which Wordsworth described in *A Guide* and in poems. An example is the strange incidence of 'erratics', boulders often of considerable size and of a rock type not found in the surrounding area. They are common in the Lake District and throughout the north of England. Modern geology finds their distribution explicable because of the theory of the advancing and retreating ice-sheets. In the 1830s there was considerable disagreement between those who espoused the theory of transport by ice-sheets and those who favoured a theory of deposition when icebergs melted. An earlier, third explanation held sway for a much longer period, that diluvial onset or retreat swept massive boulders into foreign territory. This last theory, a fluvial explanation, is the most likely to be known by Wordsworth. The most famous passage where recent researchers have found evidence of this theory is obliquely geological but sufficiently clear in its description of a stranded rock. It is in the first sighting of the 'Leech-gatherer' in 'Resolution and Independence', composed in 1802:

> As a huge stone is sometimes seen to lie
> Couched on the bald top of an eminence;
> Wonder to all who do the same espy,
> By what means it could thither come, and whence;
> So that it seemed a thing endued with sense:
> Like a sea beast crawled forth, that on a shelf
> Of rock or sand reposeth, there to sun itself;[26]

Bewell (1989) has analysed with care both the geological reference in the depiction of the erratic which is like a sea beast and the images of recovery after a night of Deluge-like rain. Yet again the poem is an example of the complexity of the use of an image. The 'sea beast' is a living image for the dead stone. What the poet first perceived as an isolated rock fragment turns into the complete man, more integrated into the world than the fragmented, fearful poet dogged by the mortality of the human condition. As Bewell noted, this is a Lamarckian transformation from inanimate to animate and then to the human.

A major example from the later poems of Wordsworth's close observation of the physical features of landscape is the sequence of sonnets on the River Duddon published in 1820. The sonnets also suggest historical causation and imply a geological theory. The Duddon and the Derwent and other Lakeland streams were identified in his early poetry as formative influences on Wordsworth's life, but this sequence from the poet's later years is markedly attentive to the actual form of the river. Wordsworth explored the valley on foot in his later years as well as in a significant moment of his childhood.[27] The poet of the Duddon and its valley was partly attracted to the river in later years because of the memory of his childhood, but by 1820 the poet had an additional interest. The publication of 1820 included the sonnet sequence, other poems, and also a long description of the human meaning of landscape. *A Topographical Description* (*A Guide* in its second edition) appeared in the same volume, along with another shorter piece of prose, a 'Memoir to Robert Walker', a figure who appears both in *A Topographical Description* and in one of the sonnets in the sequence. The text of 1820 has to be considered as a total literary experience, prose and poetry are interrelated.

The valley of the River Duddon is one of those described by Wordsworth in *A Guide* as radiating from a central area of the Lake District. It is, however, shorter than the valleys that are graced by the famous lakes and, although Wordsworth said the main valleys spread out like 'spokes of a wheel', the 'spoke' which is the Duddon Valley can hardly be said to be a major radial. The river's source is somewhat obscure. Eventually many springs form a brook, which then, as Wordsworth described in *A Guide*, swells to form a copious stream winding among mountains, from time to time between steep rock walls, then in meadows, and terminates in the Sands of Duddon. To the geologist or the geomorphologist the River Duddon and its valley are interesting for a number of reasons. The fall from source to estuary is over a short distance. The Duddon valley from Wrynose Pass to Broughton-in-Furness can be followed in a car in less than one and a half hours by driving leisurely and even stopping to admire the view. The Wordsworths seem to have taken two days on foot to cover the journey, but with frequent stops and explorations. The distance, as a crow flies, may be short, but the fall to sea-level is considerable – frequently, but not in all stretches, the Duddon has a precipitous stream path. The tributary streams are also short and rapid in flow. Wordsworth's sonnets refer to the white water and the ground bass of the river and to its contributory waters. The Duddon valley, at least until the village of Ulpha, is a mountain stream in a 'youthful' phase for much of its journey, to use the language of geomorphologists of the second half of the nineteenth century.

Like other northern rivers, such as the Derwent, Greta, Cocker, Liza, Calder, and Esk, the Duddon intrigues the geologist because it appears to have survived over long periods of geological time and through major changes in the mountains' story.[28] The Duddon Valley runs across, rather than in line with, rocks of different hardness, thus creating sections of deep cutting alternating with sections when the river gently winds, finding no obstacles to its progress. Faults, as well as the effects of glaciation, mark the structure of the surroundings' high land masses, so, in addition to the river's own dramatic path, there is, for part of the valley, a surrounding landscape of steep slopes and rocky outcrops. Overall this small stream occupies a wider valley than it might be said to deserve, again a feature of interest to geologists from the early nineteenth century onwards. There is a mystery for both geologist and poet alike in the uniqueness of the Duddon Valley. Dorothy Wordsworth made one of her few comments of a geological nature as she looked upstream along the Swiss River Aar in the Ingrund Valley. She remembered the Duddon:

Looking backward, we had a sublime view of the river, departing from the peopled and cultivated plain into a close passage between huge rocks overhung with trees! It reminded us of the Pass of the Duddon, a miniature of this Pass, – and of my brother's sonnet and, if great things may follow so closely upon little, I will add that we thought with awe of those convulsions of nature by which the chasm had been formed, for the water by its own force could never have eaten its way through such a barrier.[29]

Geologists and poet's sister alike turned to a theory of Catastrophe to account for an apparent anomaly in natural processes. In Wordsworth's notes to the sonnets there is a comment on the most striking section of the Duddon at Seathwaite. The anecdote records that a visiting stranger returned to his host's home and claimed that he had strolled along the narrow valley with its crags and 'chaotic aspect'... 'As far as it is finished'.[30]

This light touch is perhaps only a minor indication of the meaning for the poet of a landscape which has arisen out of catastrophe and continues to present a tumult in stone. A different attitude to the processes of forming the earth is gained by reading the poems as a sequence (and we follow the poet's own instructions in reading the sonnets as one continuous poem – 'together they may be considered as a Poem').[31] Read as one poem we are led to consider the poet's understanding of gradualness in the creation of a river valley. The images of the Duddon, as the sequence develops, are those of human growth. They change from 'birth-place' to 'Child of the clouds' and a 'cradled nursling'. By the nineteenth sonnet the river is 'Lordly Duddon'. Similar progressions of growth and change both diurnal and annual are to be noted in the sequence. This definition of the river's journey seems to be based on a theory of gradualness or Actualism to put alongside the 'Catastrophism' of the violent phases of the river's journey.

Contemporary in publication with the Duddon sonnets, but slightly earlier in composition, is the 'Ode: the Pass of Kirkstone'. This ode appears in the 1820 collection alongside other odes which are concerned with the theme of time, as indeed are the Duddon sonnets themselves. In 1835 the ode was published in an edition of *A Guide*, emphasizing the historical approach to the landscape which was already a theme of the prose. This ode achieves considerable attention from Majorie Hope Nicolson in her seminal work, *Mountain Gloom and Mountain Glory* (1963). Kelley (1988) considers this ode as an indication that Wordsworth was committed to Catastrophism as an overriding geological theory. Certainly the landscape Wordsworth describes is one of desolation after a disaster of immense proportions:

> Mockery – or model roughly hewn,
> And left as if by earthquake strewn,
> Or from the Flood escaped:
> Altars for Druid service fit;
> (But where no fire was ever lit,
> Unless the glow-worm to the skies
> Thence offer nightly sacrifice;)
> Wrinkled Egyptian monument;
> Green moss-grown tower; or hoary tent,
> Tents of a camp that never shall be raised;
> On which four thousand years have gazed![32]

All the properties are present for a stage littered with Catastrophic remnants: the Flood, Druids, four thousand years (a crucial date for biblical fundamentalism). The second verse stanza reminds the reader of a dominating force older than the Roman legions that traversed Kirkstone Pass. Decay and ruin predominate as themes of the ode until the hopeful message for humanity contained in the final verse.

The 'Ode: the Pass of Kirkstone' should be read with close attention to its grammar before assuming that it gives unequivocal evidence confirming geological theory. In the passage quoted above, Wordsworth's sentence constructions demand an eye for detail. The importance of 'as if' must be acknowledged. The rocks are not what they seem, they are a 'mockery' or a 'model'. There are more alternatives in this strange landscape: post-earthquake or post-flood, monument or tower or tent. The language is one of possibility. The Druidic altar has been no altar at all, except for glow worms. The ode, indeed, opens with the key phrase to guide the interpretation of the poem: 'Within the mind strong fancies work'. Catastrophe is moderated from the moment the poem begins. The final lines of the last stanza moderate the fatality of a Catastrophic position. Faith from a gap in the clouds proclaims that man's lot 'is good, thy portion fair'.[33]

Theories of the earth

Reference, however allusive, to Catastrophe provides us with an opportunity to turn attention from the details of the landscape to the major theory or theories that the majority of geologists espoused during the period of Wordsworth's youth and middle age. Considerable effort has gone into categorizing the schools of thought of a volatile period in geological history, so what follows is a bare summary and, in chapter seven, I take the opportunity to consider at more length the main controversies surrounding the questions of the age of the earth, such as whether the earth was totally covered by one or more inundations and whether the present landscape is being destroyed or renewed. 'Catastrophism' and 'Diluvialism' are the terms commonly employed in describing the dominant explanations of the geologists in the first three decades of the nineteenth century. The 'Diluvialists', as their name suggests, were 'Catastrophists' with a specific explanation, although the earth's catastrophes in the widest sense included earthquakes and volcanic action. At this stage, the geological theory called 'Huttonism' or 'Actualism' (elaborated in chapter seven), will have to be introduced briefly as a third contrasting school of thought, though for at least thirty years it was eclipsed by Diluvial/Catastrophic theories.

James Hutton proposed a theory of the earth which avoided conjecture about the beginning and the end of the world, and that the natural processes that operate in the world were sufficient to explain the forms of the earth. Hutton acknowledges that alongside these processes of river action, rain, frost, and the movements of the sea, larger activities of a volcanic type (Plutonism) produced major landforms such as dykes and sills. 'Actualism' was to take centre stage in 1832, as Charles Lyell produced a theoretical work considerably extending Hutton's thesis and making a more acceptable master theory of the earth's formation and the processes that had been at play for as long as the geologists cared to imagine. I hope to avoid two errors that some commentaries have made: that one school of thought became an orthodoxy for all geologists at any one time, and that individual geologists consistently held one single theory of geology. As in our own time, scientists are capable of absorbing ideas into master theories even though the parts they assimilate come from opposing constructs. Geologists of the early nineteenth century, although they held tenaciously to an idea, learned to adjust and even, on some memorable public occasions, to 'recant' and join the opposition.

A preliminary issue is the position taken by geologists about the biblical Flood. Undoubtedly there were fundamentalist Christians engaged as scientists in the industry of reconciling geological discoveries with biblical records,[34] but those who called themselves geologists in any serious way, members of the Geological Society, university teachers of mineralogy or of geology, had progressed well beyond the fundamentalist dating of the Noachian Flood as relatively soon after the origin of the earth, which, according to Archbishop Ussher's chronology, was 4004 years BC. As Porter's study of the eighteenth-century history of geology (1977) and Rappaport's consideration of the historical view of the Flood (1978) show, the notion of a much longer period of earth history, a depth of time, had become a commonplace for many natural philosophers by 1800. Arguments continued about whether more than one major flood occurred. Not only was it possible by 1800 to imagine a 'depth of time', it was more than possible to propose a variety of massive events within that time. This is not to say that literary references instantly adapted to this new attitude. There is a slight allusion in Wordsworth's poetry which illustrates a revision of the idea of time. In the early poem, *Descriptive Sketches*, Wordsworth alludes to a period of time:

> Alone ascends that mountain nam'd of white
> That dallies with the Sun the summer night
> Six thousand years, amid his lonely bounds
> The voice of Ruin, day and night, resounds.[35]

This reference would square with Archbishop Ussher's dating of the origin of the earth as 4004 BC. Twenty years later, in 'Ode, the Pass of Kirkstone', Wordsworth revised the date of the origin of the earth downwards ('four thousand years have gazed'). In the 1849 re-editing of *Descriptive Sketches*, the exact reference to six thousand years is dropped and the contemporary geologically orthodox phrase, 'age to age', is inserted.

Wordsworth's youthful journey to the Alps is the setting for this episode in this early poem. The Alps also stimulated ideas about the Deluge, not always directly as a piece of descriptive writing about mountain scenery. *Descriptive Sketches* provides a different allusion to the Deluge:

> O give, great God, to Freedom's waves to ride
> Sublime o'er Conquest, Avarice and Pride
> To break, the vales where Death with Famine scour's,
> And dark Oppression builds her thick-ribb'd towers;[36]

On this occasion, the Deluge is suggested by a figure of speech for the unstoppable tide of revolution. A number of critics have identified this and other references, both direct and oblique, to the biblical Flood and thereby suggested that Wordsworth was a Diluvialist and therefore a Catastrophist also. Bewell's detailed study of Wordsworth's intellectual roots in Enlightenment science and philosophy is one of the most thorough examinations of the clues left by the poet about a world-wide catastrophe. One of Bewell's theories (1989) is that Wordsworth's early friendships and his reading when combined with his direct experience of the French Revolution encouraged an association in his poetry between catastrophe in the physical world and revolution in the mental and political world of humanity. From these experiences, Bewell says, he gained a direction and a law: 'the central story told in these books [*The Prelude*] is that of how Wordsworth learned to read social revolutions in terms of geology'.[37]

Two major examples quoted by Bewell are the dream in the cave sequence (the Arab pursued by the flood) in book v of *The Prelude* and the description of the Alps in the Gondo Gorge descriptions in book vi. The description of the high Alps with their top-most peaks left untouched by the Deluge has also been cited by Jonathan Wordsworth, Meyer Abrams, and Stephen Gill as a reference to current Diluvial theory.[38] The passage is worth quoting because of its detailed references to Catastrophic history:

> The immeasurable height
> Of woods decaying, never to be decayed,
> The stationary blasts of waterfalls
> And everywhere along the hollow rent
> Winds thwarting winds, bewildered and forlorn,
> The torrents shooting from the clear blue sky,
> The rocks that muttered close upon our ears –
> Black drizzling crags that spake by the wayside
> As if a voice were in them –

The verse paragraph ends with a visionary climax, created from the dramatic components of the scene, which

> Were all like workings of one mind, the features
> Of the same face, blossoms upon one tree,
> Characters of the great apocalypse,
> The types and symbols of eternity,
> Of first, and last, and midst, and without end.[39]

The editors of the Norton edition of *The Prelude* (1979) note the closeness of this passage to Milton's *Paradise Lost*, book v. Once more we see an instance when Wordsworth appears to be drawing close to the use of scientific information, but in fact he is also making an appropriation from a literary or historical source. We shall also find this dual reference, part scientific, part literary, in the later poems.

Was Wordsworth a Diluvialist or a Catastrophist? Bewell's linking of Catastrophe with revolution is an attractive theory well supported, as the editors of the Norton edition of *The Prelude* also note by reference to the earlier poem, *Descriptive Sketches*. A longer perspective through the late poems gives partial confirmation of this thesis, but it must be placed alongside the evidence of the complexity of geological theory in the 1820s and 1830s. 'Catastrophism' is a useful umbrella word for views of earth history which assumed one or more major breaks interrupting the processes that pertain in the present. The phrase, 'one or more' should indicate that not all the geologists of the 1820s and 1830s envisaged one catastrophe but conjectured from fossil discoveries and unconformities of strata that there had been a series of catastrophes or major breaks in the geological sequence. This is a different stance from the biblical account of one major earth-consuming Deluge. As the evidence of extinction increased, chiefly from studies of fossils particularly by French researchers, Brongniart and Cuvier, and as the correlation of strata, with the assistance of fossil types, became an accepted geological practice, stratigraphy began to dominate geology. Geologists began to demand historical explanations for the visible discontinuities between one stratum and the next. World-wide hypotheses were required to explain large-scale stratigraphic phenomena. Rupke (1983) reminds historians that Buckland had produced a stratigraphic 'column' as early as 1818, which assumed continental and even world-wide relevance. English stratigraphy, Rupke continues, concentrated not on the mineral content of the column but on the clues to the processes that had caused the strata.[40] Two dominating processes occupied the attention of stratigraphers, the effect of large-scale aqueous action (Deluge), and the phenomenon of violent occurrences sundering 'normal' processes (Catastrophe).

The two terms, 'Diluvialism' and 'Catastrophism', are not simply interchangeable. 'Catastrophism' particularly should be applied in this period with circumspection. Rudwick (1971) analyses the different understandings of 'directionalist thinking', not all of which gave prominence to what he describes as 'saltatory elements'. Rupke again distinguishes between the oppositions in geological controversy on the Continent and in the British Isles. Thus studies of early nineteenth-century geology in Germany and France might legitimately oppose Neptunists to Vulcanists in explanations of world-wide catastrophic phenomena, whereas in the British Isles not all Diluvialists opposed the Plutonist theories of James Hutton (or of his colleague, Playfair). A later antithetical opposition of the early 1830s were the Fluvialists (as Conybeare described Lyellian theory) and the Diluvialists. Whatever labels are applied, the consensual basis for the period before Lyell's great work of 1832, and indeed for some years afterwards, was a recognition of significant 'revolutions' and breaks intervening between long periods of comparative quiescence, when a distinct environment (or environments) was destroyed. Violations of the earth's structure, it was assumed, were followed by periods with 'new' environments and different organic forms.

Studies of geological controversies should make us wary of defining Wordsworth as a follower of a particular school of geology. The geologists themselves were not only open to conversions from one theory to another, but also considerably nimble in assimilating rival theories and absorbing them into a major theory which they continued to hold undeterred by the demanding requirements of eclecticism. Rupke (1983) calls the 1820s 'the Diluvial decade', but also notes that William Buckland was able to reconcile Catastrophism and Huttonism into a Diluvialist position, adding that, although Buckland's stratigraphic system derived from the German geologist and mineralogist, Abram Werner, his theory of denudation owed its origin to James Hutton. Records from the *Transactions of the Geological Society* 'show a gradual shift from Wernerian stratigraphy (focused on primary rocks and on mineralogy) to Cuverian historical geology (focused on fossiliferous rocks and on palaeontology)'.[41] Humphry Davy's popular lectures on geology to the Royal Institution similarly recognized Huttonian processes, but stopped short of accepting the full Huttonian thesis.

Diluvialism associated with various Catastrophic explanations may then be accepted as the guiding geological doctrine of the period up to 1832 as long as complexities and varieties are recorded. There is an interesting direct reference to the theories of Diluvial origins in an amended poem of Wordsworth published in 1820 in one version as 'the Ode to Lycoris' ('To the same'). The poet seeks the shade of a lonely cave:

> Long as the heat shall rage, let that dim cave
> Protect us, there deciphering as we may
> Diluvian records; or the sighs of Earth
> Interpreting; or counting for old Time
> His minutes, by reiterated drops.[42]

There is evidence of a version of the 'Ode to Lycoris' in a draft as early as 1801, but without this verse with its clear reference to the inspection of Diluvial evidence. William Buckland produced 'Diluvian records' from his exploration of the Kirkdale Caves in 1823. De Selincourt and Darbishire date the version of the poem in their edition as composed in 1817 and published in 1820, three years too early for Buckland's theories of the evidence of fossil bones from Kirkdale and Paviland to have become well known. However, more recent textual study by Ketcham examines the sequence leading to the finally published form. The extract quoted above was inserted in 1827. Therefore, although the poem in its original form was unlikely to have been influenced by geology, Wordsworth made use of more recent, Diluvial geological material in the final amendment.

Other references in Wordsworth's poetry to Diluvialism or to Catastrophism are more difficult to identify as geologically 'sound' for their day. Remembering that 'Catastrophe' may include volcanic or plutonic phenomena as well as massive inundation, we may note an occasional reference by Wordsworth to internal fires of past ages. The description of the Wanderer in *The Excursion*, previously part of the characterization of the Pedlar in drafts from 1799 to 1803, includes one such allusion:

> Oft did he take delight
> To measure the altitude of some tall crag
> That is the eagle's birthplace, or some peak
> Familiar with forgotten years, that shows
> Inscribed upon its visionary sides,
> The history of many a winter storm,
> Or obscure records of the path of fire![43]

In three lines Wordsworth might be said to have shown a nodding acquaintance with actualism ('many a winter storm') and at the same time with Vulcanicity.

As illustrated previously, other instances of geological knowledge may owe more to biblical or to Miltonic origins than to scientific sources. Sometimes there is a reference to traditions other than those of Judaism or Christianity. One in particular is tantalizingly distanced from a statement of a Diluvial position by the grammatical device of a rhetorical question. In the two linked sonnets (xv and xvi) of the Duddon sonnets sequence the poet muses on the origin of the two dramatic cliff faces, Wallabarrow Crag and the Pen, which border the turbulent river. Was the niche-like rock surface made by man, perhaps in a time of pre-Christian worship as a ledge for a pagan statue, or was it a remnant of a geological catastrophe

> ...abruptly cast
> Into rude shape by fire, with roaring blast
> Tempestuously let loose from central caves?
> Or fashioned by the turbulence of waves,
> Then, when o'er highest hills the Deluge pass'd?[44]

Whereas, in book vi of *The Prelude* of 1805, the highest Alps escaped the Deluge, here in 1820, the 'highest hills' are said to be covered, a theory of world-wide total inundation espoused by some Diluvialists. A similar reference to a total engulfment by the Flood occurs in another poem of about the same period, 'Processions' in *Memorials of a Tour on the Continent, 1820*.

> And this, in order, mid the sacred grove
> Fed in the Libyan waste by gushing wells,
> The priests and damsels of Ammonian Jove
> Provoked responses with shrill canticles;
> While, in a ship begirt with silver bells,
> They round his altar bore the horned God,
> Old Cham, the solar Deity, who dwells
> Aloft, yet in a tilting vessel rode,
> When universal sea the mountains overflowed[45]

As ever in a consideration of geological allusion, care must be taken to note the rounded picture of influence. The editors of this passage suggest that there is a likely reference here to two passages in *Paradise Lost*, one refers to the Ammonite God, Cham, and the other to the Miltonic lines 'all dwellings else / Flood overwhelmed'.[46]

When all seems clear in this activity of identifying appropriation, along comes an example that is inconsistent. In *Memorials of a Tour on the Continent, 1820* in 'Desultory Stanzas', Wordsworth presents again the earlier notion that the higher Alps escaped the Deluge:

> Where Mortal never breathed I dare to sit
> Among the interior Alps, gigantic crew,
> Who triumphed o'er diluvian power! and yet
> What are they but a wreck and residue,
> Whose only business is to perish?[47]

Perhaps this verse is not as precisely Diluvian as it seems. Does it suggest that the top-most Alps escaped the floods or did they rise from the floods 'in triumph'? In *The Itinerary Poems of 1823*, Ailsa Craig, the rocky island in the Firth of Clyde, is described as emerging from a flood in a distinctively Wernerian manner: 'Since risen from ocean, ocean to defy / Appeared the crag of Ailsa.'[48] Again, these examples illustrate Wordsworth's interest in Diluvialism, but they do not register him as a member of a particular faction. Like the major geologists themselves, he retained components of knowledge from different parties. Kelley puts his position thus: 'Like many contemporaries, Wordsworth avoids taking a position in the debate between uniformitarian and catastrophic hypotheses of the earth's formation. Except for the affective power of the deluge as the sublime cataclysm of his poetry, he tends to describe processes as though they were uniform over time.'[49]

One final Diluvian image reminds us again that Wordsworth's use of geological features often combines with literary and artistic allusions. Wordsworth as a young man may have visited Yorkshire's famous caves and he refers to the region in *An Unpublished Tour*. In 1819 he published three sonnets referring to the limestone scenery of Malham and district. In these sonnets evidence of Neptunism might be deduced from a reference to waters 'far within the marble belt / Of central earth',[50] but it is an imprecise and perplexing reference to contemporary geological theory. Wordsworth's main allusion in these poems is instead to classical myth and literature. He asks rhetorically if Malham Cove, a location of typical limestone geomorphology, was scooped out by giants, who perhaps had also excavated the Giants' Causeway. Gordale Scar also provides a classical image:

> thou mays't perceive
> The local Deity, with oozy hair
> And mineral crown, beside his jagged urn
> Recumbent.[51]

The Flood is a convenient stimulator of Fancy here, no longer the threatening apocalyptic crisis of the fleeing Arab of *The Prelude*. Perhaps by 1819 Diluvialism had become so much an accepted doctrine that it could be used as a rhetorical device. A dream of flooding occurs again fifteen years later, but in a light-hearted manner directly aimed at professional Diluvialists. Wordsworth wrote to William Whewell of Trinity College in 1834, thanking him for a copy of his *Bridgewater Treatise* and criticizing Adam Sedgwick and Whewell for supporting the admission of dissenters to Cambridge. The poet in a light-hearted manner to old friends says he dreamt that the Cam's waters flooded and demolished Kings College Chapel following the serious disturbance of new university statutes.[52]

The theory called Neptunism was cited earlier, and it introduces the question whether Wordsworth knew of Werner's theories of the formation of the world, other than through absorption of a general Diluvial hypothesis. Werner's thesis, a world created by the gradual deposition of material in suspension in a universal ocean and the emergence from the waters of the continents already configured into mountain and lowlands, held a commanding position in European geology until the 1830s. As with any persistent scientific theory it had an advantage of being able to absorb new discoveries, such as palaeontological evidence from research in the Paris Basin or from stratigraphy in the British Isles. Werner's theories were based on a construct of primitive or original formation with a succeeding rock formation of younger origin. This division into 'primitive' and secondary conveniently confirmed the theoretical underpinning of the work of the English stratigraphers of the 1820s, a point I shall return to later. We have seen in quotations already used that Wordsworth was familiar with terms like 'primaeval' or 'primitive'.

In one particular respect, Werner's stratigraphical hypothesis, probably through English translation in an encyclopaedia or a guidebook, may have provided for Wordsworth a small, but revealing technical detail of nomenclature. Werner's geological 'column' proposes a division of the youngest rocks of the world into 'diluvial', produced during the Flood and 'alluvial', produced by 'modern', post-diluvial forces of sea, rivers, and weather. Wordsworth demonstrates his awareness of the meaning of 'alluvial' in his description in *A Guide* of the formation of the valleys and the lake shores of the Lake District. He accurately uses the term to describe the continuing deposition of 'gravel and soil' by rivers as they enter the smaller lakes: 'Alluvial promonteries are created which eventually will reduce these lakes to numerous and insignificant pools; which, in their turn, will finally be filled up.'[53]

PRIMITIVE SUBLIME AND SECONDARY BEAUTIFUL

A Guide also provides one of the most substantial examples of Wordsworth's understanding of the notion of a two-fold division of geological history that was largely accepted in late eighteenth-century and early nineteenth-century geology in England, if not unanimously in Edinburgh. The following passage about the origin of the larger lakes employs two technical terms: 'primitive' and 'secondary': 'That uniformity which prevails in the primitive frame of the lower grounds among all chains and clusters of mountains where large bodies of still water are bedded, is broken by the *secondary* agents of nature, ever at work to supply the deficiences of the mould in which things were originally cast.'[54] This passage distinguishes between the primitive, original structure of the earth and the secondary processes working on that structure. There are more examples, such as when the vales are described: 'And, it may be observed, that, in one circumstance, the general shape of them all has been determined by that primitive conformation through which so many became receptacles of lakes.'[55]

Wordsworth assumes that Nature has continuing beneficial effects, as if the first form of the landscape was somehow awesome but authentically inadequate. Picking up his own word which implied a criticism of nature's actions, he continues:

Using the word *deficiencies*, I do not speak with reference to those stronger emotions which a region of mountains is peculiarly fitted to excite...Sublimity is the result of Nature's first great dealings with the superficies of the earth; but the general tendency of her subsequent operations is towards the production of beauty, by a multiplicity of symmetrical parts uniting in a consistent whole. This is every where exemplified along the margins of these lakes.[56]

Wordsworth does not invariably see the 'secondary' powers of Nature as benign. For instance, lakes may be slowly silted up and eventually lost. It is worth noting that these geological references in *A Guide* are followed by the admonition to check 'these intrusive calculations' and to be 'content with appearances as they are'. The recording of negative, 'secondary' changes in landscape is not always regarded as intrusive, particularly in comparisons between the Lake District and Switzerland:

Havoc, and ruin, and desolation and encroachment, are everywhere more or less obtruded; and it is difficult, notwithstanding the naked loftiness of the *pikes* and the snow-capped summits of the *mounts*, to escape from the depressing sensation that the whole are in a rapid process of dissolution; and, were it not that the destructive agency must abate as the heights diminish, would, in time to come, be levelled with the plains. Nevertheless, I would relish to the uptmost the demonstrations of every species of power at work to effect such changes.[57]

This passage is paralleled in Dorothy Wordsworth's journal of their tour of the Alps in 1820:

In passing through the Rigi valley, perpetual marks of falling ranges or decay of mountains are visible, yet no fearful devastation; scars gradually wasting – and fragments tumbled down. Threads and ribbands of cataracts were now gently performing their work; but their paths on the declivities told a plain tale both of perpetual and fitful wasting.[58]

The consequences of avalanches, not only of ice but of rock, were immediately visible to the travellers at Goldau because of the effect of the major flood of 1806. Similar catastrophes were perceived at the Lake of Uri. These examples suggest that 'secondary agents' are ambiguous in their implications for the student of landscape. According to *A Guide*, the Lake District appears to benefit by secondary agents. They improve landscape rather than precipitate the cataclysmic decay all too clearly visible in the Alps; yet even in *A Guide*, Wordsworth clearly recognizes that major alterations of scenery may continue to occur. He notes: 'the sea appears to have been retiring slowly for ages from this coast. From Whitehaven to St. Bees extends a tract of level ground, about five miles in length, which formerly must have been under salt water.'[59] The phrase 'slowly for ages' conveniently allows me to turn to the theoretical context which modern critics have proposed as the source of Wordsworth's knowledge.

Two important frameworks of thinking are revealed by the references above. First, there is an implicit acceptance of a long process of time during which erosion shapes and alters the earth's landforms, even though in some areas, such as the sea coast and the high Alps, the effects of erosion are recent and visible in historic time. Although volcanic activity also occurred in recorded history with an immediately dramatic effect on landscape, geological processes usually act throughout an extensive span of time. From this first presupposition follows a second geological viewpoint, a distinction between primary forms and secondary processes. Secondary processes are contradictory and difficult to comprehend in simple terms. Sometimes they lay waste, at others they add to the environment. Wordsworth may have been reflecting here a basic division of opinion about the long process of secondary action. Some geologists suggested a balance of nature with secondary erosion replaced over time by secondary deposition. Others saw erosion as a dominant force, eventually reducing the mountains to a vestigial landscape. The nature of the primitive is the most intriguing of concepts and it occupied the attention of major British geologists for a period co-terminous with Wordsworth's lifetime.

As a concept of aesthetic significance, the primitive landscape has considerable power in Wordsworth's thinking. The most impressive argument about a literary influence on Wordsworth's ideas about primitive and secondary formations of the earth is in the study, *Mountain Gloom and Mountain Glory* by Marjorie Hope Nicolson (1963). The central purpose of her thesis is to explain the major change of taste and aesthetic attitudes to mountain scenery throughout western cultural history. The shift, she records, was from mountains being seen as disorderly and worth avoiding to the Romantic quest for inspiration in lonely mountain regions. A major thinker in Nicolson's intellectual route-map was Thomas Burnet (1635–1715) whose *Telluris Theoria Sacra* of 1684 represents both a continuation of a classical and Christian tradition and a new direction in theorizing about the earth.[60]

Burnet faced up to a long-standing dilemma in Christian and Hebrew theology: what did God create out of chaos, a beautiful world or a world which subsequently became fallen and imperfect? The doctrine of Noah's Flood provided one answer but raised another question. Was the post-Edenic world before the Flood flawed and redeemed when the Flood's waters receded? Did God's covenant imply a new start? These arguments were confused because of disagreements about whether the Flood actually covered all the higher mountain ranges. If it did not, then the old unredeemed territory persisted. A further issue to be taken into account in any explanation of the purposes of the Creator was the likelihood of a final Deluge or apocalyptical disintegration. Burnet attempted an argument to reconcile all these questions. Gould (1988) has persuasively argued, in an illuminating study beginning with an imaginative analysis of the frontispiece of *Telluris Theoria Sacra*, that Burnet's theory of geological progress is arrow-like, yet with an implication that the world's history would return to the point where it began: 'In other words, Burnet displays his narrative (time's arrow) in the context of time's cycle – an eternal divine presence at the top, a circular arrangement of globes beginning and ending in Immanence, a complex set of correspondence between our past and our future.'[61]

Burnet's starting point was a near-perfect sphere: 'As to the form of it, it was all one smooth continent, one continued surface of the earth, without any sea, any Mountains or Rocks; any Holes, Dens or Caverns: And the situation of it to the sun was such as made a perpetual Equinox.' The surface of this perfect 'continent' was composed of a layer of life-giving substance ('terrestrial liquors'). Adam and Eve shared this Eden. With the Flood, however, a total environmental disaster occurred and its aftermath was to leave the 'ruins of a broken world', which we have largely inherited. Layers of rock below the liquid layer were projected upwards as the arch of the outer layers of the previously perfect sphere cracked open, with sectors of strata collapsing inwards. Great ranges of mountains were thrown up and the inner fires of the earth were released with dire results: 'We suppose the great Arch or circumference of the first Earth to have fallen into an Abyss at the Deluge, and seeing that it was larger than the surface it fell upon, it is absolutely certain, that it could not all fall flat, or lie under the water.'[62] The waters that had also been released from fissures at

first deluged the land and then receded, but created an oceanic
territory distinct from and even antagonistic to terra firma. All was not
permanently ruined. Human will, encouraged by God's forgiveness,
permitted a reconciliation to be effected. Human labour cleared
forests, drained marshes, and rendered the ruined earth habitable. The
softer agencies of rain and rivers smoothed the harsher edges of the
ruin and washed down eroded remnants which became fertile soil.

The evidence that Wordsworth was acquainted with Burnet's work
is undeniable. One text was in the Pinney Collection at Racedown,
Dorset and two others in his own library or in Coleridge's housed at
Rydal Mount.[63] Whether Wordsworth uncritically took on board the
geological theory is doubtful. One of the chief arguments put forward
by Nicolson to establish a direct influence on Wordsworth's idea of the
origin of the earth is the passage in *A Guide* quoted above, where
Wordsworth compared 'that uniformity which prevails in the primitive
frame of the lower grounds' which 'is broken by the secondary agents
of nature'. Nicolson also finds supporting clues in 'Ode: the Pass of
Kirkstone'. Earlier in 1813, in *The Excursion* book II, from which the
following excerpt comes, is a further example to support Nicolson's
argument.

> Far and near
> We have an image of the pristine earth,
> The planet in its nakedness: were this
> Man's only dwelling, sole appointed seat,
> First, last, and single, in the breathing world,
> It could not be more quiet.[64]

The word 'primitive' in these instances bears a considerable weight of
hypothesis in Nicolson's argument. 'Primitive' is, however, not a term
confined to Burnet's theories. It is used by Otley, for instance, in the
much more technical and Wernerian sense of the lowest component
of the stratigraphical column. Indeed, Otley applies 'primitive' to a
region: 'We have in this district none of those granite peaks which are
described as occurring in other primitive countries.'[65] James Hutton,
from a different position than Werner, in 1795 weighs and considers
the appropriateness of the term 'primitive' and finds it wanting, not
because it is inappropriate in a geological text, but because his theory
challenges the existence of evidence of first origins.[66] However, he
and his close colleague, John Playfair, both continued to use the
word. In short, 'primitive' as a geological term may have originated

with Burnet, but was no longer solely his. *The Encyclopaedia Britannica* of 1797, for instance, was owned by Wordsworth. In the section entitled 'The Earth' there is an extensive summary of Hutton's work and that of other geologists, providing a rich source of geological terminology and theory from British and European sources for the non-specialist reader.

The excerpt from *The Excursion* quoted above appears to me to be slight evidence to support a view that Wordsworth was wholly captivated by and committed to Burnet's geological theory. The passage is one episode amongst many in *The Excursion* about a hidden glen or secret, high-level, wooded valley, set apart like a modern Eden. The words 'pristine earth' are preceded by the phrase, 'an image of'. Wordsworth's careful employment of this comparative distancing phrase to introduce a description is worth critical attention. We can interpret the passage either as a justification for belief in Catastrophe, or it can be taken at its surface linguistic meaning: 'this is like the Flood or an image of the Flood'. Add to this argument the literary context in which Wordsworth composed. In writing of any aspect of the primitive form of the earth, he was always conscious of the seminal Miltonic Eden and Milton's evocation of its loss. In short, Wordsworth employed a wider array of sources than one late seventeenth-century theologian. Coleridge's famous dictum in a letter to Southey in 1803, 'Wordsworth's words always mean the whole of their possible meaning',[67] certainly applies here. My argument is not to deny the effect of Burnet on eighteenth-century geologists who, in their turn, contributed to the intellectual environment in which Wordsworth lived. As Roy Porter (1977) has commented, Burnet belonged to a group of natural historians who assisted the development of geology by setting an 'agenda for solutions to the problems of the Earth'. It is with this ancestry in mind that one could agree that Wordsworth was an inheritor, but it is not necessary to trace direct linguistic connections with Burnet's own works in order to live comfortably with that line of influence.

One important strand of Nicolson's thesis is however much less contentious, that of a tradition of aesthetic theory. I believe that both Coleridge and Wordsworth enjoyed reading Burnet, not for 'scientific' explanations, nor indeed for an aesthetic doctrine of sublimity and beauty, but because he was a stylist. Coleridge preferred Burnet's Latin to his English style.[68] Wordsworth in his middle years found poetic satisfaction in his Latin passages. In the published letter of December

1844, *The Kendal and Windermere Railway*, Wordsworth specifically commends Burnet's Latin:

In the *Sacra Telluris Theoria* [*sic*] of the other Burnet there is a passage – omitted, however, in his own English translation of the work – in which he gives utterance to his sensations, when from a particular spot he beheld a tract of the Alps rising before him on the one hand, and on the other the Mediterranean Sea spread beneath him. Nothing can be worthier of the magnificent appearances he described than his language.[69]

By 1810, Burnet was, for Wordsworth, an antiquarian, a distinguished, stylish antiquarian, but hardly a source book for the kind of geological and geographical information that he wished to convey in his 'scientific review', *A Guide*.

Theresa Kelley's analysis (1988) of the opposition between 'primitive' and 'secondary' in *A Guide*, as well as in other prose works, approaches the aesthetic dimension of landscape description with subtlety. She correctly identified stratigraphy as a dominant interest of the early decades of English geology, but she advances from that field of interest into a perception of Wordsworth engaged in a form of description which includes the struggle between sublimity and beauty, between the depths and surfaces of the world: 'It is as if Wordsworth had inscribed an aesthetic figure on a stratigraphic map whose layers have been fused together or laminated.'[70] Kelley's valuable insight into the permeation of Wordsworth's prose by contemporary geological interests is applied not only to *A Guide* and prose works, but also to instances in the later poems, particularly where 'the unstable character of the sublime' is apparent in violent, disturbing scenes and dramatic views. A close examination of 'The Jungfrau and the Fall of the Rhine near Schaffhausen', published with the poems written after the European tour of 1820, reveals to Kelley the survival of a perception of the sublime in eruptive opposition to softer, gentler forces of nature. She also identifies the resurrection out of Wordsworth's youth of political forces of disturbance and revolutionary opposition. An important source for Kelley's theories of Wordsworth's attention to geological description of primitive origin and secondary processes as well as to the political condition of Europe was Ramond's translation of William Coxe's *Travels in Switzerland in a Series of Letters*, a text to which reference has already been made. Possible literary sources of Wordsworth's geological knowledge are the subject of the next chapter.

Before leaving this chapter, with its instances of geological allusion and reference, it is worth reminding a reader of the relevance of this evidence from the later poems. What has perhaps appeared to be scattered and uncoordinated in Wordsworth's prose and later poetry presents a pattern when read in the context of the history of geology in the early part of the nineteenth century. The pivotal position of the prose work, *A Guide*, between the early and later poetry, should be acknowledged. *A Guide*, as Jonathan Bate says, 'invites all kinds of appropriation', because it is a 'multi-purpose text'.[71] Bate also reminds us that *A Guide* stands as a marker for a new route of landscape description, 'The geologist's hammer has replaced the Claude glass.'[72] From 1810 onwards, in his first popular prose work, the poet who was to be judged as the leader of the early Romanticism, became a writer with a consciousness of a different way of describing nature, which was systematic and orderly in its methods, in contrast to the disturbing, catastrophic events and processes which it described. 'Control' became a word not only describing his prose style, but also his developing social, moral, and literary theory. Before turning to these major philosophical matters, I shall examine the ways that Wordsworth gained access (or rather could have gained access) to contemporary geological knowledge.

CHAPTER 3

'Pronounce their benediction; speak of them as powers':[1] the wider context of geological information

The previous chapter was about what Wordsworth knew about geology. This chapter speculates on how he knew about it. Peter Manning (1990) has called the range of circumstances, events, authorities, and the general commerce of intellectual trade, 'the context of Romanticism'. The approach of this chapter is to examine a wider range of contexts in which Wordsworth carried out his literary life than is usually addressed in seeking influences on a writer. Foucault castigates the term 'influence' as 'too magical a kind to be very amenable to analysis...it attributes an apparently causal, but unexamined process to the phenomena of resemblance and repetition'.[2] In its place he proposes an examination of different types of discursive formation. Of the four types he recommends, the fourth, the mapping of transformations, for my purpose is the most useful for describing the geological activities to which Wordsworth had access and from which in different degrees his poetry produces 'resemblances' or transformed elements of discourse.

The 'mapping' of patterns of geological activity and its transformation into literature is complicated by dating. An author of Wordsworth's period, and particularly a reader of a wide range of literature, made up his or her intellectual portfolio of information about science from works of the distant past as well as from the scientific output of the rapidly changing present. Wordsworth's reading of Thomas Burnet's *Telluris Theoria Sacra*, a seventeenth-century work, had some effect on *A Guide*. The poet was not alone in listening to a voice from the distant past. Burnet continued to be a figure in the geologists' intellectual landscape for many years after his theory had been superseded by late eighteenth-century notions of the formation of the earth. *The Transactions of the Geological Society* record that the President, George Bellas Greenough, donated the 1719 edition of Burnet's work (together with a book by the eighteenth-century medical practitioner John

Woodward) to the Society. This instance is one strand in a pattern of continuity, a thread of tradition continuing over one hundred and twenty years, not only in a literary environment but in a scientific setting. In the early Romantic period, the new does not totally replace and dissolve the old. Recent studies of Romanticism (such as Butler 1981 Porter and Teich 1988) emphasize the diversity rather than the unity of the experience of writing in the period on which later ages have imposed a unity. Similarly, studies (such as Brooke 1991a of the relationship between science and religious belief have progressed beyond simplistic polarities of antagonism and harmony.

Another example of shared discourse across ages is found in one of Wordsworth's direct communications with a geologist about geologizing. In 1828, Wordsworth wrote to William Whewell in a light-hearted manner. Whewell, Sedgwick, and their Cambridge colleague, George Airy, had been conducting investigations at Dolcoath in Cornwall to attempt to measure changes in gravity at different levels down a deep mineshaft. Wordsworth was skittish about their field work, which nevertheless could produce 'great things':

For my part, as a little bit of a Poet, and still less of a Philosopher, I am looking for a new Edition of Kircher's Mundus Subterraneus [*sic*] with Emendations and large additions to be printed at the University press. No doubt you will be able to add largely to his enumeration of subterraneous animals, a Subject eminently important to naturalists, and not indifferent to Poets, who are much at a loss how to do these things correctly. e.g.: as one of the body I should like to know whether the figure of the Dragon delineated on page 117 Edit. Amsterodami 1678 is to be depended upon. . .[3]

Athanasius Kircher (1602–1682) wrote a 'fabulous geography' about 1665. His works were in the Rydal Mount library. This reference is not to suggest that Wordsworth indiscriminately preferred a fabulous geographer's understanding of what went on below the earth's surface to the scientific explanations of his geological friends. Like them he was conscious of a continuity of fable and of meaning into an age of scientific discovery. As a poet, he saw the creative advantage of mingling the explanations of the past with the answers of the present. Wordsworth's geological 'moments' are often tinged by a mythical colour, because his sources and those of his readers spanned the discourses of the two previous centuries. An example previously quoted is the invocation of observant spirits in the Duddon sonnet describing the high rocks of Wallabarrow Crag overlooking the rapids at Seathwaite.

If the continuing flow of the past complicates the study of correlations, then the present, in the sense of the poet's (and the geologists') lifespan makes the position more involved. For a writer, literary or scientific, there is not one moment of awareness of a fact or theory sufficient for a lifetime. The geologists were progressively changing their views of the nature of geology during Wordsworth's life. The information available to him was always in the process of change. The previous chapter has given some small 'incidents' of a shift of geological information in Wordsworth's geological vocabulary as the years passed. An example from a well explored and well documented source underlines this point. The importance for Wordsworth's first description of the Alps of Ramond de Carbonnière's translation of William Coxe's travellers' guide to Swiss history and geography cannot be denied. Thorough analysis of Ramond's French text and its assimilation into Wordsworth's poetry of the Alps has been carried out by Sheats (1973), Kelley (1988), and by earlier critics.[4] The contemporary Swiss physicist and geologist, de Saussure, was Ramond de Carbonnière's own source and he was not an obscure authority. Saussure's work was well known in Britain and is extensively quoted by Hutton in his *Theory of the Earth* of 1795.

Sheats puts much emphasis on a phrase of Ramond's, 'L'abyme du tems', the abyss of time. Wordsworth, Sheats concludes, appropriated the image of a gulf of time in *Descriptive Sketches* of 1793, in 1805 in *The Prelude*, book VI, and in 'Desultory Stanzas' in 1822. Sheats is not only interested in tracing appropriation of descriptions of scenery. He suggests that Ramond's reading and reinterpretation of de Saussure led to a renewal of creative forces in the poet. By 1790, Wordsworth had already read the conjectures of his own countrymen, Woodward and Ray. The British natural historians were able to give some verifiable geological evidence of the Flood, justified by what, for their day, was orderly collecting of fossils. What Ramond's work contributed to the young poet, according to Sheats, was an emotional colour to the geological phenomena: 'The imagination...seems to glimpse an image of eternity which it receives with religious terror...What Ramond offered the militant republican of 1792 was a way of reconciling this traditional scriptural interpretation of the Alps with a lofty and philosophical conception of "nature" and with the humanitarian ends of the French Revolution.'[5] We should, however, note a broader significance of Ramond's 'abyme'. It is a term with a wide significance in literary and theological language of the period. Goethe used the powerful word 'abyss' (Abgrund) in *The Sorrows of Young Werther* when the hero compares a vision of a landscape which had been serene with the landscape he feels he sees in his despairing moments: 'It is as if a curtain had been drawn from before my soul, and this scene of life had been transformed before my eyes with the abyss of the grave, forever open wide!'[6] Goethe's novel was widely read and popularized a heroic type of romantic aspiration combined with tragic youth. The abyss, as Sheats has pointed out, has evocations of Scripture, but also of Dante and Milton. There is also an intriguing reference to 'the infinite, which. . .is an abyss' in Kant's *Critique of Judgement*, significantly at the point where Kant refers to the sensation experienced by travellers in mountain regions.[7] The authority for Kant's aesthetic judgement is none other than de Saussure's account of the Alps, on which Ramond and, through him, Wordsworth drew for their descriptions.

How far Wordsworth was possessed by an Apocalyptic vision when he contemplated the Alps is not a simple matter to be confirmed only by occasional references to last things or to catastrophic events. Rupke (1983b) has given interesting examples of the frequency of the 'Apocalyptic Denominator' in art and science in the early nineteenth century. The fashion for Catastrophe and for geological links with revolution and the break up of stable societies is only one dimension of the period after the Reign of Terror and during the period of Reaction in Europe. Meyer Abrams' study, *Natural Supernaturalism* (1973), proposes a deeper understanding of apocalyptic vision in Romanticism, an understanding which seems to be particularly appropriate for appreciating the intellectual and spiritual journey of Wordsworth into his maturity and old age: 'Faith in an apocalypse by revelation had been replaced by faith in an apocalypse by revolution and this now gave way to faith in an apocalypse by imagination or cognition.'[8] Abrams also reminds us that the modern sense of apocalypse may be disintegration and destruction, but the older biblical sense is one of new beginnings.

Extending Sheats's valuable study of the effect of Ramond's translation beyond Wordsworth's poems of the 1790s is not difficult. As well as *The Prelude*'s description of the highest Alps of 1805 and the previously quoted 'Desultory Stanzas', there are further references to 'the abyss of time' in the later poems. I shall concentrate in chapter seven on the correlation between the geologists' concept of 'deep time' and the poet's sense of time in his later works, but one example illustrates another aspect of the sense of a chasm and catastrophe inspired perhaps by Ramond. This is the paradoxical image of an abyss in reverse, like Ramond's depiction of the highest Alpine peaks. In *The Excursion*, the conversing friends have withdrawn into a remote upland valley:

> – and lo! while in this strait
> I stand – the chasm of sky above my head
> Is heaven's profoundest azure; no domain
> For fickle, short-lived clouds to occupy,
> Or to pass through; but rather an abyss
> In which the everlasting stars abide;
> And whose soft gloom, and boundless depth, might tempt
> The curious eye to look for them by day.[9]

There is a difference between this glimpse of depths and the feelings conveyed in the poems of 1790 and re-composed in 1805. The older poet is no longer looking into an abyss with religious terror, but to seek a stillness. The words that follow this description of depths are 'Hail, Contemplation.' The later poems are not without ambiguity, nor even without fear and glimpses of personal and natural catastrophe. Note, for example, in this stanza the word 'tempt', and the natural pause at the line end with its faintly hovering threat of seeking something dangerous in the abyss. Yet the predominant impression is that the observer is detached. Only the 'curious eye' might be tempted to look for stars in daylight. The 'abyss' here is a depth of understanding not a depth of terror.

Ramond de Carbonnière appears once more in Wordsworth's later writing, but with a curious deflection, close to a casting off of his previous influence – even of his geological credentials. Writing to Crabb Robinson in 1828, Wordsworth asks him if he had read 'Raymond's' [*sic*] account of the Pyrenees: 'It is well worth looking over, more for the beauty of particular passages, than its general interest, or its merit as far as I am able to judge, as an acquisition to geology. It is however on this account that the author seems to pride himself. His translation of Coxe, I think, I recommended to you before.'[10] Crabb Robinson attended lectures on geology and would presumably concur with his friend's assessment from the vantage point of the relatively advanced geology of the late 1820s.

Attention to Wordsworth's later years, the main focus of this book, should not blind us to the continuing influence of Wordsworth's childhood education. Indeed, the older poet's friendship with scientists like Whewell and Sedgwick was rooted in the early schooldays of the Lake District. Both scientists had the benefit of an education in northern grammar schools. Sheats places weight on the foundations of Wordsworth's openness to early radical scientific interests in the schooling he received at Hawkshead. He concludes that the Pedlar, who eventually came to rest in *The Excursion* but appeared in a draft almost fifteen years earlier, exemplifies the rounded, well-educated north countryman of intellectual interests, whom the young Wordsworth would not have found out-of-place in Keswick or Ambleside or in even more remote parts of the north:

> Therefore with her hues,
> Her forms, and with the spirit of her forms,
> He clothed the nakedness of austere truth.
> While yet he linger'd in the elements
> Of science, and amongst her simplest laws,
> His triangles – they were the stars of heaven
> The silent stars![11]

The passage continues to describe the contrast of these 'lonesome' sciences with the direct influence of nature upon the Pedlar's growing feelings. Some of the sciences, notably geology, were not so 'lonesome'. Quarrying and mining added to rural discourse a new register, the language of practical geology. In the early poem, *An Evening Walk*, sounds of slate quarrying are recorded, with trains of loaded horses, and the 'chissel's clinking sound'. Later in the prose work, *An Unpublished Tour*, there is a long description of quarrying.[12] Miners' dictionaries circulated and were consulted by early nineteenth-century geologists as they struggled to establish a systematic nomenclature. Wordsworth was far from isolated from geological activity in its commercial guise.

Sheats and other commentators on Wordsworth's early life have identified Erasmus Darwin as a literary source of his understanding of Natural History. The most direct poetic appreciation of theories of the earth was in *The Economy of Vegetation* and *The Botanic Garden*. King Hele (1986) claims that, when Wordsworth was a Cambridge student, *Zoonomia* was an admired text and he is confident that Wordsworth acquired knowledge of Natural History including what became known as geology from that source. Wordsworth's youthful reading was, however, very wide ranging and, if he did read and digest a theory of the earth from the copious footnotes of Darwin's poetry, he also had access to Continental authors, and particularly to major French philosophers who drew no boundaries between political, economic, or

Natural History. Late eighteenth-century thinkers strongly felt the need to explain the contemporary position of humanity, either to justify the *status quo* or to propose reform. To do so they encouraged historical enquiries which led them into theories of the formation of a world which seemed to serve humanity so well or so badly according to their political stance. Bewell (1989) has thoroughly examined the philosophical sources for Wordsworth's radical sympathies when he visited France in 1790 and 1792. Wordsworth's reading of anthropology opens up a wider perspective of literary sources, including Buffon and Montesquieu, than earlier critics have assumed. Nicholas Roe (1988) has filled out the picture for that period of Wordsworth's life with documentation of Wordsworth's friendships with English scientific radicals residing in France, before and after the Terror. In brief, we have no need to search for one source of geological knowledge which inspired poetry. The house of intellect in Wordsworth's formative years and in his maturity had many doors and a richness of rooms.

THE ENCYCLOPAEDIA BRITANNICA

Mention of the variety of philosophical texts to which Wordsworth had access should remind a modern reader that compartmentalization of access to knowledge is a modern phenomenon. Philosophy, literature, travel, science, mythology, and anthropology are now classified separately and taught in different departments to distinctively identified students. A modern student wanting to know about geology would seek out that section of the library. The eighteenth-century seeker after intellectual interest would more naturally consult an encyclopaedia. The late eighteenth century and early decades of the nineteenth century were times, like our own, with a consciousness of the 'explosion' of knowledge. One ideal for Wordsworth's period was the organization of knowledge, particularly a unified system which kept together the rapidly dividing branches of knowledge, hence the importance of an encyclopaedia. The Wordsworths owned the 1797 edition of the 'Scottish' *Encyclopaedia Britannica* and Coleridge had access to its volumes in a neighbour's library in Keswick.

The 1797 *Encyclopaedia* is a text worth attention in establishing the context of Wordsworth's knowledge. The geological reference is the section entitled 'The Earth', not, it should be noted, 'Geology'. Thirty pages of double columns are devoted to a detailed account of theories of the earth, starting with the Ancient Greeks, skimming through mediaeval and modern authors and listing the theories of Burnet, Woodward, and Whiston. Buffon's theory is given eight columns of attention, quoting extensively in English. James Hutton's theories are also extensively examined in over twelve columns. These excerpts give a reasonably comprehensive view of what contemporary geologists were writing, often by direct quotation accompanying critical analyses. It is interesting to note the dismissal of earlier natural historians, Burnet, Woodward, Whiston, and Buffon. Their deficiencies, the contributer writes, 'must be exceedingly obvious, even to the most superficial reader'. Wordsworth's contemporaries were therefore not likely to be receiving Burnet without reservation. Hutton, despite his extensive coverage, is not acceptable to the contributor. Particularly damaging was Hutton's assertion that there was no evidence of a beginning or an end. The anonymous writer is strongly directionalist, firmly convinced of the Divine purpose displayed in the world:

what we call the laws of nature were given to preserve the earth in that shape which the Deity thought proper to give it originally by his own power; and by no means to form it in any particular way, much less to put it out of the form which he had already given it, thus the world, according to the best accounts we have, is very little altered in its appearance, and also, according to what we can judge, will continue unaltered for ever, unless the Creator thinks proper to interpose in such a manner as to supersede all the laws he hath given it, and change it to some other form.[13]

It is perhaps a trick of our own twentieth-century perspective to imagine that Wordsworth assiduously pursued knowledge by engaging in systematic study through primary sources. Scientific knowledge for the first half of the nineteenth century continued to be dispersed amongst a variety of written contexts of which the *Encyclopaedia* was only one. I shall now turn to other sources which Wordsworth would have accepted as a normal part of his mental surroundings. They reveal how open to the new science of geology were members of a social class who read, travelled, and talked with others about their reading and travelling.

GUIDES FROM HOME AND ABROAD AND OTHER PRINTED SOURCES

Maps for general travellers' use rapidly developed in the middle of the eighteenth century, changing from simple charts to useful devices for exploring the countryside. Hill shading and the use of symbols for natural as well as for human features of the landscape rapidly became accepted conventions. Hand in hand with the adoption of more or less standardized cartographic symbols were improved surveying techniques which made orientation more reliable creating confidence in travellers such as Wordsworth who frequently made long journeys on horseback, often deliberately avoiding highways. In the recently discovered correspondence between Wordsworth and his wife there are serious words of advice on the value of maps.[14] A good guidebook (such as Otley's) normally contained a map, indicating that the region could be appreciated as a whole. Maps ceased to be devices for estates' surveyors safeguarding property, but became tools to investigate common property available to all curious travellers.

Guidebooks in the early nineteenth century had progressed from identifications of stations for painting or for viewing to useful handbooks, with descriptive texts on local economic and natural features. Wordsworth's request to Adam Sedgwick to add geological information to *A Guide* was neither novel nor solely applicable to geology. The edition of 1842 that included Sedgwick's 'letters' also introduced notes on botany by Mr Gough. Guidebooks for the British Isles which conveyed geological or other scientific information in a systematic manner were not confined to the Lake District nor to the early decades of the nineteenth century.[15] Ramond de Carbonnière's translation of William Coxe's tours of Switzerland has already received attention, but, in case Wordsworth's own commendation makes us think that Ramond's work was a unique source, it is worth remembering that Coxe untranslated also provided geological information. In the original, English version there is a long explanation of the construction of General Pfiffer's model of the Alps exhibited in Lausanne. Memory of the model provided Wordsworth with the opening lines of *A Guide*. Another good example of the encyclopaedic guide which covered the sciences as well as topographic, economic, and human geography, was Richard Sulivan's six-volume work, *A View of Nature in Letters to a Traveller among the Alps* of 1794, which John Beer (1977) considers may have been consulted by Coleridge.[16] The Wordsworths accumulated guidebooks from home and abroad as the catalogue of the Rydal library indicated (C. L. and A. C. Shaver, 1979).

Guidebooks are written to assist travellers who wish to visit accessible regions. Travellers who write about places where they are unlikely to be followed by the majority of their readers produce more discursive and speculative texts. The temptation must be strong to emphasize the exotic and the mysterious, if few are likely to check your accuracy.

Travellers' tales have always been difficult to classify as fact or near-fiction, and today they are hardly the domain of scientific writing. In the eighteenth and early nineteenth century, however, travel accounts were exactly that. They were a source of information for collectors and classifiers and for home-based scientific enthusiasts. The Wordsworths were inveterate collectors of travel journals. Their collection, as we know from the records of their library, was catholic in taste and generous in selection from across the years. Most of the texts in the Wordsworths' collection were from the eighteenth century, rather than the more formal, modern accounts (such as Charles Darwin's records of the *Beagle* voyages) intended as reports back to sponsoring learned societies. Wordsworth's use of myth and legend in his poems has often been traced to these early accounts of the New World or the Southern hemisphere.

The accounts of journeys published within Wordsworth's own lifetime became progressively more factual; in certain instances they were systematic topographical descriptions and in some cases they contained directly recorded geological observations. Alexander von Humboldt, the distinguished brother of the equally distinguished founder of the University of Berlin, is a good example of the scientist recording geology as well as cultural information in his travel accounts from North and South America. We know that Wordsworth was, at the very least, aware of Humboldt's journeys and he may well have acquired one text, for in a letter of 1815 to Southey, Wordsworth made a specific request for 'Humboldt's books on South America'.[17] The same letter also contained a request for the works of James Montgomery (1813), who produced a dramatic poem about the Deluge and Cain's offence against the Law. Yet again the dual message of myth alongside empiricism is heard. What could Wordsworth have acquired by reading Humboldt on the geology of South America? Humboldt engaged with geology and Natural History under the tuition of Blumenbach at the University of Göttingen, a few years before Coleridge, Greenough, Carlyon, and Chester studied there. If Humboldt had accepted his studies uncritically he would have exported the theoretical position of Blumenbach, an admission of the evidence of extinction from fossil studies and a Neptunian framework for the history of the earth. Humboldt found in the New World plentiful vestiges of extinction. The palaeontological record at this stage confirmed Blumenbach's and Cuvier's theories. Humboldt's exploration of formidably difficult and vast tracts of territory served to justify one

branch of Diluvial theory, that the earth had suffered a total engulfment. The Americas had not been exempted from the Flood. Putting
together the two tenets of European scientific belief, Diluvialism and
the extinction of species, he came to the same conclusion as men who,
like Buffon, had stayed at home in Europe in their libraries: that nature
suffered periodical phases or epochs of destruction and regeneration.

Humboldt's accounts and records of landscape, geology, botany,
zoology, and human geography, and those of travellers to Africa and
Australia provided Wordsworth and his contemporaries with wonders
of an unknown world, but they also served to justify already well-
known theories. The news from the newly discovered lands in the early
nineteenth century delivered evidence to confirm European scientific
hypotheses rather than to shatter European-centred science. It was
travellers of a later generation, such as Charles Darwin, collecting and
recording more systematically and from wider locations, who presented
information that disturbed. Phenomena such as coral reefs and atolls, a
wider range of fossils, evidence of a vast scale of mountain building
across continents, all when combined with a theory of Natural
Selection, shook the complacency that was associated with Directionalism, but that is an account appropriate for the period after Wordsworth's death.

What I have been describing above as springs of scientific information arose from texts which later generations would classify as
belonging to another, literary culture. These texts would eventually be
consigned to the subcategory of 'not-quite-science' or popular science.
A glance at the contents pages of the early nineteenth-century
intellectual reviews such as *The Edinburgh Review* shows how the
scientific, the literary, and the political at this stage were closely written
and read together. It is true that early in its history, the Geological
Society began to publish *Transactions* and scientific societies followed the
practice of producing specialist texts for increasingly specialist readers,
but the separation of journals into the literary and scientific was many
years away. The division of readership into distinct, non-communi-
cating sectors was also yet to come. Although at times of destructive
reviewing of the poet's work they were banned from their home, the
Wordsworth family was keenly aware of the reviews, which later
generations have somewhat simply described as 'literary reviews'. The
publication in the major intellectual journals of work by friends of
Wordsworth, such as Coleridge, Hazlitt, Lamb, and many others, not
to mention valiant attempts to initiate new journals such as *The Friend*,

should indicate to us the importance of these texts to literary groups. As Marilyn Butler (1993) reminds us the reviewers' role was to act as 'culture's medium' in a wider sense, bringing together readers with wide interests, political, economic, and scientific, as well as what we narrowly define as literary.

Roy Porter (1977) has described the partisan publication of geological information in rival journals. *The Edinburgh Review* and *The Quarterly Review* took up different stands on the controversy of Wernerism and Huttonism, yet the contributors to the reviews were not wholly partisan. Playfair, for instance, reviewed Cuvier's *Essays on the Theory of the Earth* for *The Edinburgh Review* in 1814. In the successive editions of *The Edinburgh Review* from 1813 to 1830 there are fourteen articles specifically indexed for geology and topography (including major 'keynote' articles on Cuvier, on fossil fishes, on French geology, and on mineralogical systems) and twelve long accounts of travellers' scientific expeditions to various parts of the world. The thesis of separated literary and scientific culture cannot be sustained in the period up to Wordsworth's death, if published sources and a reading public with broad interests, are anything to go by.

Foucault warns his readers that in the quest for cultural influence, books, documents, letters, and other texts have been read as 'monuments' which give evidence of the 'heart of man'. He advises: 'the history of knowledge can be written only on the basis of what was contemporaneous with it, and certainly not in terms of reciprocal influence but in terms of conditions and *a prioris* established in time'.[18] His warning deserves attention by searchers into the intellectual context of the ideas with which a writer operates. We have been accustomed to seek the distinctive, individual human hand behind the text that influences an author. The quest has been for the passage that acted as a pale forebear of the more famous literary episode. In many ways the literary historian is a detective pursuing respectable, non-criminal plagiarism. Foucault reminds us that the context in which a writer operates is wider than literary texts and, if read with care, rich in traces of discourse. The search for context has therefore to be taken beyond conventional sources of ideas, such as books and pamphlets, into a variety of other written discourses. A small but revealing example of this phenomenon is the physical text in which a poem appears. Wordsworth's 1820 publication included 'The River Duddon: a sequence of sonnets' and other poems and a re-publication of *A Guide*, with long prose notes on a collector of Natural History, (Wonderful)

Reverend Walker. What is not so immediately observable until the actual copy of the first edition is studied is that the end papers include an advertisement for Natural History and particularly for mineralogy and geology, including works by Greenough, Playfair, the mineralogist Mawe, and even a comic poem on geology.[19] To classify this page as merely a publisher's end paper advertisement, an item of ephemera, is to miss the true experience of the book of newly published poems in 1820 and so to neglect an aspect of the audience of poetry of that time.

'WITH VIRTUOUS FRIENDSHIP'S SOUL-SUSTAINING AID'[20]

Studies of 'influence' may aim to enquire into the human beings hidden behind the artefacts they create but often the enquiry remains fixed on the monument, the literary text, and not on the hand that fashions it. So, in tracing sources of a poet's material, the discovery of a text behind a text has been a full-time research occupation and, indeed, produced a growing industry of studies of intertextuality. These studies have recently acknowledged that the range of texts from which a major poet may 'borrow' is wider than literary genres. The point of the last paragraphs has been that in Wordsworth's contextual background there were many different texts and a comprehensively available scientific culture deployed in them. Our interest in these enquiries into published sources is, of course, conditioned by our own literary culture. What is less easy to discover is the voice silenced by time because it was not given permanence by publication. Reconstructing a circle of friendship, a 'network' to use a modern sociological term, is made possible by diaries and letters, themselves semi-permanent extensions of a long dead discourse. To understand the full range of information about geology available to Wordsworth and to answer the question, how he could have known about geological hypotheses, we should consider the kind of people with whom, over his long life, he held serious conversations. What we can trace of the contribution of a poet's circle of friends to the workings of a poet's mind is in one sense literary, since its record is the written document, but the literary record is inevitably only a vestige of the dialogues and exchanges from an age that talked at length and valued discussion on serious matters.

The identification of Wordsworth's circle of friendship and its links with science in his early years has been well studied in works such as H. W. Piper's *The Active Universe* (1962) and by Lovejoy (1960) and Durrant (1970). More recently, there has been a careful uncovering of Wordsworth's early contacts with the work of radical experimental philosophers such as Priestley and Beddoes particularly through Coleridge, by Levere (1981), Fitzgerald (1984), and Roe (1988). One reason why Wordsworth's later years have been neglected from the point of view of science is because of a reasonable presumption that Wordsworth abandoned science along with his political radicalism. His mature and older years, it is assumed, were a retreat into literature rather than a reaching out from literature. Such an approach neglects the tremors of geological study that were felt in the Lake District. One does not need to say 'even in the Lake District' because it is an argument of this book that the Lakers were not cut off from the main currents of intellectual energy. The remaining chapters examine the major geologists who figured in Wordsworth's network of friendships in his middle and later years, but other names, familiar to students of Wordsworth's correspondence, can be enlisted at this point in the ranks of geological interest. Thomas Arnold, for instance, who brought his young family for long holidays at Fox Howe near Rydal Mount, with such a profound effect on his son, Matthew, was a keen amateur geologist. The minutes of the meetings of the Geological Society record that Arnold was present at a meeting as early as 1822. It was William Buckland, Reader in Geology at Oxford, who organized the election of Arnold to the Chair of Poetry. Another figure of literary society, Henry Crabb Robinson, was even more close to the poet. Usually described as a literary and philosophical commentator who introduced European thought into many literary circles, Robinson was also fascinated by geology and attended lectures by Buckland and Lyell. He described his attendance at Buckland's lectures to Mary Wordsworth in a letter of 1844. Wordsworth's growing connection with Cambridge, after his brother was translated to Trinity College in 1820, meant a new circle of friends, this time of admiring younger members of the university. The younger dons, such as Julius Hare were not only part of an informal Wordsworth admiration club, they were often amateur geologists; Julius became a fellow of the Geological Society in 1828. A more impressive literary–geological connection from Wordsworth's life was Sir Walter Scott. Dennis Dean (1968) makes a large claim that Scott was keenly aware of Huttonian and Wernerian theories of the Earth. In 1805 George Greenough dined with Scott in Edinburgh after a day inspecting geological sites. Adam Sedgwick, Professor of Geology at Cambridge, was active in fund-raising for a Scott Memorial at Abbotsford.[21]

A substantial, scientific figure who appears in Wordsworth's younger life as well as in his middle years is also a likely source of geological information. Humphry Davy became known to Coleridge in 1799. Returning from Germany to the south-west of England, Coleridge renewed contact with Beddoes and other members of the experimental club that met in Bristol. Humphry Davy had joined this group as an employee or scientific assistant, but quickly established leadership in chemical and electrical studies. Coleridge joined in experiments with enthusiasm and even proposed establishing a laboratory in the Lake District to be operated by Wordsworth, Davy, and himself. Certainly by 1801, Davy had become well known to Wordsworth, although at a distance, for he was engaged in proof-reading the second edition of *Lyrical Ballads*. Roger Sharrock (1962) persuasively proposed that it was Davy's lectures at the Royal Institution in 1802 with their argument for a noble role for the Man of Science, that inspired Coleridge to write to Wordsworth about the theme. Wordsworth's rejoinder, Sharrock states, is to be found in the expanded 'Preface' to the second edition of *Lyrical Ballads*.

Davy's knowledge of geology, judged from records of his lectures to the London audience, was extensive and like other members of the new Geological Society, as we have seen in chapter two, he included a range of theories in his studies. If Coleridge and Wordsworth were learning about geology from Davy, then they were learning up-to-date geology and a range of theory. Like his contemporaries, Davy is a Directionalist. His geology confirms his faith:

And by means of a few, simple laws, displaying one great and perfect design, all the changes of matter are rendered subservient to the well-being and happiness of man, and of the whole living creation...By wise and beautiful laws the equilibrium of things is constant. Life is preserved by operations which appear destructive, order and harmony arise from what at first view seems derangement and confusion, the perfection of the work is perceived the more it is studied, and it declares, in distinct language, the power and the wisdom of the author.[22]

The most direct association of Davy with the Lake Poets was in their youthful years. Davy's earliest literary link was with Southey, who published some of Davy's poems in the *Annual Anthology* for 1799. Like many of the early nineteenth-century geologists, Davy's intellectual interests were wide. His brother's biography mentions notebooks containing religious and philosophical subjects as well as original poems and copies of poets' work. George Greenough, a founder member with Davy of the Geological Society, made similar collections throughout his life. There are two main groups of references to Davy in Wordsworth's letters; the first dates from 1802 to 1808. Davy is seen as a good influence on Coleridge 'his valuable friend, Davy').[23] There are also waspish comments on the social class of Davy's second wife. By 1812 Davy's social position had risen and he had married a wealthy widow, who was not to Wordsworth's taste. The second set of references comes from the recently discovered correspondence between William and Mary Wordsworth edited by Beth Darlington (1981). During Wordsworth's long stay in London in that year during a period of reconciliation with Coleridge and close acquaintance with London literary society, he met the Davys frequently. By this time Davy was a Fellow of the Royal Society and fully acknowledged as a genius of science. There is no record of literary, much less geological exchanges between them. When Davy died, Wordsworth made a telling comment in a letter: 'His scientific pursuits had hurried his mind into a course where I could not follow him, and had diverted it in proportion from objects with which I was best acquainted.'[24] This note of 1830 could be taken as a text for the growing division between the language of scientists and the language of men of letters. The chemists were beginning to write in an exclusive register of language; the geologists, at least for a few decades, continued to be understand-stood by most readers.

Coleridge confessed at one point that he was not sure whether he was entranced by science or by Davy himself.[25] Coleridge's interest in science in general, and in geology in particular, must claim some attention in any study of Wordsworth's intellectual interests. As in all areas of collaboration between the poets most attention has been paid to that fruitful period of their friendship, from 1797 to 1805. Research into these wonder years has increased awareness of the origins of Coleridge's scientific interests. Levere's major study (1981) of the young poet's absorption with all kinds of science, reveals a range of fields of science: chemistry, electricity, and medicine. Coleridge's scientific interests in the 1790s were particularly inspired by Beddoes. Levere (1981) identifies Beddoes as, amongst many other things, a geologist who combined in his studies a mixture of hypotheses, as did many other famous enquirers into nature. 'His lectures were essentially Wernerian, his papers Huttonian.'[26] Beddoes was at the centre of the new organizations of geology, being admitted as a member of the Geological Society in April 1808, sponsored by his former pupil,

Humphry Davy. At a different level, Wordsworth knew Beddoes as a medical adviser, consulting him about his brother-in-law's health in 1808.[27]

Whatever intellectual luggage Coleridge and the Wordsworths took with them to Germany in 1798, it was certainly Coleridge who added to his scientific stock of knowledge while he was at Göttingen. It is sometimes suggested that Coleridge acquired an interest in geology from vacations in the mineral-rich Harz Mountains. It was more likely that he received theoretical teaching before he undertook those excursions. Coleridge had intended to travel further than Göttingen in order to sit at the feet of Schiller in Jena, but the revised stop at Göttingen and his remaining there was no accident. There he studied under Blumenbach who was to have a long and powerful influence on the development of studies in palaeontology and on the relationship between biological studies and geology. Göttingen also represented an interesting meeting place for literary and classical studies inspired by the late Enlightenment's interest in historical texts and the thriving school of geological enquiry associated with Werner at Freiburg. Laudan (1987) suggests that 'Wernerism was uniquely matched to the study of historical texts, being in its own sphere an extension backward in time.'[28]

Levere's thesis is that Coleridge's attention to geology matured and enlarged in his middle age, when he had taken up residence in London. He was able to experience the public excitement about the subject in its years of expansion. In 1821 Coleridge commented on Buckland's *Vindiciae Geologicae* to Crabb Robinson. Ten years later there is a record of Coleridge reading Poullet Scrope's review of Lyell's *Principles of Geology* in *The Quarterly Review*. He was hostile to Lyellian Actualism, because when it is 'applied to a world of growth and imperfection (it) necessarily leaves a craving void for every philosophic Mind'. Without a beginning or an end to the formation of the world, Coleridge complained, the earth 'loses all pretension to the name of *Geology* – not to speak of the yet higher Geognesy – it is merely *Geography*'.[29] Coleridge's mention of 'geognesy' can be easily traced to its most famous German source, Werner. The mature philosopher may have remembered a youthful intellectual acquaintance with Werner, but Levere believes that Coleridge's attention to geology after 1820 was derived from a different German source, Naturphilosophie: 'Coleridge in the years before his death, had come to see geological debates as of the most fundamental importance.' Levere quotes from Coleridge's notebooks to demonstrate that he was aware of 'the German and thence the French Hypotheses of a progressive Zoogeny'.[30] This last reference to the French hypotheses is to Cuvier's researches, which, Levere argues, reconciled Werner with Catastrophism. Hypotheses about successive geological eras became incorporated into Coleridge's theory of the ascent of life. These theories were proof of the inherent vitality of the Creation, reaching ladder-like to the supreme creation: humanity.

Although there is no evidence that this late philosophizing about geology by Coleridge was conveyed to Wordsworth, for one practical reason I believe that they may have had more to share in this field of science than has usually been conjectured. We should note that, despite the breach in their friendship, that was never wholly repaired, there were significant periods of meeting and renewal of old interests after 1810. Not least we should attend to the strangely conceived and unplanned visit to Belgium, Holland, and Germany in 1828, a barely researched section of biography, but surely an episode of some significance because of its destination. By that time Coleridge was immersed in German philosophy and his absorption was a matter of public knowledge either through his written work or through lecture series. The other likely harmony between Coleridge as an amateur geologist and Wordsworth's interests is not the stuff of documentation. It lies in the ability of both poets to assess landscape with an appreciation that was, in part, a geologist's. Wordsworth's perceptions of the shape of the hills and the valleys of the Lake District has already been the subject of chapter two. Coleridge's eye for the shape of the hills was acute. The notebooks of his extraordinary journeys on foot in the Lake District and in Scotland contain detailed descriptions which are close to the craft of the topographer. Furthermore, he made pencil drawings of the crest-lines of various hills, very similar in style to those found in the sketch books of professional geologists, such as Adam Sedgwick, twenty or more years later. Literary and geological resonances of this kind are faint. They rely on intuitive attention to different registers of language which demand an ear attuned to the details of scientific language, a skill which the literary critic could claim. A major example of this quality of reading, rich in the appreciation of the language which permeated literature and science, is Gillian Beer's study (1983) of the evolutionary narrative of Darwin's 'plots' and their family relationship with nineteenth-century fiction.

The last section of this chapter has sketched the performers in a parade of people who formed a circle with Wordsworth as its centre. This theme of social networks now occupies the main emphasis of this book. The identification of friendship networks with their common interests and values has not previously been closely considered in Wordsworth's middle and later years. The richness and vitality of the 'wonderful decade' from 1797 to 1807 and the intensity of the relationships that nurtured the poetic collaboration of those years have very properly engaged the attention of scholars. This study now turns to a different level of friendship and to the unexplored areas of interest that united the older poet and a group of geologists.

CHAPTER 4

Trinity men

When admiring the rapid growth of organizations for the advancement of science in London, Edinburgh, and Dublin in the first four decades of the nineteenth century, it is easy to neglect the supporting and equally significant growth of small provincial societies. Centre and periphery were both in expansive moods; furthermore, they were often in an articulated system. Morrell and Thackray (1981) have documented the phenomenon of what they describe as a 'trade in natural symbols' in the early years of the British Association for the Advancement of Science. The Association's early leading figures, including geologists like Greenough and Sedgwick and polymaths like Whewell, encouraged the dispersion of scientific knowledge together with the dissemination of scientific practice. The power and energy for this evangelistic mission to the provinces came from the provinces themselves (Cannon, (1978)), from wealthy men of science based, like Greenough in his new Regent's Park villa in London, but also, to an extent not previously acknowledged, from an out-going attitude from natural philosophers in Oxford and Cambridge. A common misconception is that the ancient universities in the eighteenth and early nineteenth centuries had no significant influence on scientific learning. The period from 1820 to 1850 was one when the universities were not alone in enlarging the scientific empire, but some dons played a major part, an organizing staff officer role, in science's successful campaign for the mind of the literate.

For generations before the 1830s, Natural History in England and Scotland had been a dispersed activity. The late eighteenth-century scientific parson, an amateur enthusiast collecting for the greater glory of an Enlightened God, is a commonly accepted figure, yet even in the period of Wordsworth's boyhood, such characters were not isolated from national scientific discourse. Recent research into Gilbert White's letters, for example, reveals a correspondence stretching from the rural base at Selborne to distant parts of the British Empire and, in England, linking the two universities.[1] Wordsworth's hero, the (Wonderful) Reverend Walker, appearing in the series of sonnets on the River Duddon was, like White, a collector of botanical, mineral, and fossil specimens. He is a romanticized, lonely enquirer, but many of his contemporaries at the turn of the century had established networks of like-minded natural historians who helped each other to develop their techniques of collecting and identification.

The study of geology from 1807 onwards illustrates how these dispersed enthusiasts were drawn into an organized, though distant scientific institution. A mission statement of the first meeting of the Geological Society on 4 December 1807, with George Greenough in the chair, read: 'that there be forthwith instituted a Geological Society for the purpose of making Geologists acquainted with each other, of stimulating their zeal, of inducing them to adopt one nomenclature, of facilitating the communication of new facts and of ascertaining what is known in their science, and what yet remains to be discovered'.[2] The 'zeal' is acknowledged, but it requires organization and the advantages of standardization. The Society set out to enable the distant collectors and observers to work with a shared methodology. Greenough's only book *A Critical Examination of the First Principles of Geology* of 1819 was a doctrinal text. The word 'critical' in its title stood for a sifting of vague theory from observable data, particularly encouraging techniques for the collection of specimens on a common basis with other well-schooled and inducted collectors. An anonymous text, *Geological Investigations*, in which Greenough is assumed to have had a hand, was widely circulated to draw the attention of provincial collectors to the value of methodical note-taking, labelling, and the use of acknowledged nomenclature. Of course, the Geological Society gained from standardization. Map-making, stratigraphic correlation and identification of fossil beds were all improved by nationally agreed standardized techniques.

The Geological Society and eventually the British Association, were not dependent on a metropolitan membership. In this chapter, I shall suggest there was a third location between London and the provincial Natural History societies which had a profound significance in geological studies. This was the University of Cambridge in the period 1820 to 1860 with one college in particular, Trinity, exercising a distinctive influence on geological organization. I shall consider two Trinity men, Adam Sedgwick and William Whewell, and, where it is possible to do so, draw some analogies and resemblances between them and William

Wordsworth, who knew them both. All three in different ways illustrated the theme of centre and periphery of the previous paragraph, they all represented three centres of linked intellectual endeavour in early nineteenth-century England, the provinces (in all their cases, the Lake District and the northern Pennines), London, and Cambridge.

Wordsworth's Cambridge is very properly taken to be his undergraduate days at St John's College recorded in book III of *The Prelude* and, in a less often quoted passage in praise of a democratic academic community, in book IX. Studies by Schneider (1957), Moorman (1968), Sheats (1973), and Secord (1986) have reminded us of the variety of the early intellectual influences of Cambridge on Wordsworth. Garland (1980), writing about Cambridge before 1840, has noted the study of mathematics as an essential feature of the Cambridge education which Wordsworth and the men who became his Cambridge scientist friends shared: 'At least, in part out of respect for Newton and his memory, the subject was endowed with a mystique which made it an object of near religious veneration.'[3] Mathematics was to colour the type of geology for which Cambridge became famous.[4] The other undergraduate 'core' studies, moral philosophy (and specifically the moral philosophy of Paley) and classical poetry are further intellectual links between the Cambridge of Wordsworth's youth and the Cambridge of Trinity College, which Wordsworth rediscovered after 1820.

Both for the history of geology and for a full comprehension of Wordsworth's later life, it is important to recognize the crucial turning point in the family's fortunes in 1820. Already Wordsworth had achieved recognition in his own right, rather than as one amongst other 'Lakers', after the publication in 1814 of *The Excursion* and then the editions of new and revised poems from 1818 to 1820. There was, concurrently, an encouraging improvement in family income. William and Dorothy from the time of their brother, Christopher's appointment as domestic chaplain to the Archbishop of Canterbury at Lambeth Palace, in 1805, had a close relative in a high place. Christopher then saw the most important development in his career, when he was appointed from Lambeth to be Master of Trinity College, Cambridge, in 1820. Although the salary was not in the league of many of the families who sent their sons to study at Trinity, the prestige and security of a Royal appointment were considerable. No longer were the Wordsworths solely linked for preferment to the fickle interest of great northern families, although William never neglected to be conscious of their power and influence. The series of sonnets on the River Duddon opens with a dedicatory poem to Christopher reminding him of their common Lakeland heritage and indicating the importance of his brother's career. From 1820, Christopher Wordsworth and his family had 'arrived' in a place which had personal significance as well as national prestige for William Wordsworth. It was a spiritual station in the poet's own journey. In November 1820, after a fortnight in London on returning from their European Tour, William, Dorothy, and Mary called on Christopher at the Master's Lodge at Trinity and William and Mary stayed there for some time. Dorothy left to spend December in Ipswich, but returned to Cambridge in January 1821 and began a pattern of visits, playing her gladly accepted role as caring sister for an overworked brother. William too was to return frequently and by doing so to enter a world of men of science.

Wordsworth's Cambridge acquaintances and friends included Airy (mathematician and astronomer), Peacock (mathematician), and John Herschel (the Johnian astronomer). Later, as his visits to Trinity became more widely known, he was lionized by a slightly younger generation, many of them Trinity men. The intense theological debate occurring in Cambridge and Oxford in the 1830s and 1840s involved scientists as well as theological scholars. In any case, many scientists were ordained men with an intense interest in their Church and the teaching of their faith. Julius Hare was a case in point engaging at Trinity College with a wide range of intellectual issues, but, more significantly, placing poetry and the imagination high in his list of values. He was also a member of the Geological Society and stands as a good example of the then open door between literature and science.

The world of Cambridge in the first forty years of the nineteenth century and its disturbed reaction to the Age of Reform has been well documented in histories of the university by Tillyard (1913), and, in terms of scientific developments, by Garland (1980). What has not been attempted in detail is the reaching out to other intellectual fields such as literature by many eminent academics who were to influence Britain's standing as a centre of world science. Morrell and Thackray's studies (1981 and 1984) of the British Association and its rapid establishment give fascinating examples of the determined ways in which Cambridge and Oxford men established the reputation of the universities at a time when there were more amateurs (and provincial amateurs at that) than university professionals engaged in science. Two geologists predominate in the early years of the Association, displaying

Figure 2. Portrait of the poet's brother, Christopher Wordsworth,
as Master of Trinity College, Cambridge.

vigour and political astuteness of a high order, Adam Sedgwick and William Whewell, both Trinity men. By this time, both had become friends of William Wordsworth and I aim to describe how this connection came about. Moreover, I explore how the circle of friendship was maintained not only by social background and a culture of Anglican orthodoxy, the argument commonly put forward by sociologists of science,[5] but by a shared intellectual history composed of a common educational background, a respect for literature, and a reverence for poetry.

ADAM SEDGWICK: 'THAT GOOD MAN'

In 1847, the eminent geologist, the Reverend Professor Adam Sedgwick, recovering from a period of ill health in Bath, enjoyed a chance encounter with a dear, old friend: 'I have been interrupted nearly two hours, very pleasantly by Mr Wordsworth. I hope to spend the greater part of tomorrow in his company.'[6] We know nothing about their discussion. Although there is a commonly accepted record about what they discussed when they met in the Lake District about twenty-five years previously, we are not really much better off for reliable information about earlier conversations. There are chance references in letters, with clear expressions of affection and undoubted warmth. One important source, rich in the evidence for the way geology was presented to the poet, is Sedgwick's series of 'letters' on the geology of the Lake District published with the sixth edition (1842) of Wordsworth's *A Guide*. Unexplored minor sources of information are to be found in Sedgwick's field notebooks, now in the Cambridge University Museum of Geology, and in his unpublished notes for an autobiography.

In many ways, Wordsworth and Sedgwick were similar in both their origin and education. Sedgwick was born and raised in Dent in the Yorkshire Dales. He too attended a good local grammar school, before changing to Sedgburgh School at the age of sixteen. One passage from his unpublished attempt at an autobiography is Wordsworthian in its description of a country boy's life. We have to remember that, although the geologist might not have read *The Prelude* until after 1850, he would for many years have known Wordsworth's shorter poems which paint an idyllic child-life of a similar kind to his own:

One of my early employments in a half holiday, when nutting in Dent woods was, as I well remember, collecting the conspicuous fossils of the mountain limestone...I almost lived out of doors. At fourteen years old I was trusted with a gun and coursed over the heathey moors the whole autumn day. I was a fisherman too at this age and was particularly careful to obtain the exact feathers from the smaller birds which were considered the most killing flies for trout grayling...Nor, though I ought to confess it with some reluctance – save that I never had an unworthy selfish thought in the matter beyond the joy of sport – was I quite free from the crime of poaching snares for rabbits, hares, pheasants. But to this day I like to hear the click of the fowling piece and as I pass a mountain burn can I scarcely help speculating in what holes the trout lie.[7]

In the same fragment of autobiography Sedgwick is proud to identify his ancestry with the 'statesman' of the Yorkshire Dales, 'Yeoman living on their own property'. Like Wordsworth's family before bereavement and debt dispersed the children, the Sedgwicks were independent northerners. He noted that a rural childhood implied no separation from cultural life, claiming that his father had met Samuel Johnson and Christopher Smart.[8]

The development of the friendship between the two men did not spring directly from a common origin in the north of England, although it may have encouraged affinity to grow. They met in the Lake District after Wordsworth's first visit to his brother at Trinity College but exactly when is not clear. It has been common practice to accept Sedgwick's published account of the date (1822) when they first met in the Lakes, but the evidence from the notebooks is contradictory. Whatever the date, the geologist remembered the start of his friendship as 'the happiest summers of my life'.[9] The first recorded meetings were preceded by the reputation of the Lake Poets. Although Sedgwick visited the Lake District on three occasions after becoming a fellow of Trinity College, in 1813, 1817, and 1819,[10] he does not appear to have made his first contact with the poet before the 1820s. He had, however, met John Wilson (alias Christopher North) and he may have visited Southey. His letters tell us that he was fully aware of the Lake Poets. In a letter of 1827 to Miss Isabella Sedgwick, he mentions meeting Crabb Robinson in 1811 at the home of Thomas Clarkson, who was well known to the Wordsworths. Mr and Mrs Clarkson told him about Wordsworth, Coleridge, Southey, and Lamb: 'I afterwards became acquainted with the Lake poets and I honoured them much, tho' never an idolater of them.'[11] He also records some frustration at failing to meet Wordsworth in 1817.

Sedgwick devoted the summers of 1822, 1823, and 1824 to long field excursions in the Lake District and during these excursions he met the poet and discussed important philosophical issues. Sedgwick was later to write, in vigorous Victorian style, about these meetings. All the evidence intriguingly is from Sedgwick, almost nothing from Wordsworth. The poet gives confirmation at least that a commitment was made by writing to Sedgwick almost twenty years later to ask him to fulfil a promise of the 1820s to write some geological material to add to *A Guide*. The first three 'letters' were produced for the 1842 edition of *A Guide*; two more geological 'letters' accompanied later editions. They reveal not only that the commitment entered into in the period between 1822 and 1824 was serious, but also that the themes the two men discussed continued to be relevant to the geologist in 1842 and onwards. Sedgwick applies a significant phrase, the 'universality of nature' to his own beliefs and to Wordsworth's in the opening remarks to the first 'letter'. We can presume this topic was part of their earlier discourse. Some geologists, he has to admit, have closed their eyes to the loftier purposes of science: '...and this I know, is no part of your philosophy, for no one has put forth nobler views of the universality of nature's kingdom than yourself'.[12] In correspondence he refers to the passage in book III of *The Excursion* where Wordsworth condemned field geologists.[13] Wordsworth's reply was reassuring and good humoured. He meant to refer only to mineralogists and in any case was writing through a character.

For one modern historian of science the correspondence of the 1840s produces a pleasing picture: 'He [Sedgwick] loved to roam in the hills as much as did the poet himself, and he loved to have Wordsworth with him...So we have the romantic but true picture of the aged sage and the young geologist tramping over the Lake District together, the geologist quietly geologising, while the poet tried out romantic thoughts.'[14]

Since, in 1824, the poet was only fifty-four, and the geologist all of thirty-seven, it may be necessary to reduce this picture in emotional scale a little. The truth is that we do not have much direct evidence about the frequency of their meetings during those summer months. Sedgwick's letters and reminiscences give us a tidy version of the discussions that took place in a sporadic, unplanned manner, over dinner, on the road to Keswick and, even more poetically, as they climbed the high peaks. Sedgwick, years later as he prepared the 'letters' to accompany *A Guide*, remembered, or even perhaps reconstructed, the experiences when Wordsworth joined him in:

Figure 3. Portrait of Adam Sedgwick as an old man.

...many a lusty excursion and delighted me (amidst the dry and sometimes almost sterile details of my own study) with the out-pourings of his manly sense, and with the beauteous and healthy images which were ever starting up within his mind during his communion with nature, and were embodied, at the moment, in his own majestic and glowing language.[15]

This rich memory is, of course, about twenty years after the events. What contemporary evidence is there for the actual meetings and their significance at the time?

Sedgwick's field notebooks, from 1819 to 1846, are a source of information, however partial. They are working field-notes with dates, locations and lists of angles of geological 'strike', with occasional comments on mineralogy.[16] The sections of the notebooks devoted to the Lake District excursions occasionally record his meetings with friends and colleagues and it is to these references that I have looked for evidence of the dates of meeting Wordsworth on his home ground. Although Sedgwick's own statement in letters to the Lake District guide and geologist, Jonathan Otley[17] or in the 'letters' accompanying *A Guide* identify 1822 as the first recorded encounter, the notebooks' evidence is that the first meeting in the Lake District was during the summer of 1823. In any case in 1822 Sedgwick was working in a different section of the Lake District, a long way from Rydal and Grasmere, visiting Eskdale, Bootle, Whitehaven, St Bees, 'Wastdale', the Duddon Valley, and Kendal. In 1823, a singularly wet year ('toujours il fait mauvais temps' 14 August 1823), he records: 'dine with Mr Wordsworth' on 24 August and 'breakfast with Mr Wordsworth' on 26 August, before travelling along Great Langdale Valley and returning to Rydal. After various outings to Coniston, in 'furious tempest and heavy rain', Sedgwick returned on 6 September to Grasmere to 'drive with Mr Wordsworth to Keswick', from whence he walked to Bassenthwaite Lake and met 'Mr and Mrs Southey'. He was accompanied by Jonathan Otley at this period and, after various travels across high pikes, completed the season at Penrith, leaving for Cambridge on 23 September.

The 1824 geological season in the Lakes began early for Sedgwick. By 8 June he arrived in Kendal and, after riding on 10 June to Little Langdale and ascending 'Wrynose', he returned down to Rydal. He may have stayed with the Wordsworths, because on 11 June he notes, 'ascend with Mr Wordsworth from Rydal Mount, noting the angles of slate beds with the aid of a compass and descending to Grysdale Tarn'. On 12 June he drove to Easedale and the next day, a Sunday, he 'attended Grasmere Chapel with Mr Wordsworth'. The 14 June was a day of 'mauvais temps' again, but on 15 June he called on 'Mr Wordsworth' and a Mrs Watson 'dined them at Kendal' (corrected to 'Ambleside'). The following day he and Wordsworth ascended Lough-rigg Fell where he may have noted Wordsworth's philosophy, but certainly recorded 'indications of dip are contradictory near Kirkstone at top of pass'. The rest of June 1824 took him to Patterdale, Halstead, Shap, Bampton, and Keswick where again he worked alongside Otley, but took time on 28 June to walk down to Derwent Water with Southey in order to see one of Otley's geological specialities, a Floating Island. That evening he dined with Southey. On 3 July, he and Otley took detailed observations of a Floating Island and confirmed 'that all the facts agree with Otley's observations'. A little later that month, on 12 July, he again dined with Southey. After a month around Skiddaw, Buttermere, Scale Force, Ennerdale, and Bassenthwaite, he packed up his specimens and left the Lake District on 5 August.

These records of contacts between Sedgwick and Wordsworth are incomplete. The notebooks are not personal diaries, but working records of geological observations; nevertheless, they give some substance to the view that the two men met in the summers of 1823 and 1824, not in 1822. However they do little to answer the question of whether Sedgwick had met Wordsworth in Cambridge or elsewhere before dining with him on 24 August 1823, although it is unlikely that he went unannounced or unprepared for supper at Rydal Mount. What is useful is the evidence in the notebooks of the intermixture of close, objective observation of stratigraphy alongside social and, from time to time, architectural observations. The notebooks' main interest for historians of geology must be their record of field techniques and the gradual development of regional geological mapping and surveying, but they are also records of the establishment of a network of literature and science.

At this time Sedgwick established lifelong friendships with other Lakelanders. In addition to the notebook references already indicated, there are a number of letters to Jonathan Otley. Sedgwick and Otley worked together determining technical features such as cleavage in slates and the direction of strike. The mention of Otley, whose work was known by the Wordsworths and who may have accompanied Greenough in the Lakes,[18] should remind us that Sedgwick was not short of company on his travels. The Lake District at this period was as popular a location for natural scientists as it was for tourists, and sometimes the two roles coincided. As well as Sedgwick's meeting with professional guides, such as Otley and McCulloch, there are records of distinguished parties visiting the by now famous landscape. Sedgwick's Trinity College colleague, Whewell, enquired after Sedgwick in 1824 a few days after his own party had visited the Wordsworths at Rydal Mount and the Southeys at Keswick. Sedgwick also remembered an historic meeting with John Dalton near the summit of Helvellyn, and, on a visit to Southey, he shared in 'the simple intellectual pleasures of his household, and profited by his boundless stores of knowledge'.[19] These were years of richness – 'the happiest summers of my life',[20] not only because Sedgwick was establishing a reputation in the growing scientific field of geology, but also because his health was improving. The ever-widening circle of stimulating friendships for this gregarious geologist probably contributed more than any other factor to his sense of well-being.

The list of the recorded meetings between the two men after the 1820s is not continuous, although it spans a long period of their lives. We are not in the fortunate position of having letters referring to all these occasions; for instance, we do not know how many times Wordsworth met Sedgwick at Trinity College during his visit to the Master's Lodge after 1820. In a letter written in the winter of 1830 to William Rowan Hamilton, Wordsworth records a visit of over a month to Trinity College and of meetings with the mathematician, Professor Airy, and with politicians and literati; but 'of science I can give you no account though perhaps I may pick up something for a future letter'.[21] A similar letter of a few months later, also to William Rowan Hamilton, confirms that he met Sedgwick ('that able man, the Geologist, Professor Sedgwick'[22]) and other Trinity scientists in Cambridge. Wordsworth was involved in correspondence with Whewell in 1834 and, indirectly, referred to Sedgwick in respect of reforms of the university's regulations.[23] The poet was sufficiently in good standing to feel confident in expressing severe disagreement with the proposals which were supported by Sedgwick for widening student admissions to Cambridge.[24] In March 1842 there is the necessary correspondence between Wordsworth and Sedgwick about the 'letters' to accompany *A Guide*, followed by occasional meetings in the last years of the poet's life.

Direct face-to-face meetings are not the only ways by which old friends keep in touch. The people with whom the geologist was familiar, and from time to time conversed frequently, coincided with

many of Wordsworth's circle. I have already referred to Sedgwick's
early connection with Crabb Robinson, the Clarksons and Southey in
1811. One friendship which Sedgwick shared with Wordsworth, was
with Sir Walter Scott. To Sedgwick, and to many of his contemporaries, Scott was a figure of heroic proportions. As I mentioned in
chapter three, Sedgwick was one of the organizers of a fund to
purchase Abbotsford as a memorial to Scott, a project which must
have pleased Wordsworth.[25] Other people known to Wordsworth, in
Sedgwick's letters or notebooks, are Samuel Rogers and Hartley
Coleridge.[26] One different strand in the fabric of friendship comes
from a much higher social sphere. In later life Sedgwick was able to
proceed on field studies from the socially elevated base-camp of
Lowther Castle. The connection of the Lowther family with the
Wordsworths' fortunes and their later patronage of the poet is well
documented. Less well known is the close friendship with the middle-
class Marshalls of Hallsteads. In their civilized Lake District home,
William Rowan Hamilton, William Whewell, Sedgwick, and the
Wordsworths met, as I shall illustrate later.

It is possible to continue constructing specific friendship networks
linking the two men. What is more important to recognize is their
shared presumptions and the social culture in which they both
engaged. Particularly because of the Wordsworths' close connection
through Christopher with Trinity College, with the university and with
the complicated culture of Anglicanism, the family would have been
very familiar with Sedgwick's non-geological life, the world he knew as
Canon of Norwich Cathedral. The power of this connection arose
from something which could all too easily be simplified with a phrase
such as 'spirit of the times'. Cannon (1974) and Allen (1978) have
identified 'the Cambridge Network', represented prominently by
Herschel, Babbage, Peacock, Airy, Whewell, and Sedgwick himself.
Morrell and Thackray (1981) describe the 'Broad Church' associations
of this group.[27] We can be reasonably certain that, although all the
scientific activities of this group were probably not of detailed interest
to Wordsworth, their general stance in relation to religious belief and
to social issues was within his range of interests. These thinkers were
not disruptive of the older poet's world-view; they trusted Divine
wisdom, rejected materialism, and held a modestly progressive but far
from revolutionary social philosophy. More positively, the Cambridge
scientists' theories of natural phenomena appeared to confirm and to
stabilize Wordsworth's own world-view, a point which will be further

elaborated in respect of Adam Sedgwick's general philosophy in a later chapter.

Like other contemporary geologists such as George Greenough, Sedgwick read widely. As a good uncle, he recommended standard authors to his nieces. As well as the Bible, Goldsmith and Cowper were particularly commended for young women. His own taste was broader. He admired Burns and Swift as well as Wordsworth. Unlike Whewell, Sedgwick was not a frequent writer of poetry. I have only discovered two pieces of verse in Sedgwick's own hand, both from 1833. In one of his sketchbooks (that is to say a slim booklet wider than the field notebooks, largely used for field sketches and cross-sections) Sedgwick had written on the inside cover in pencil:

> Jesus permit thy gracious name to stand
> As the first effect of her infant hand
> And as her fingers in the sampler move
> Engage her tender heart to seek thy love
> With thy dear Children may she have a part
> And write they [*sic*] name their all [supporting] heart.

In a smaller field notebook of 1833, again in pencil, there is another piece to a young needlewoman:

> The springing Fair whose gentle minds incline
> To [all] lovely innocent and fine
> With admiration in your works are read
> Of various textures of the twinning thread.
> Let then your fingers their charming skill impart.

Information on Sedgwick's connections with Wordsworth is only one level of interest. Opportunity will be taken in later chapters to trace the influence of Wordsworth on Sedgwick's writing on the activity of science, on the values inherent in practising geology, and on larger matters of faith, but the biographical dimension must now move to consider Sedgwick's colleague, William Whewell, in order to complete the account of Wordsworth's link with Trinity College and geology.

WILLIAM WHEWELL: 'THE CONVERSATION OF ANIMATED FRIENDS'

Whewell himself acknowledges the value of friendship: 'It has always been my wish that, as far and as long as men might know anything of me by my writings, they should hear of me along with the friends with whom I have lived, whom I have loved and by whose conversation I have been animated to hope that I too might add something to the literature of our country.'[28] To move from reading Adam Sedgwick's work to reading William Whewell's is like first visiting a large house, then moving on to a mansion of intellect. Sedgwick demonstrates the wide range of interests of a nineteenth-century scientist, but Whewell is the 'all-rounder' on an even vaster scale. In the context of studies of Wordsworth the chief interest inevitably must be in Whewell's major works on the history and nature of scientific activity and on moral philosophy, but a full picture of the man would include his work as a theologian, a philosopher, a writer on Gothic architecture, on philology, on European law, and on university education. He was also an administrator of distinction in the University of Cambridge, planning and managing a considerable expansion programme. Isaac Todhunter, the academic biographer of Whewell, quotes no less an eminent scientist than Sir John Herschel as extolling the amount and variety of Whewell's knowledge 'never in the same interval of time accumulated by any man'.[29] In the twentieth century, Whewell's reputation as a philosopher of science has been in eclipse. It has been difficult to appreciate his stature amongst his contemporaries until the recent publication in 1991 of two studies on Whewell, which have achieved a reappraisal of his value not only to his colleagues but also for our own understanding of the history of knowledge.[30] The comparison between Sedgwick and Whewell is put by another friend of Wordsworth, Sir William Rowan Hamilton: 'While Sedgwick has undoubtedly a more poetical imagination than Whewell, I sometimes doubt whether he has also an equally comprehensive intellect.'[31] Imagination and poetry were, however, never far from Whewell's mind. Far more than Sedgwick, he engaged in literary criticism as well as in writing verse. As early as 1814, he won a university prize for a poem on the subject of Boadicea. In terms of academic reputation he outshines Sedgwick. He became Master of their College, after Christopher Wordsworth's retirement, and he was twice Vice-Chancellor of the university. He was elected for a term as President of the British Association and he served as President of the Geological Society of London. In Europe, he was highly respected, particularly for his major work on tides. Pinnacle of pinnacles, the Queen and the Royal Consort favoured his college and university with visits during his period of tenure. Despite all these distinctions, he never lost the friendship of Adam Sedgwick, although they were not always of one mind on university reforms or on national politics.

Figure 4. Portrait of William Whewell as Master of Trinity College, Cambridge.

For most of his life, Whewell was a faithful friend to colleagues from his undergraduate days. Two of them, Hugh James Rose and Julius Hare (later Archdeacon of Lewes) were regular correspondents with him. More pertinent to this study, they were both known to Wordsworth. Not all the meetings of this circle were in Cambridge. With Thomas Arnold, Captain Thomas Hamilton, and a brother of the geologist, William Buckland, Julius Hare, and William Wordsworth ascended Helvellyn in 1832.[32] Hugh James Rose appears to have met

Wordsworth at Trinity College, but there is also a reference in Wordsworth's letter of 13 March 1837 to meeting him in the Strand. The contacts between Wordsworth and Whewell's younger, intimate friends, though perhaps generated in Cambridge, extended more widely and survived time, distance, and even political differences.

Whewell's own circle of friendship also included more central figures of the scientific establishment. Two who were known to Wordsworth were John Herschel and George Airy, but there were also relationships through families in marriage.[33] The strength of affection between these very active talented men is testified to by their warm correspondence. Lifelong relationships were not damaged by the occasional plain admonition, awarded usually to Whewell for his autocratic temper. The tone of Whewell's letters to Wordsworth was always considerate and warm, although on subjects such as university reform they found little to agree. Wordsworth is always the seer, the elder visionary to whom even the masterful Whewell deferred, at least in writing. Whewell's correspondence reveals not only the range of influential people with whom he was involved; it demonstrates again that English intellectual society was not at this stage of the century concentrated in London. Cambridge, London, and the Lake District are three settings in which Wordsworth maintained an intellectual discourse.

The Lake District played a significant role in the network of high culture in the period from 1810 to 1850 in a less obvious way than Cambridge and London. Whewell, like many successful scholars who went to Cambridge in the early years of the century, spent his childhood in the northern counties. He was born in Lancaster, and after a demonstration of early talent in mathematics, he was sent to a Westmorland grammar school, not unlike Wordsworth's own school. As in the poet's case, his mother died when he was young. At Heversham school his classical studies and mathematics developed considerably. He was taught for a period by the blind scientist and mathematician, John Gough, who is mentioned in book VII of *The Excursion*[34] and by Coleridge in *Omniana*. In October 1811, Whewell entered Trinity College where he was to make his home for virtually all his life.

Whewell returned to Lancashire for a number of family occasions and, as his fame grew, for civic functions and ceremonies to celebrate his achievements. His earliest excursions to the north as a young Trinity Fellow were scientific in purpose. Specifically they were to join Sedgwick and to add to his own experience of field-work in mineralogy and geology. It was during this period in the early 1820s that he met Wordsworth on his home ground. These were not, however, chance encounters. By 1820, when Christopher Wordsworth had been appointed Master of Trinity, Whewell was already looking forward to meeting the famous brother. On 1 July 1820 Whewell wrote to Hare about the vacant mastership: 'The general opinion gives it to Wordsworth. If this turn out so, he shall invite his brother here and you shall come and meet him, and we will be the most poetical and psychological college in the universe though certainly some of us are bad material for such an edifice.'[35]

The combination of poetry and psychology is significant. Whewell already identified Wordsworth with moral and mental ideas as well as with imagination. Whewell's anticipation was rewarded quickly because, by the autumn, William and Mary Wordsworth had visited their brother and his college. It was therefore not remarkable that the Cambridge man took a positive step to consolidate an acquaintance in the following summer as the field-work season commenced. In September 1821, he dined with the poet at Rydal Mount.

This first visit impressed Whewell in an unexpected way. It was not so much the poetical that he found attractive, but the intellectual. He found someone who, to his surprise, talked his own language. Soon after the visit, he wrote to a friend:

I was with Wordsworth part of two days and was very much gratified with his company. The only thing to complain is that he is not half as Wordsworthian as his admirers, and I am more and more puzzled that a man of his acuteness and good sense should write poems with white rabbits and wagon drivers for their heroes. I have since seen him here on an expedition somewhere or other among the hills, which he has great propensity for climbing whenever he can get a fine day.[36]

Many other visits to the Lake District, either for social or field-work reasons, followed in subsequent years. In June 1823 he planned to meet Sedgwick who was 'geologising in the Lakes'. Sedgwick's notebooks do not confirm that this meeting took place. In 1824 there is clear evidence of contacts between poet, stratigrapher, and Whewell. Both Wordsworth from Rydal and Southey from Keswick were able to direct Whewell where to find Sedgwick, who was busy with his hammer 'at the back of Skiddaw'. Whewell stayed with his college friend for three energetic days collecting minerals, finally leaving him somewhere between Penrith and Carlisle. Other visits to Wordsworth in this period may have occurred but have not been recorded.

In the 1830s the friendship with Wordsworth had become very firm, cemented by links with other mutual acquaintances. On 21 August 1834, on the way to Scotland, Whewell called on the poet and took time to sail with him on Windermere.[37] The previous year Sedgwick and Whewell had carried out a geological study of Charnwood Forest in Leicestershire. This is an interesting area even for modern geologists since it is a denuded outlier of older rocks within the younger rocks of the Midlands Plain. For literary purposes, it is an even more interesting location, being close to Coleorton where Sir George Beaumont, Wordsworth's patron had lived. It is conceivable that the contact with that wealthy family was made through Wordsworth and his sister. The connection between Whewell and Coleridge in the early 1830s has been noted by Fisch (1991) and Schaffer (1991). Whewell corresponded with his friends about a memorial prize to commemorate Coleridge in 1834.

The Marshall family of Leeds, London, and Hallsteads by Ullswater played a very significant part in Wordsworth's and Whewell's life. I do not know if this connection has been remarked on in any detail previously, other than in Rimmer's study (1960) of the economic rise and fall of the family, but it is a very good example of the unified social environment generally noted by Annan (1955), and by Rudwick (1976), Porter (1977), and Gaull (1979) in their different approaches to early nineteenth-century geology.[38] On 12 October 1841, William Whewell married Cordelia Marshall, daughter of John Marshall, a wealthy linen manufacturer, who had been a Member of Parliament for Leeds. Cordelia Whewell died in 1855 and Whewell married a second time, to become a widower again ten years later. After his second wife's death, he was looked after by a member of the Marshall family (Cordelia's niece) who became his biographer (Mrs Stair Douglas). The large 'holiday homes', where Marshall's first wife and family spent much of the year, were first at Ullswater at Watermillock and then at Hallsteads. It was from this last Lakeland retreat that Whewell was married. Stair Douglas and Isaac Todhunter, the major biographers of Whewell, are somewhat coy about how Whewell came to know his bride-to-be because discretion on such matters was in the Victorian spirit of biography. Our curiosity about the marriage is justifiable because it reveals a long-standing family friendship from the Wordsworths' early years.

John Marshall, Whewell's father-in-law, married Jane Pollard of Halifax. Jane Pollard is the earliest known correspondent of Dorothy Wordsworth and remained a friend and intimate letter-writer for as long as Dorothy was capable of writing letters. They had met at Halifax when, as a child, Dorothy was living with her grandmother. Their exchange continued to be warm and even sisterly in character. It is to Jane Marshall that Dorothy wrote about the arrangements for William's marriage and, a few years later, expressed her heart-rending account of the death of the Wordsworths' daughter, Catherine. William met John Marshall as early as 1800 and they walked round Rydal and Grasmere with John Wordsworth, and then dined with Coleridge at Keswick – 'My brothers quite took to him.'[39] Dorothy spent time looking out for property for the Marshalls when they wanted to buy a home in the Lake District. It had to be a house large enough for a growing family, in a scenic area. The Marshalls' decision to live in the Lake District made the bond between Dorothy and Jane tighter and the families visited and widened the circle of friends to whom they introduced each other. Jane Marshall eventually gave Dorothy an allowance of money. Only a gift from someone so close could have been acceptable to the independent Dorothy Wordsworth. William Wordsworth was a welcomed visitor at the well-provided Marshall home at Hallsteads and occasionally corresponded with Mr Marshall. Dora Wordsworth became a close friend of the Marshall daughters. In 1829, Wordsworth was accompanied by John Marshall and his son, James, to Ireland.

As the Marshalls prospered, they also acquired a town house in London at 41, Upper Grosvenor Street, where the Wordsworths and Dora stayed for long periods when they were in town. According to the partial record of Wordsworth's pocket notebook, the poet dined or had breakfast on eight occasions with John Marshall at his London residence, between 14 May and 8 June 1839. This period also included a visit to Cambridge.[40] Hallsteads and Grosvenor Square may have respectively represented rural retreat and urban duty for the well-to-do, but both places in fact had a busy social life, in which the Wordsworths and their friends shared. In October 1838, William Rowan Hamilton stayed at Hallsteads and was moved to compose a sonnet on the experience of 'the Elysian fields of Lowther'. Whewell must have been there also, because, in a letter to Hamilton, Sedgwick jocularly mentions the incident: 'Whewell told me a good story of your fit of inspiration on the banks of Ullswater which did not work in unison with Mr Marshall's spit and smoke jack.'[41] Whewell, according to Fisch (1991), acted like an intellectual patron to the younger Irish mathematician. Fisch asserts that Whewell met Hamilton first in 1832, after a visit to Coleridge, and that both Coleridge and Hamilton in different ways introduced Whewell to German philosophy. The Marshalls plainly acted as hosts to a culture that included literature and science and incorporated European learning.

Rimmer (1960), the biographer of the Marshall family, claims that Whewell met the Marshalls directly because of the Wordsworths but offers no evidence to support this.[42] It is possible that James Marshall may have met Whewell at the Geological Society in London, of which they were both members. It is obvious that, in visiting Hallsteads, Whewell was circulating in a bright, encouraging, intellectual atmosphere with which Wordsworth frequently engaged. At least for this social group, a home by the Lake was no rural retreat. This was generally true of the region or at least of its populated parts, which attracted people who, although their purpose was to make a pilgrimage to the hills or to satisfy a collector's or a scientist's curiosity or even to worship at Rydal Mount, also brought with them the news and ideas of Oxford, Cambridge, and London's great houses. The Lake District had become an intellectual centre by early Victorian times, with as rich a gathering of educated and influential writers and artists within a short carriage ride of each other as could be found anywhere outside London. A small but interesting point is that some of this 'set' were also members of the Geological Society. The names of Julius Hare, William, Arthur and James Marshall, and Thomas Arnold appear in lists of Geological Society members.

THE POETIC MAN OF SCIENCE: 'A LAKE POET AMONG TOWNS AND CITIES'

When Whewell was only seventeen he wrote to his younger brother giving advice on composition and metre. In later years, a love of poetry remained: 'I agree with you that the love of natural scenery lasts undiminished better than most other pleasures; but I am not yet weary of poetry, only rather fastidious, and I suppose this is what you are. I have however, of late found a new way of enjoying poetry by reading it to my wife every evening which at any rate prevents it putting me to sleep.'[43] Becker (1991) gives an impression that Whewell's interest in writing poetry was assumed in later life. My reading of Whewell's work is that his critical fastidiousness about poetry was not a late acquisition. Indeed, as a young man, his first approach to Wordsworth's verse was discriminating. In July 1817 he corresponded with Hugh James Rose, about the recently published *Biographia Literaria* and its views on Wordsworth's poetic language. Whewell's opinion was that the theoretically-driven elements were only a small part of the value of Wordsworth's poems. These components (his 'prosaic style, his puerility, his mystical and inflated language and his attachment to pedlars, his deification of children et cetera') have an undesirable effect on the whole:

nevertheless it has always appeared to me so woven and matted in with the rest as to give a tinge to the whole mass; it was in consequence of that, that I never entirely got over the repulsion I felt to Wordsworth, for there were so many passages, obviously favourites of the poet, where I could not feel any sympathy with him, when I appeared to have.[44]

He continues with an argument of self-reassurance. If Coleridge's own criticisms of Wordsworth's theories of language are correct, then Whewell's poetic tastes are reconfirmed, for the Lake Poets and their following do not mark a revolution in English poetry, 'but a little furbishing and beautification (as the churchwardens call it) of the parish church. Just get rid of the stale epithets and the stale personifications and one or two other errors that have crept in, and all our poets will turn out to be good poets.' The *Biographia Literaria* therefore relieves Whewell's mind. Pope, one of his firm poetic heroes, can continue to be admired unreservedly and admitted into the top rank of poets for admiration. Not all of Coleridge's theoretical statements on the nature of poetry are pleasing to the young don: 'they are, as before, muddy with their own turbulence. I can make nothing of them.' Nevertheless, *Biographia Literaria* has done its job well, for Whewell resolves to send for a book of Wordsworth's poetry.

In August of the same year he takes up literary criticism again with Rose and reveals clearly that Wordsworth has now become as important to him as Pope, but not for 'theoretical' reasons: '...if you think it inconsistent to admire both Wordsworth and Pope, you will do me the favour to believe that it may nevertheless be my case: nay, more, that I may admire one or the other, or neither according to the state of the barometer'.[45] To a different Lake Poet enthusiast, Julius Hare, Whewell commented on the 'solemn bleat of *The Excursion*', yet in 1824 he gave a copy to his sister, Martha. What then made Whewell look forward with excitement when he heard of the appointment of Christopher Wordsworth to the Mastership of Trinity College with the consequence that he might meet his brother at high table?

The answer to the shift of view is that Whewell selected from *The Excursion* and from earlier works of Wordsworth the kind of poetry that he and a growing number of friends and acquaintances wished to read. Their interest in the theories of composition, as expressed in the 'Preface' to *Lyrical Ballad*, was minimal. Whewell writes to Rose in 1817: 'What has a poet to do with theory? Let him mind his business, or it will be the worse for him.' For the new generation of Cambridge Fellows the voice of the great poet of Nature harmonized with their own appreciation of the natural landscape. As for Whewell, he had the special privilege of knowing the poet as a friend. Despite Whewell's sense of disappointment as the mystery of the great poetic figure dissipated, the reality of the man in his native setting became stronger and more influential. In 1822, writing to the Reverend H. Wilkinson, Headmaster of Sedbergh School, Whewell can still be critical of his new friend's poetry. His sonnets in particular

aggravate his faults and they concentrate his harshness of expression and his determination to dwell upon feelings which are very sincere and vivid in himself...Since I saw him I think I admire his beauties as much as ever, but I have lost that mysterious respect with which I used to look at his faults with a sort of suspicion that there might be something in them.[46]

At this time, Whewell had recently read or re-read the 'Ode: Intimations of Immortality' and found it difficult to discover any Wordsworthians who could explain 'the strange stanza in the ode which in other respects I admire as you do'. From this time on, as the friendship developed, there is no criticism of Wordsworth's theories or of his style. Indeed, by 1828, he wrote to the poet for advice on prosody in connection with Uvedale Price's book on metre.[47] One episode in later years reveals his complete conversion. The Edgeworths (friends of Sir William Rowan Hamilton) said to Whewell that Wordsworth was 'only fit for the nursery'. His loyal response was a confident rebuke: 'Well I should be glad to go into the nursery with him.'[48] There were, in the end, no critical reservations.

Perhaps the best way to illustrate the developing influence of Wordsworth's poetic themes on the scientist is to compare two excerpts from Whewell's correspondence. The first is in August 1821 when he wrote to a friend that he intended to take 'a regular Cockney tour' to the Lakes. The tone is gently mocking. He knows the cultural attitudes to pack in his baggage and that they are fashionable, although he fully intends to participate in the fashion:

You have no idea of the variety of uses to which I shall turn a mountain. After perhaps sketching it from the bottom, I shall climb to the top and measure its height by the barometer, knock off a piece of rock with a geological hammer to see what it is made of, and then evolve some quotations from Wordsworth into the still air above it. He has got some passages when he has tumbled the names of those hills together till his verses sound like the roaring of the sea or like a conjuration which would call the spirits of them from their dens.[49]

This, despite its light touch, is a carefully constructed piece of writing. 'Evolve' is used in the technical sense of 'to give off, to emit as vapours'.[50] The sensation, not the poetic theory, the field-work taken lightly and without pomposity, that is the early style of Whewell's feeling for the mountains of his childhood years. Compare this with the older man and his strength of feeling for the landscape of his past. The occasion was his speech at Lancaster in the summer of 1842 when he was guest of honour at a dinner in his home town:

The early scenes of youth – the castle towers – the waters of the Lune – have haunted me when absent, and have been a source of especial pleasure to me when present. My heart has leaped up when I revisited them, with a delight wholly different from that which other scenes, not devoid of enjoyment, have brought to me. We owe to the early years of our boyhood, influences which remain with us through all the years of succeeding life. The poet, Wordsworth, with whom I have within the last few days had the advantage of associating, says:

> The child is father to the man
> and I could wish my days to be
> Bound each to each by natural piety.

So I feel that the boy is indeed the father of the man – that the early sympathies he may enjoy – the love of poetry among school fellows – the facilities he meets with in the persecution of his favourite studies and pursuits – that these have more power than when his nature is more matured and his mind more expanded. His must be a hard nature indeed who does not feel this 'natural piety' on reverting to the scenes of his boyhood. I feel it with joy every week of my life.[51]

To add to this episode one further quotation is only to drive home the poetical source. In a letter of September of the same year from Hallsteads he writes to his sister: 'Since my return here I have had some grand long mountain walks with William Marshall and with Mr

Wordsworth while he was here. I am now beginning to know this neighbourhood pretty well, and shall be able to walk on the sides of Helvellyn in imagination, when I am confined in body to the level banks of the sluggish Cam.'[52] Not only are there echoes of sentiments directly from the poetry of Wordsworth, such as the theme of childhood's extra 'facilities' and the expression of 'emotion recollected in tranquility', the language used – 'scenes of youth', 'haunted me', 'my heart has leaped up', 'the early sympathies', 'confined in body' – is so directly influenced by Wordsworth's poetry that it is hard not to believe a paraphrase is being attempted. Perhaps even more haunting are grammatical constructions with a Wordsworthian tone, such as the negatives 'not devoid of enjoyment' or 'who does not feel'.

The last quotations belonged to the highly-charged emotional years of Whewell's marriage to Cordelia Marshall. At this time, poetry, and poetry of one poet in particular, assumed a special, personal significance, but the record of his own creative writing goes back to the days of his youthful university prize. He is not unusual amongst writers of his time in directing verse to young ladies. In 1826 he composed a long ballad called 'The Spinning Maiden's Cross', based on an Austrian folk-tale, for the birthday of a young girl in Lady Malcolm's family.[53] In 1832, he addressed a more formidable feminine subject, a sonnet to Mrs Somerville on her scientific work, *Mechanism of the Heavens*. Most courageous of all, he composed and delivered a sonnet to Dora Wordsworth, containing, diplomatically, generous praise to her father. Then in 1841, Mrs Douglas related, he composed a poem on his wife's 'chain of hair'. In addition to poetry, Whewell wrote at least one piece of imagination, a curious piece of prose 'science fiction'. Todhunter records that it was contemporary with Whewell's theological work, the *Plurality of Worlds*. It is about a visitor from the moon who searches for a lost brother descended to earth by meteorite. The opportunity for philosophical dialogue between moon-man and an intelligent British friend is not lost.

Whewell was obviously up to date in fashionable reading of a certain kind. There is no record of a taste for Byron or for Shelley. Todhunter records an incident which suggests that, if Whewell were alive today, he would have taken the literary weeklies: 'In those pre-Tennysonian days, every person of taste in the University was delighted in the works of Henry Taylor, and Professor Whewell was found engaged in the perusal of *Philip van Artevelde* with Froissart by his side – carefully comparing the modern drama with the ancient chronicle.'[54] It was

Henry Taylor (1800–1886) who first introduced Isabella Fenwick to the Wordsworth family. A further indirect connection with Wordsworth is that Taylor married Theodosia Alice Spring Rice, the daughter of Lord Monteagle. Monteagle became Chancellor of the Exchequer and Wordsworth corresponded with him about the Copyright Bill for which the poet wished to encourage support. In the 1830s, as Spring Rice, he was Member of Parliament for Cambridge.

If the above activities were conventional for a literary-minded gentleman, however busy, there were other more serious poetic commitments. Whewell was passionately interested in metre and rhythm in poetry and music. In *The Philosophy of the Inductive Sciences*, book 2, chapter VIII, on the fundamental idea of time, there are long passages on poetic rhythm. Whewell quotes examples in Latin and English to justify his theories. Later in the explication of the so-called 'secondary Mechanical Sciences', he similarly uses poetry to illustrate the theory of waves. Poetry is more than a mere illustration, although in common with other scientific writers of his time he freely used 'tags' from classical and contemporary authors to head chapters. Gillian Beer has noted that the early Victorian scientists claimed an authority from poetry: 'thus they claimed congruity with poetry, perceived as the authoritative utterance within current language'.[55] This is as true of Whewell as of any scientist of the time, but he is doubly involved in the authority of poetry, because of his personal interest in prosody. In November 1845, Whewell corresponded with Julius Hare on the possibility of gaining public attention for 'a fair hearing for English Hexameters'. Previously, in 1840, he had published and circulated privately 'The Isle of Sirens', a long poem in hexameters.[56] He translated Goethe and Schiller and attempted to retain the principle of their metre. In this intellectually demanding exercise he was not alone. At the same time, he was corresponding on the subject of translation with Sir John Herschel, who had himself translated Schiller's *Spaziergange*.

These serious engagements with the craft of poetry are, however, not the most telling indication of the poet hidden within the scientist. Shortly after his wife's death on 18 December 1855, he composed a sequence of long elegies. One was inspired by a painting by Horace Vernet, representing the Angel of Death carrying away a wife from her husband. In the same cultural environment in which 'In Memoriam' was written, perhaps this elegiac sequence is not surprising, and indeed the tone of verses, such as 'The Monument' is Tennysonian:

There the body is laid, away from the din of the city,
There in the Place of the Tombs. Such is our burial use.
Stand on every side memorials of neighbours departed;
Modestly there on the ground lies the memorial of her.[57]

Not all the themes are so redolent of Victorian funerals. Earlier in the same poem there is a Wordsworthian ring as Whewell is reminded of the Marshalls' Lake District home 'in the lap of Helvellyn':

  that happy mansion of Hallsteads
Lies off the rocky shore, scatters its shrubberies around
There around it swell the heathy summits of mountains,
Yew-crag, Hallen, and Place, Swarth-fell and Catchedicum,
There opes Kirkstone Pass, and Patterdale shines in its valley,
There leaps Aira's Stream into the beautiful dell
O how oft in those happiest days of growing affection,
Roamed we the bank of the lake, clomb we the breast of the hill!
Every turn of the shore, every crag of the hill-side
Lives in my memory yet; gleams to the eye of the mind.[58]

It is not remarkable that a well-read man should pick up the cadence and the vocabulary of classical tradition and contemporary poets, but it is striking that this sequence of elegies is a sustained composition by a man heavily weighed down by grief added to an awesome load of teaching, writing, and administration. Poetry was a serious matter for this and other geologists, not a light relief.

The origin of this poetic seriousness is too often claimed to be mysteriously meteorological with the frequent use of dead metaphors such as 'cultural atmosphere' or 'climate of the times'. Undoubtedly, Whewell, Sedgwick, Rose, Herschel, Hare, and their circle of friends were sons of the early Romantic period inheriting the achievements of what a few years previously had been revolutions in literary taste. Literary work, which in its first editions had been radical and shockingly new, by the 1820s had become an accepted mode of thought and sentiment. Poetry aired important subjects and in turn poetry itself was a common subject for discussion. As Charles Lyell's letters reveal, the conversations in the houses of the rich patrons of the sciences were about religion, the arts, and contemporary literary figures. When Whewell was in London he participated. Lyell records one such social occasion in 1837 when Whewell was present with Samuel Rogers and other literary men. As well as listening to Whewell giving opinions on Scott, Trollope, and Harriet Martineau, they discussed more mundane matters – Wordsworth's income from writing poetry.[59]

There is, however, at least in Whewell's case, a more identifiable and traditional source of poetic interest than fashionable literary gossip, a source which he shared with Wordsworth. Both poet and scientist were educated in the same classical tradition. Furthermore, they continued to read from that literature throughout their adult lives. The Latin poets in particular provided Whewell with an additional authority for the laws generated from scientific observations. This continuing thread of learning emerged first in a respect for poetic expression and second, in an often bizarre fascination with new words and with a language for science. Poetic 'tags' from Pindar, Virgil, Lucretius, Nonnus Dionysus, and Lucan are used to head the chapters of *The History of the Inductive Sciences*, as well as short passages from Spenser, Milton, Pope, and Wordsworth. The convention of poetic references elevates the tone of the scientific theory that follows. The scientist claims a continuity with the voices of the past. There is therefore a conscious verification of modern scientific work by the classical poets. Gillian Beer relates this authority to a paternal sanction: 'not only the mother-tongue but the father-tongue shaped the dominant educational ideology'.[60] In 1836, Whewell wrote to John Herschel, taking issue with him about the value of the study of ancient languages in the education of the young:

For I am fully persuaded that the study of Greek and Latin authors, in the original mode of presenting themselves, can never cease to be an essential part of the liberal education of the present age...[Men will never become] independent of the history and antiquities of literature. The process of seeking and finding groups and reasons for assumptions, rules and methods is always the peculiar character of a liberal education and a study of literary antiquity supplies this.[61]

If Whewell clearly saw a never-diminishing relationship between scientific and classical (and therefore literary) learning, his clarity was not dulled about the distinction between poetry and science. He knew there were two separate discourses, but they were interrelated, whereas some of his contemporaries were prepared to merge the distinction without conscience. In an interesting exchange with Julius Hare, Whewell had argued that Hare adopted the philosophy of certain writers because he admired their poetry. 'Hare replied, emphasising every word, "But poetry is philosophy, philosophy is poetry."'[62]

The second firm thread of connection with the literature of the past is Whewell's interest in, even fascination with, scientific terminology, a quality which was widely acknowledged by his peers. This topic has received scholarly attention from Schaffer (1991). In 1834, Michael Faraday wrote to Whewell for advice on nomenclature for his discoveries in electricity. Whewell could claim credit from that exchange for introducing the scientific terms 'anode' and 'cathode'. Lyell and Whewell had similar consultations resulting in permanent additions to geological language. Sometimes however, the advice was, perhaps fortunately, disregarded. 'As to your *luviality* I hope you will not adopt such a beastly compound as protoalluvium which is wrong at both ends. I cannot image, however *alluvion* got its termination. Primalluvium would be tolerable.'[63] Both *The History of the Inductive Sciences* and *The Philosophy of the Inductive Sciences* contain long sections of guidance on classical languages and scientific nomenclature. Whewell acknowledges that advance along the paths of scientific truth depends upon observation and the process of induction, but also that progress is assisted by the systematic use of technical terms. A further elaboration of the good practice of using classical roots for modern scientific nomenclature is a long section of *The Novum Organon Renovatum* of 1858, with a particularly interesting set of examples from the development of terms in geology. Lyell, always conscious of the importance of the link between geology and linguistics, required new terms to surmount the problem of the unsatisfactory variety of terminology left in the wake of the abandonment of Werner's theories. The term 'transition' rocks (between 'primary' and 'secondary') had been pragmatically introduced to modify simple Wernerism. Lyell turned to Whewell for advice and so the term 'hypogene' for 'nether-formed' rocks was introduced. These rocks in their turn were subdivided into unstratified or plutonic rocks and stratified hypogenes or metamorphics. 'Hypogene' has largely disappeared, but 'plutonic' and 'metamorphic' remain in the language of geology. Whewell would have argued that their strength was twofold, in their continuity with previous nomenclature in the history of science and in the assurance provided by their Greek and Latin derivations.

A lifelong personal involvement in composition, a common grounding in the classics and a fascination with language and its history account for Whewell's dwelling in the same domain as the poet. There is one further major sharing of values which we should bear in mind in thinking about the power of poetry for the scientist. It is the place of poetry in the scale of intellectual values. To Whewell, the most intellectual of the scientists, poetry stood on a very high pinnacle indeed, and correspondingly the status of poet was accorded great value. At a simple, practical level of broadening the base of knowledge, poetry and imaginative literature were regarded as important for self-development. In a letter to his sister, Martha, in 1821, he recommends a course of fiction 'for those with a retired life'. Such works, he says, enable the reader to understand, in a manner that could not conceivably occur by any other means, the 'principles and feelings which appear in human affairs, and the manners of different classes of society'. A year later, writing to his sister, Ann, he recommends the writing of Maria Edgeworth and, in so doing, makes a fundamentally Romantic judgement about the range of human experience: 'I can never believe that the imagination, the fancy, the taste of man, would have been so exquisitely constituted, as they are, if it could be a duty not to exercise them.'[64]

As Whewell engaged year by year in what became his major task of justification for, and explanation of, the scientist's task, he became more explicit about the place of poetry in the order of humanity's best activities. It is accorded a distinctly lofty station, but for procedural reasons, a place separated from science in the hierarchy. This is well illustrated by a long passage in the tenth book of *The Philosophy of the Inductive Sciences*. As on other occasions, it stems from an agreement with Cuvier's statement that the geologist is 'an antiquary of a new order'. The geologist and the antiquary are both readers of a text provided for us to understand the richness of Divine Creation. The geologist's endeavours belong to a range of studies including the human experiences of 'Government, Law, Poetry, Art':

we now perceive that there are several large provinces of speculation which concern subjects belonging to man's immaterial nature, and which are governed by the same laws as sciences altogether physical. It is not our business here to dwell on the prospects which our philosophy thus opens to our contemplation; but we may allow ourselves in this last stage of our pilgrimage among the foundations of the physical sciences, to be cheered and animated by the ray that thus beams upon us, however dimly from a higher and brighter region.[65]

THE CAMBRIDGE IDEOLOGY

There are two risks in attempting to understand a period such as the time from when Sedgwick became Woodwardian Professor of Geology (1819) to Wordsworth's death in 1850; it can be dangerous to accept, uncritically, two accounts – one ideology created in the period by the chief actors and the other generated by the research itself. In respect of the former, the Trinity men were as diligent as most members of the Geological Society to present a united front against scientific materialism on the one hand and, on the other, against fanciful and eventually threatening hypotheses such as biological transmutation or a godless creation of a never-commencing and never-ending physical world. The Truth which they wished to protect was that the world had been created with a purpose in God's mind and they asserted that their studies would do nothing to reduce that belief in the public mind. However, they stoutly defended the rights of their science; it should not be ruled out of court because it dealt with apparently threatening forces.

The Trinity geologists were not unusual or distinctive in espousing Directionalism in the period from 1820 to 1850 and in claiming that their studies confirmed Divine Providence at every step. When we read their assertions of confidence in the Maker's purpose we have to look beneath the surface for evidence of differences between the subgroup of geologists and, in particular, between Sedgwick and Whewell, otherwise it is too easy to record and acclaim a unity, which was true at one level, but not at another.

In the first place Cambridge geology did represent a different approach to the subject from that of Oxford and of many members of the Geological Society particularly those who were leading clergy of the Church of England. Secord (1986) analyses these differences. Oxford's intellectual background was in classical and theological studies and so men like Buckland and Conybeare present a geology concerned with historical processes and anxious to justify itself in relation to the Bible. Cambridge geology was primarily concerned with the practice of geology, charged by the influence of mathematics and Newtonian principles. 'Sedgwick, Whewell, Henslow, William Hopkins and John Herschel were all determined to bring geology's innocence to an end.'[66] Sedgwick's notebooks with their details of angles of dip and strike are instances of a new sophistication in the subject. He and Whewell were more disposed to measure patterns in the landscape, than to turn, as Buckland did, to attempts to write an account of the Deluge, tested in the caves and rock faces of England. Furthermore, Cambridge geology sprang from a strong mineralogical tradition which though it faded in priority order compared with geology, produced a link with European geology and practicality. Whewell was in fact a collector of minerals and a Professor of the subject before his duties widened and his polymath career developed.

It is important too to penetrate below the surface presented by the geologists themselves – a surface of bluff, robust controversy, ending when the Chairman had formally closed the meeting in convivial meals and manly good humour. Many of the controversies were deeply felt and passionately fought. The intensity of geological argument was more than a social habit, it rested upon urgent feelings for the moral implications of the theories being knocked about in debate. Dean (1992) explains why so much attention was given to Hutton's theories at the same time as the geologists who referred to him were urging readers to ignore his theory of the earth. They felt that the implication of Actualism were so serious for theological reasons that only an elaborate analysis and defence was possible. The enemy was identified as rationalism and atheism and the vigour of the attack was considerable. Another example of deeply argued geology was the argument between Sedgwick and Murchison on the correct stratigraphic division of the Devonian. Secord (1986) describes Sedgwick's passionate commitment to opposing his former friend's judgement as 'a moral crusade'. Sedgwick's conviction was that the facts of geology had to be securely constructed so they could be used as weapons in the battle against Utilitarianism, materialism, and the concept of transmutation of species. It is only when controversy is understood as an essential part of the process of science (and not as a pathology of science), Secord argues, that we shall understand how science was built. This statement is, I believe, particularly true of the period when the Trinity men debated geology. The modern researcher has to accept the common policies, such as Directionalism and a belief in providential order, as well as the divisions of their methodology and their diverse conclusions.

An ideology that we create for ourselves as modern observers can arise from living too closely with the material and seeking patterns of unity in it. This chapter, and indeed the subsequent chapters, will be guilty of endorsing a unity which arises from looking for it, unless, from time to time, balance is preserved by reminding the reader of diversities and contradictions. The concluding chapter will comment on the delicate task of hearing what was said over one hundred years ago and at the same time listening to it – a different act of perception. One device used in this text is the introduction of a slightly different voice, George Greenough's, to provide a contrasting colour to the two other main contributors to the dialogue. He has necessarily been little in evidence in this chapter, but is introduced for the reasons adduced in the subsequent chapters. At this point, in a chapter on Trinity men, one correction to an impression gained from continuous attention to Trinity voices may be necessary. Although unities are there to be identified, there were differences between the geologists themselves.

I have referred already to Sedgwick's Churchmanship – a form of Evangelicalism which Marston (1984) argues was comfortably tenable alongside what would now be called a liberal theological position in relation to science. In politics, Sedgwick was Liberal unlike the older Wordsworth. Whewell was of a different breed of Anglicanism, in some ways an older, more traditional kind, rooted in the plain faith of the parson of the previous century, the solid virtues of parish and associated Church. Brooke's study (1991) of Whewell's unpublished sermons suggests that he was a survivor of natural theology. Both Whewell and Sedgwick were united with Wordsworth in a broad front against radicals and utilitarians.

Neither Sedgwick nor Whewell should be confused with other Church or State political movements within Cambridge and specifically in Trinity College. Although Julius Hare and some of his contemporaries could justifiably regard Whewell as their patron in respect of Fellowships, he was not of their persuasion in Churchmanship or philosophy. Hare's espousal of the new European historiography, of Niebuhr in particular, was of little interest to the older Fellows. Similarly, Coleridge's studies of Church and State which attracted the attention of many of Trinity's young Fellows was not within Whewell's or Sedgwick's sphere of interest. Trinity was one of the biggest Colleges in early Victorian Cambridge and thus had the potential to contain a variety of positions on intellectual and theological matters. The researcher must ensure that, although there are shared visions, the varieties of belief are also recorded.

In many ways, Whewell's and Sedgwick's standing as cautious innovators, with a secure intellectual basis in the past intellectual traditions, may have been exactly what cemented the friendship with the mature Wordsworth in his conservative years. Their geology was part of this package of assurance – not threatening, on the contrary reassuring. The hypothetical issues of Deluge theory emanating from Buckland and others may have been less attractive for the poet than careful analysis by the trustworthy men whose education had been similar to his own. Certainly the poetic record contains little of interest in the Diluvial debate after 1820. The Trinity geologists' orderly description of landscape, their attention to the continuum of geological history, rather than to the catastrophic breaks or break of the earth's story, related much more closely to Wordsworth's own practical interests: the sense of the present patterned landscape and its great scale.

This chapter has been concerned with the social interconnection between two leading scientists and Wordsworth. The evidence so far rests on their record of shared social activities over a long period complemented by shared values and shared education. In part Sedgwick and Whewell grew to admire Wordsworth the man as well as Wordsworth the poet because of social opportunities. As this chapter has argued, we recognize these opportunities existed when we cease to think of Wordsworth as exiled in a northern remoteness. The literary and intellectual 'triangle of trade' of Cambridge, London, and the Lakes was of significance in the dissemination and interpretation of a national high culture. The last part of this chapter has focused on one aspect of that high culture, a common attention to poetry and to its wide-ranging values.

To explain how poetry and its related human arts were so elevated in the landscape of human achievements and why they are said by Whewell to dwell in a 'higher and brighter region', I shall have to turn to the major scientific work of Sedgwick and of Whewell, where, in historical and methodological terms, they pursued human intellectual activity to its frontier and on into the realm of morality. If we follow them on this quest, we shall understand better why they claimed a common intellectual and emotional companionship with Wordsworth.

CHAPTER 5

Order, clarity, distinctness

One of the most revealing comparisons of a shift in geological theory is between the explanations of the formation of the earth of Thomas Burnet's *Telluris Theoria Sacra* of 1684 and James Hutton's *Theory of the Earth* expounded in 1785 and 1795, later rewritten by Playfair in 1802. Even bearing in mind that by 1810 Hutton's theory itself smacked to contemporaries of antique geologizing, there are profound differences between the two theories in respect of the way they understood and how 'understanding' they approached Natural History. Burnet's theory was wholly study-based and theoretical, whereas Hutton's, though not as empirically founded as some of his followers claimed, was at least followed by observation and recording of phenomena such as igneous sills and dykes and unconformities in cliff faces, quarries, and other exposures. Hutton made records which have passed into the history of geology as landmarks of field observation. More contrasting still is the comparison of the two theoreticians' sense of the message conveyed by the landscape in its present state. To Burnet, the world is a ruin, softened in part by God's grace and by the sweat of human brow, but basically a wrecked vestige of a former Eden, which had been an ideal, smooth, and serene globe. Hutton's view prepares the way for a Romantic appreciation of a world which, far from being fallen, is enriched and has a history. For the faithful it is a living testament to God's Divine purpose. 'We perceive a fabric erected in wisdom to obtain a purpose worthy of the power that is apparent in the production of it' is the way in which Hutton expresses his confidence in the created world.[1] In other passages Hutton does not wholly abandon the conventional eighteenth-century metaphor of the machine; however, the machine he celebrates is not a wreck. It is like a living body which has a constitution in which natural decay is naturally repaired.[2] He expressed the notion of repair even more clearly in an early paper of 1785 presented to the Royal Society of Edinburgh: 'This is the view in which we are now to examine the globe; to see if there be in the constitution of this world, a reproductive operation, by which a ruined constitution may again be repaired, and a duration or stability thus procured to the machine considered as a world sustaining plants and animals.'[3]

To find an echo of that particular sentiment in Wordsworth's writing we shall have to consider examples which illustrate the balance or tension between duration and decay, which I consider in a later chapter. In this chapter, I wish to dwell on a shift of literary attitude to the natural world, which the geologists endorsed. The world, far from being a wreck of former glory, was alive and well, praised for its powers by poets, described by natural historians, specifically commended for its long-term stability, and sustained in its order by laws which were available for discovery by the new generation of geologists. This is not to say, however, that the human mind always found this ordered universe immediately explicable or predictable. The geologists and the artists of the early nineteenth century were fascinated by the evidence of disturbance, by eruptions of volcanoes, by meteors, and by vestiges of catastrophic events. Rupke (1983) and Pointon (1979) illustrate this absorption with the violence of nature, chiefly in the past, but from time to time in the present. Essentially the generation that led geology in the first forty years of the nineteenth century trusted that, whatever the surface appearance of chaos and physical confusion patently visible to anyone travelling outside the areas tamed by human efforts, there was a discoverable order, underpinned by discoverable laws, whose clarity would emerge through patient hard work and study. It is these features of order, law, and clarity which Wordsworth's natural universe also displayed in the poems of his middle and later years.

Along with a belief in the essential lawfulness of the physical world, despite the history of natural calamities, came an array of techniques and methodologies of study with the purpose of realizing orderliness. The collection and systematic recording of data, methodical observations, and logical explanations of laws of cause and effect were all orderly systems. Once a veil of obscurity had been lifted by systematic methodology, all would be clear. Taking on board observation of geological phenomena meant the abandonment of speculation about the origin of the earth, since such mental exercises could not be justified by methods and techniques of observation. Laudan (1987) gives a detailed analysis of this fundamental shift from eighteenth-century geology to that of the early nineteenth century. This reorientation did not, however, always mean the total avoidance of grand theories of explanations and origins. Hutton, Werner, Buckland, Lyell, and Darwin all offered universal explanations. Catastrophes of past times demanded a theory of history. What was being rejected was the ending of speculation in scholars' libraries supported imprecisely by collections of minerals in display cases. What was newly acceptable was a procedural system of field studies, measurements of strikes and dips across regions, and the systematic collection of fossils marked accordingly to location in strata. Hutton's famous sentence: 'The result, therefore, of this physical inquiry is, that we find no vestige of a beginning, no prospect of an end' is not a rejection of theories of the earth.[4] The sentence occurs in a text on that very topic. It is a statement of the limits of methodology and procedure. 'Vestige' and 'prospect' are about evidence and forecast based on experience. If no evidence is available, speculation on origins and forecasts are fruitless.

The axiom, 'To reason without data is nothing but delusion',[5] was firmly part of the agenda for most geologists after 1800, preparing the way by 1832, for the widely accepted concept of 'Actualism' in the popular work of Charles Lyell. The quest for data was not a sterile collecting obsession, substituting measurements of angles for the collection of minerals. Assumptions based on systematic collection were intended to reveal natural order and the ways by which laws operated to maintain that order. Statements of the inherent order of the world are not confined to the geological domain of thought. Hutton's substantial work of philosophy, *An Investigation of the Principles of Knowledge and of the Progress of Reason from Sense to Science and Philosophy*, is also a text about order. Chitnis (1976) links the two activities of Hutton thus: 'If the theory of the Earth is seen against this background, and then it can be viewed not as a work of a mere observer of rocks but a demonstration of the human mind achieved through an exposition of the order of the natural world.'[6] Hutton's statements are consistent with those of the geologists who followed him, who not only felt it a duty to find order in the natural world but also commended the endeavour of seeking it. Those who sought order avoided the discomfort of disorder. Order and law are natural to the scientist. Hutton wrote, 'the purposes of life lead naturally to those of science...In like manner, his mind is either displeased with or hates the thought of inconsistency and contradiction.'[7] Man, unlike the brute, who is satisfied with the surface of 'things as they are', seeks to know the past and the future. 'It is with pleasure that he observes order and regularity in the works of nature, instead of being disgusted with disorder and confusion.'[8]

The scientific description and explanation of landscape is pre-eminently an organizing, regularizing activity. To the untrained eye, there is little organization in any immediately graspable sense in any landscape which includes a variety of physical features. It was a striking quality of the great names in the early years of the Geological Society, that they addressed themselves to particularly difficult, varied land-scapes, such as the mountains of Cumbria, North Wales, and Scotland. It was as if they took up the challenge of the most chaotic, with a missionary zeal to bring order into the areas which had the fiercest resistance to system. William Whewell's major work in producing world tide tables similarly strove to regularize a large-scale universal phenomenon. Adam Sedgwick perhaps more than any early geologist except for his friend, and later rival, Murchison, is the best example of this zest for clarity when confronted by complexity. Secord says of him: 'Sedgwick's geological fame rested above all on his insight into structures, an ability to visualize rock masses in three dimensions and interpret their interrelationships after only a few traverses.'[9]

Of course, order and law have values written into them. Putting aside the most obvious links that sociologists of science from Structur-alist schools have made about geological strata and social hierarchies, there is an inextricable relationship at this period between a desire to find laws that demonstrate order and a religious belief in Direction-alism. The world is established not just to be a tidy, systematic place, but as a visible sign of a greater Divine system; it has been created in this way for a purpose. The time of the growing reputation of geology was also the time of *The Bridgewater Treatises*, a major activity devoted to justifying God's purpose by scientific argument. We should not over-simplify the Directionalism of the period. Buckland's contribution to the treatises, on geology, did not gain universal acclaim. George Greenough had serious reservations, not on the grounds that God had no observable plan, but because of the simplicity of Buckland's argument: 'Their contrivance has often the appearance of failure.'[10] In the field of morality, Sedgwick and Greenough are sceptical about Paleyianism. Both geologists appear to share with Wordsworth a distrust of over-simplified Divine determinism. Whewell's arguments in his own *Bridgewater Treatise* (1834) on astronomy and general physics and natural theology were considerably more complex than Buckland's straightforward apologetic. Whatever the depth of rationale and the reservations and twists and turns of the argument that led to a foregone conclusion of God's beneficence, there was little scepticism about what appeared as self-evident, namely that, although the universe might appear chaotic, there was a hidden pattern to be read.

One particular aspect of the change in the nature of the quest for order was the relative importance of geology itself in the scale of prestige of Natural History. David Allen (1978(1976)), amongst others, has described the attractions of geology to the early Victorians and noted the corresponding diminution of mineralogy. Mineral collecting in cabinets is an emblematic science for the eighteenth century. The 'cabinet' collections – so derided by the outdoor types, the field geologists of the next century – were essentially hierarchies, small samples of the earth's products in ranked and tidy drawers. They were 'wonders of nature' and evidences of strange circumstances from overseas or from deeper mines in the home country. Geology assumed a different kind of order in two ways, a description of geographical regions and an historical explanation. Adam Sedgwick's address to the Geological Society in 1831 on the structure of that complex area, the Lake District, illustrates the geological 'eye' at work. The quotation from his Presidential Address, cited in chapter two, is at one and the same time a topographical description (the map-maker seeing the region), an analysis of types of rock with a taxonomy of description (the three well-defined groups of Otley), and a system of technical terms associated with historical explanation ('carboniferous', 'superior (secondary) strata').[11] Wordsworth's own description of the Lake District in *A Guide* only differs from this in the amount of technical, geological information. The sweep of analysis of a landscape puts it in the same family as Sedgwick's description.

Mineralogy was an altogether different order of observation. Roy Porter says, 'By the early nineteenth century, for practitioners and the general public alike, geology was assuming the image of a more popular, profound and spiritual science than mineralogy or than orthodox Natural History.'[12] Wordsworth was aware of the hierarchy of the two sciences. In 1828 he wrote to Whewell, who had consulted him about Sir Uvedale Price's text on metre:

Your strong impression of the dryness of the subject somewhat reminds me of a tenet of Sedgwick's who maintains that a person may be too good a mineralogist for it to be possible for him to be a good geologist. In the same way, I suppose a person may be too good a writer of verses to be a good critic of versification or rather I should say a good anatomist of verse.[13]

Geology had ascended to a rank above mere technicality. A further reminder of the rejection of attitudes associated with eighteenth-century mineralogy is to be found in Wordsworth's use in *The Prelude* and in *The Excursion* of that most dated mineralogical epithet 'cabinet', to describe an attitude of detachment from nature, a withdrawal from life into the study.[14]

Geology is not only expansive in terms of the spaces it surveys, it is also more generous in spirit than 'cabinet' studies. As in astronomy, the subject whose leading position in the hierarchy of the sciences geology emulated, the ordering of nature was no routine business. Grand scales created grand emotions. Whewell, justifying the study of astronomy and physics in his *Bridgewater Treatise*, remarked on the intensity of scientific experience. Science is not a cold analytical activity dealing with a mechanical universe. Whewell quotes evidence from the biographies of past scientists such as Kepler, Galileo, Pascal, Boyle, and Newton, as well as from scientists he has himself known. At the instant when each thinker saw 'a law emerging from the mass of previously unconnected things', he experienced an unforgettable moment of belief in Divine beneficence, not unlike a Romantic vision or a Wordsworthian 'spot of time'. Whewell distilled from his study of great scientific predecessors a moment of truth, important enough for these thinkers to record it with joy and thanksgiving. These vivid occasions in the history of scientific discovery endorsed the aspirations of the nineteenth-century men of science at a time when there were many adverse criticisms of the paths pursued by their curiosity. It is in instances like this, when Whewell extolls the energy and zest for learning of past figures of science, that one can appreciate Cantor's recent statement that Whewell can be understood 'in terms of two opposing historiographical traditions – one rationalist, the other romantic'.[15] A great poet of the end of the preceding century, Goethe walked the same tightrope. In his *Italian Journey*, he writes of the revival of spirits that methodical scientific observation can stimulate: 'The truth is that, in putting my powers of observation to the test, I have found a new interest in life. How far will my scientific and general knowledge take me? Can I learn to look at things with clear, fresh eyes? How much can I take in at a single glance? Can the grooves of old mental habits be effaced? This is what I am trying to discover.'[16]

In *The Bridgewater Treatise*, Whewell engages with the emotional problems created by ordering and systematizing knowledge. A superficially depressing response could arise because of a scientist's attempts to order the vast scale of the universe. Wordworth's figure, the Solitary, in *The Excursion* has been made melancholy in this way. He has toyed with science and concluded that the world is a dead system. On the contrary, the effect of the researches of Whewell and the geologists is to affirm God's interest in humanity, because science will 'excite a desire to be able to contemplate more steadily and conceive less inadequately the scheme of his government and the operation of his power'.[17] Whewell argues that, although some may think that the revelations of the telescope make us feel the Almighty's care does not stretch down to such insignificant levels as human society, there is the opposite end of the natural scale revealed by the microscope: a 'teeming, rich world in the smaller paths of life':

It appears then that, if the first flash of that view of the universe which science reveals to us, does sometimes dazzle and bewilder man, a more attentive examination of the prospect by the light we thus obtain shows us how unfounded is the despair of our being the objects of Divine Providence, how absurd the persuasion that we have discovered the universe to be too large for its rule.[18]

WORDSWORTH AND ORDER

I have already made the point that *A Guide* is 'scientific' in the sense that its the aim was to order the apparently random and chaotic. The sequence of sonnets on the River Duddon gives a further instance of a systematic description of a river based on observation of its successive phases from source to sea. In the same decade of creativity, *The Excursion* was, amongst other things, a major apologia for an orderly world with a benevolent intention. The Solitary in books II and III or Margaret in book I, are characters who demonstrate the dire consequences of failing to trust in an ordered, benign universe. When Margaret gives up hope, her housekeeping deteriorates. Similarly, the Solitary's cottage is an untidy, disorderly collection of half-forgotten interests and hobbies. When order has been neglected, despair ensues. The Wanderer's stratagem for neutralizing the Solitary's deep despair is to reassert the orderly nature of the universe. 'The calamities of mortal life' are not denied. It is obvious that human beings may be 'sad or disturbed' (the last word again an epithet of disorder). Whatever their circumstances humans have experienced, the 'procession of our fate, howe'er / Sad or disturbed, is ordered by a Being / Of infinite benevolence and power.'[19]

Both aspects of God's actions, orderliness and benign intention, are frequently discussed in the works of contemporary geologists. They found affirmation for their religious faith in providence and confirmed their faith by reading *The Excursion*, for they found in the poem an argument for design and good order, which they too might have glimpsed in Nature as they undertook their own specialist studies. Even the most convinced Catastrophists in Great Britain – and by 1814, according to Gillispie (1951), there was a growing conviction in Great Britain and in France of not one but of successive phases of Catastrophe – were certain that there was, despite major breaks in geological history, an order associated with intention. 'Directionalism' was possible to hold hand in hand with a belief in successive extinctions and renewals of the earth's processes. Similarly, the Wanderer in *The Excursion* is able to acknowledge individual catastrophe at the same time as maintaining a belief in the general progress of the human condition, a progression which was intended and Divinely dispensed. The barest ridges and fells, formerly the emblems of the decay and ruin of the world, become in *The Excursion* the setting for order. For Burnet, and for those who followed or modified his work, the cultivated parts of the world represented order partially imposed by the human beings on disorder. In a doctrine of pre-lapsarian order, cultivation was also an attempt to restore what had been ruined. For Wordsworth the high fells are the places where renewal occurs in the human heart. The mountains, monuments of ruin and decay for Burnet, became for the older Wordsworth the texts of avowal of faith and, above all, of law.

The word 'law' is used in *The Excursion* in a variety of ways. 'Law' in the following passage means fixed and unvarying principles or regularity in different species or in different contexts. Contemporary scientists used 'law' in this sense, for instance when comparing species:

> Happy is he who lives to understand,
> Not human nature only, but explores
> All natures, – to the end that he may find
> The law that governs each.[20]

At least, as far as this poem is concerned, Marjorie Nicolson's assertion that Wordsworth, Byron, and Shelley had 'delight in irregularity' is not confirmed.[21] There is another wider sense of 'laws' which Wordsworth prefaces with the word 'general' in the next quotation. It is an overriding, major condition of life on earth laid down by the Creator, affecting the past, the present, and the future:

> Trust me, that for the instructed, time will come
> When they shall meet no object but may teach
> Some acceptable lesson to their minds
> Of human suffering, or of human joy.
> So shall they learn, while all things speak of man,
> Their duties from all forms; and general laws,
> And local accidents, shall tend alike
> To rouse, to urge. . .[22]

This level of law or laws is eternal. In the section when the friends take simple lessons from the graveyard with the help of the Pastor, they are confronted with the depressing threat of change. What are they to learn from the memory of the long-dead Elizabethan knight? Despite the inevitable changes and revolutions in society, the Wanderer reassures his companions, there is a law of direction, a doctrine of gradual conservation. The 'vast frame of social nature' is always changing; there is 'restless generation' and 'restless decay'. 'And by this law the mighty whole subsists: With an ascent and progress in the main'.[23] In book IX of *The Excursion*, the word 'law' occurs seven times. According to de Selincourt and Darbishire, it was used three times more in the lines omitted from the final text of that book. It is too easy to suggest that the frequency of the word confirms the growing conservatism of Wordsworth and his expression of anxiety about civil and social disorders. I believe this is an over-simplified reading of the essentially complex issues that law and orderliness raised for Wordsworth and to which he devoted a never-completed enquiry.

The word 'law' is not confined to the middle and later years of the poet's life. In *The Prelude* of 1805 Wordsworth writes as characteristically as he is to do in 1814 in answer to a question of doubt and despair:

> What then remained in such eclipse, what light
> To guide or chear? The laws of things which lie
> Beyond the reach of human will or power,
> The life of Nature, by the God of love
> Inspired – celestial presence ever pure.[24]

In book VII of *The Prelude*, dispersion and confusion are the opposite of law:

An undistinguishable world to men,
The slaves unrespited of low pursuits,
Living amid the same perpetual flow
Of trivial objects, melted and reduced
To one identity by differences
That have no law, no meaning, and no end.[25]

Gillian Beer, in her seminal study of Charles Darwin, writes that the early Victorian 'tracking of fixed laws' was: 'part of the comforting inheritance of Romantic thought in Victorian science which seemed to assure a continuance of natural truth through the action of permanent discoverable laws'.[26] By arguing that *The Excursion* acted as a comforting authority to scientists, I am not suggesting that Wordsworth simply took from scientific studies a system of order, turned it into verse, and endorsed it. With such a poet there remained ambiguity behind most assurances. There is more than one meaning in his statements on both law and order. They are never opposed to happiness nor do they override joy.[27] *The Excursion* is a text asserting moral as well as physical laws and reaffirming that they underlie the good life. Law becomes an assurance in the later work and a source of admiration and of sustenance, encouraging faith in the individual, but it is not invariably comforting in the sense of providing small-scale daily solace to the troubled mind. The power of the Almighty is awesome in its enforcement of regularity on vast physical forces:

How beautiful this dome of sky;
And the vast hills, in fluctuation fixed
At thy command, how awful![28]

If the laws of nature are there to be discovered, how best can they be pursued? Although Wordsworth presented a distinctively orderly method of description in *A Guide* and elsewhere, there is in the poetry an undeniably mixed attitude to enquiries that seek to impose order on nature. The classic instance of a dismissal of one style of scientific conduct is in *The Prelude*. Addressing Coleridge, Wordsworth writes:

Thou art no slave
Of that false secondary power by which
In weakness we create distinctions, then
Deem that our petty boundaries are things
Which we perceive, and not which we have made[29]

Consistent with this criticism of mentally created categories and false systematization is the statement in *The Excursion*:

> Enquire of ancient Wisdom; go, demand
> Of mighty Nature, if 'twas ever meant
> That we should pry far off yet be unraised;
> That we should pore, and dwindle as we pore,
> Viewing all objects unremittingly
> In disconnexion dead and spiritless.[30]

Not only is the ordering function of the human mind dangerous because it generates mental (not actual or natural) categories, its character is evaluated by that most condemnatory Wordsworthian negative, 'joyless'.

Left at that point, it would be understandable to consider Wordsworth as a Romantic writer who delighted in the unity of Nature but who was constitutionally opposed to its analysis. Reading in greater detail in *The Excursion*, and even in preparatory passages to *The Excursion* to be found in *The Prelude* of 1805, we can find the opposite tendency, one that gives due recognition to discriminating methods. Any serious student of nature (and we can include geologists) would require not only to see natural reality but to understand it. Their reward is happiness: 'Happy is he who lives to understand / Not human nature only, but explores / All natures.'[31] The promise of joy continues for the discriminating, distinguishing mind. Unlike the false objectivity of the deadening observer, the understanding discriminator is granted a bonus of heightened feeling: 'for knowledge is delight'. There is more benefit still. Delight 'breeds Love' and thence access to adoration of the supreme Creator, the highest form of love. This ladder of ascending reward is remarkably similar to the satisfaction claimed by the geologists, an ascending emotional and moral quality as their studies advance.

The two lines following the last quotation from *The Prelude* are worth more examination ('Where begins / The Union; the partition where'). The activity of perceiving nature is both 'union' and 'partition'. Partition is not the dissection of a dead thing. The difference between the perception of difference and the scalpel-like process of 'prying' lies in the attitude of the observer, who pursues his task not out of curiosity but with an element of worship and purposeful enquiry. God's divine plan is there to be perceived, not merely by abstract ingenious apologetics or by arguments of design. Wordsworth was as sceptical of crude Paleyanism as Greenough, Sedgwick, and Whewell.[32] We can not reorder Nature, making it a plain map with a convenient pattern. Greenough in his notebooks put the essential complexity thus: 'In the works of nature we see everywhere proofs of design – but not unity of design. We find variety of purpose, inconsistency, frailty counteracting design, perishable, insufficient provisions – useless precaution.'[33] Greenough is no despondent Solitary. He believes, from his Unitarian, Nonconformist base, as firmly as Sedgwick, Whewell, and Wordsworth from theirs in the established Church, that God's purpose could be discerned by patient careful discrimination. Eighteenth-century plain sense as the route to appreciating God's plan had dispersed into the complex routeways of a more elaborate age, yet still an age of continued confidence in that plan. Surface clarity had given way to complexity. The quest for order leads to a different level of the appreciation of what is presented by Nature to our eyes.

THE AMBIGUITY OF CLARITY

In Wordsworth's writing after 1810 clarity assumes an ambiguous and conflicting position. In *A Guide* there are a number of points where Wordsworth takes pains to illustrate how the traveller may perceive transitory visions of the mountains particularly when they combine with mist and sunlight. Thus, in the section 'Miscellaneous Observations', Wordsworth relates the appearance in Ullswater of a 'magnificent Castle', which, his previous knowledge tells him, is only the reflection of a ruined tower. Earlier ages, he adds, may have believed in 'subaqueous palaces, gardens and pleasure grounds – the brilliant ornaments of Romance'. Modern man knows, however, 'the actual processes of Nature'. In an earlier section describing the lakes, he notes that their very surface can be so clear that someone in a boat might imagine that it was 'suspended in an element as pure as air, or rather that the air and water were one'.[34] Mists and vapours exhaling from the lakes and meadows give a visionary character to everything around them. The inverted image of a large bird, such as a raven or heron, may be seen in the lake amongst reflected clouds. These visions have a powerful effect on the feelings of the spectator, yet Wordsworth is not concerned merely to shock and amaze the traveller; he is also acting here in a scientific manner in that he carefully describes, but also explains phenomena. He aims to show how 'other elegant fancies may have had their origin, less in invention than in the actual processes of nature'.[35]

A good example of Wordsworth's role as a demystifier, yet as a poet who wants us to be as equally aware of mysterious visions as of natural phenomena, is the description of what appeared to be a 'newly created Island' in Grasmere one winter's day. Wordsworth and his companion behaved at first like Gray's or Gilpin's travellers. They were 'alarmed'. They then recovered and in a different mood began to examine and describe, creating a map of the island in prose. Then came the apostrophe: 'Marvellous was the illusion! Comparing the new with the old Island, the surface of which is soft, green and unvaried, I do not scruple to say that, as an object of sight, it was much the more distinct. "How little faith", we exclaimed, "is due to one sense, unless its evidence be confirmed by some of its fellows!"'[36] The 'island' gradually disappeared, having been revealed as a reflection in a bed of ice. Wordsworth gives a technical explanation. The ice 'had produced the illusion, by reflecting and refracting (as persons skilled in optics would no doubt easily explain) a rocky and woody section of the opposite mountain named Silver-how'. This is the country both of illusion and of the emotions that accompany illusion, yet also the country where rational explanations are given and accepted.

In a later edition of *A Guide* there is a section directly borrowed from Dorothy Wordsworth's journals where we best see the combination of a visionary interpretation of the landscape together with a correcting steer of reality; the apparent is clear, the reality is obscure. From the summit of Scawfell Pike, Dorothy sees what she believes is a ship at sea. The wise, experienced old guide who conducts the party points out that what she sees is also like a horse. Then reality takes charge – it is in fact a changing cloud. Minutes later the guide's experience and good sense enabled him to interpret the meaning of the phenomenon and to warn his charges of their danger. He sees a storm imminent when the party only sees the clear light of the sun and intriguing shapes in the sky.

In the poetry of the period after 1820 what is at first sight plain and simple is not only deceptive in visual terms; it may also be deceptive morally. Clarity becomes dangerous. In the Duddon sonnets there is a sequence beginning with 'Tradition'. This is the folk-tale, half told rather than fully concluded, of the 'love lorn Maid' who drowns reaching for the perfect rose reflected in the deep pool. The sonnet which follows 'Tradition' puts aside 'sad thoughts' and passes on to the mundane activities of sheep-shearing. In the later poems written after 1820, clear water is not always what it seems. The River Rhine makes its appearance briefly in *Memorials of a Tour on the Continent*, 1820 and more substantially in *Ecclesiastical Sonnets* of 1822. In the last-named collection the Rhine is used as an elaborate analogue for the reign of Charles the First which changed from political content to revolutionary rage. The river like the State has only an illusion of stillness. Like the Jungfrau 'where men below / Wonder that aught of aspect so serene / Can link with desolation', the waters appear 'at a little distance' to be calm, but the reality is soon very different:

> but on they go
> Fretting and whitening, keener and more keen;
> Till madness seizes on the whole wide Flood,
> Turned to a fearful Thing whose nostrils breathe
> Blasts of tempestuous smoke.[37]

The Rhine appears again in the concluding sonnet of the series, but it is then progressing out of its obscure condition to a transformed clarity:

> Look forth! – that Stream behold,
> THAT STREAM upon whose bosom we have passed
> Floating at ease while nations have effaced
> Nations, and Death has gathered to his fold
> Long lines of mighty Kings – look forth, my Soul!
> (Nor in this vision be thou slow to trust)
> The living Waters, less and less by guilt
> Stained and polluted, brighten as they roll,
> Till they have reached the eternal City
> Built for the perfected Spirits of the just.[38]

Clarity and turbulence, peace and strife, often associated with water which is deceptively still or clear, are strangely mixed in these later poems. 'Musings near Aquapendente; April 1837', a poem by a water-fall, has markedly shifting moods of repose and anxiety, sadness and nostalgia, together with a forward-looking commitment to poetic power. In the same sequence there is a sonnet, 'Near the Lake of Thrasymene', which also opposes peace and disturbance and, in so doing, employs emotions associated with the stream that flows in an historic place, for this was the location of the battle between Rome and Carthage. The river, aptly named Sanguinetto, once flowed with blood but now is a 'Sweet stream! as crystal pure'. The cleaned river stands for the eradication of an evil past. Immediately afterwards in the thirteenth sonnet, the memories of bloodshed are again invoked. Wordsworth first creates a purified place, then raises a haunting by the chief and the men who perished in the famous battle. Calmness and clarity are once again revised and qualified. Still, clear water is, as it were, muddied by violence.

The Itinerary Poems of 1833, based on Wordsworth's journey to the Isle of Man, provide another example of the alternation of clarity and turbulence. In the nineteenth poem, 'By the seashore, Isle of Man', the poet praises the clarity of the sea:

> Why stand we gazing on the sparkling Brine,
> With wonder smit by its transparency,
> And all-enraptured with its purity? –
> Because the unstained, the clear, the crystalline,
> Have ever in them something of benign;
> Whether in gem, in water, or in sky.[39]

There is a falseness in this benignity however. The sea is not as divinely pure as it appears, for 'Temptation centres in the liquid calm'. We are fascinated and tempted to plunge in 'revelling in long embrace with thee'. The next sonnet illustrates the effect of surrendering to that temptation. It is the story of a young man who, mistaking clarity for shallowness, had to be saved from drowning. Incidentally, the note in de Selincourt's edition tells us that in about 1828 the poet's son, William, saved the youth's life. The point is not, however, biographical. A moral lesson is preached. The youth, being innocent, knew nothing of human deception. His action in stepping into seductive purity is only recovered by Divine intervention; 'He survives to bless / The Power that saved him in his strange distress.'[40]

DISTINCTNESS

Wordsworth's middle and later poems, so often assumed by their surface message to be sermons of compromise and of acceptance, of conservatism and stillness, retain the younger poet's ability to render an ambiguous emotional commitment, or, more plainly, to present a contradiction, never more so than in those passages concerned with the interaction between the human observer and the observed outer world. From *The Excursion* onwards the reader is made aware of humanity's subtle mental power, the ability to comprehend unity and, conversely, to distinguish between objects in Nature, to separate out from a mass its component elements. The distinguishing facility, conflicting and uncomfortable in its application though it may be, is pre-eminently a scientific set of mind. An example would be the predisposition of the geologist who patiently distinguishes strata in a cliff or quarry face or the discrimination of the palaeontologist who plots the incidence of fossils or fossil traces across strata and distinguishes between minute variants in appearance. The early geologists clearly recognized that theirs was a task involving contrasts or oppositions between phenomena. Equally, they required to be satisfied about what was similar as well as about what was different. There is an early Romantic source for this dual ability. Goethe rejoiced in his new-found skill of separating the part from the whole yet, by separation, encompassing the whole. In a classic statement of the physical geographer's craft, he notes in *Italian Journey*: 'I find I can quickly get a topographical idea of a region by looking at even the smallest stream and noting in which direction it flows and which drainage basin it belongs to. Even in a region which one cannot overlook as a whole, one can obtain in this way a mental picture of the relation between the mountains and the valleys.'[41] Hutton in his painstaking analysis of how the human mind proceeds in a scientific enquiry writes in *An Investigation of the Principles of Knowledge*: '[It is] by the Knowledge of identity and difference that is first formed the science of ourself, by knowledge of quality and inequality that the science of external things is made to proceed in our mind.'[42] Greenough similarly faces the dilemma of the observer of nature. In Nature, he writes in his notebook (UCL, 29/3), there are no demarcations or even clearly-edged shapes, everything passes away by almost imperceptible gradations. To Greenough, science 'is not a picture of nature', it is an activity committed to making distinctions where on the surface few appear. This is precisely the descriptive challenge for Wordsworth in *A Guide*'s first paragraphs, as he considers the complex mass of Lake District mountains when approached from the south. The human mind and eye have to discriminate and separate in order to describe.

At a less descriptive, more epistemological level, Whewell also contemplates the essentially scientific activity of separating identities from a mass. As we have seen, he associates this special process with the thrill of discovery a scientist enjoys when he observes 'a law emerging from the mass of previously unconnected things'. In a minor publication, *Two Introductory Lectures to Two Courses of Lectures on Moral Philosophy* (1841), there are passages parallel to those in other major works, but in addition the progressive clarification generated by scientific method is addressed. Experience is the origin of speculation, but the intellectual process that follows experiential learning is not only cumulative in the sense of an accretion of ideas, it is also cumulative in 'distinctness', an interesting word:

But gradually by the acting and reaction of man's practical and speculative nature upon each other the ideas unfolded from this rude and latent form, contemplated by the reason with more and more distinctness, the man ever trying to understand more and more clearly the things which he himself does, till at last since nothing is inconsistent with itself can be fully realized, the constant effort which he makes to realize his thoughts and to understand his actions, brings the idea before him in the perfect clearness and distinctness which constitute science.[43]

Whewell gives an example of this cumulative process from the development of the scientific idea of force, unfolding from the first crude notions in Aristotle. Scientific knowledge ascends by a series of steps, a succession which leads to 'distinctness of ideas'. Whewell refers to the history of geology for a precise example. 'The period of classification' out of the unformed perception of the apparent chaos of natural landforms produced much clearer patterns such as 'the general form of mountain chains, the relation of the direction and inclination of different chains to each other, the general features of mineral veins, faults and fissures; the prevalent characters of slaty cleavage'.[44] The last named instance of geological clarification was, of course, one of the achievements of his friend and colleague, Adam Sedgwick. In their turn these geologically identified patterns become available for the generation of new ideas. Clarity and 'distinctness' are progressively at work.

Is this quest for 'distinctness' exactly what Wordsworth castigates as false clarity, murdering by dissection, 'secondary powers' creating false schemata? To answer that question, we shall have to pursue the word 'distinctness'. Though obviously related to 'distinctions', 'distinctness' has a life of its own, stronger two hundred years ago than now. There is a particularly good example of Wordsworth's own use of 'distinctness' in *The Excursion*, book IV, made more striking by the narrative context in which it is placed, a direct statement of a vision for science. In the following passage, Wordsworth is writing about science in the original, non-modern meaning of a general area of organized knowledge, but the emerging meaning of science in its modern sense is also apparent. The Wanderer sets out a long argument to correct the Solitary's despondency. His message is one of the gradual education of the mind in its communion with 'the Forms of nature'. He proposes a gradual development, a moral education, which will grow into 'the glorious habit by which sense is made / Subservient still to moral purposes, / Auxiliar to divine'. The newly clothed and no longer dejected spirit will then be prepared for a subsequent enhancement:

Science then
Shall be a precious visitant; and then,
And only then, be worthy of her name:
For then her heart shall kindle; her dull eye,
Dull and inanimate, no more shall hang
Chained to its object in brute slavery;
But taught with patient interest to watch
The processes of things, and serve the cause
Of order and distinctness. . . [45]

Dr Johnson's *Dictionary* gives eight different meanings for the word 'distinction', including social distinction and a variety of shades of sense gathered around the idea of the individual identity of things or people, but it only offers two narrowly differentiated meanings for 'distinctness'. One of those meanings is concerned with clarity and unimpeded vision. Johnson supported this definition by a quotation from the seventeenth-century thinker, John Ray's *The Wisdom of God Manifested in the Works of Creation*. His other meaning is 'such separation of things as makes them easy to be separately observed'. I believe that Wordsworth in the passage from *The Excursion* is conscious of both meanings when the Wanderer commissions science as the 'precious visitant'.[46]

Following first the meaning associated with clarity, there is a substantial reason for pursuing Johnson's reference to John Ray's use of 'distinctness'. Wordsworth at various times either owned or had access to Ray's *The Wisdom of God*. It was in the library at Racedown and, later, the Wordsworths held Coleridge's copy of Ray's *Travels in Europe*, 1673. The most interesting connection between Ray and Wordsworth in this context is the function of the eye in the pursuit of a form of clarity which means something more than 'clearness'. It is concerned with seeing things as they really are, rather than what they first appear to be. There are, Ray says, two reasons why all the membranes and humours of the eye are perfectly pellucid and void of colour; first for clearness, secondly for the 'Distinctness of Vision'. If the eye had been itself 'tinctured' with a colour it would 'refund the Colour upon the Object and so it would not be represented to the Soul, as in itself it is. So we see, that thro' a colour'd Glass things appear as well more dim and obscure, as tinctur'd with the Colour thereof.' The eye is not only a beautiful organ in itself, it is the means of conveying such qualities as beauty to the soul. Ray employs a lively set of images to convey the eye's functions and in so doing adopts again the word 'distinct'.

As the Eyes are the Windows to let in the Species of all exterior Objects into the dark Cells of the Brain for the Information of the Soul, so are they flaming Torches to reveal to those abroad how the Soul within is moved or affected. These representations made by the Impressions of external Objects upon the Eye are the most clear, lively and distinct of any other.[47]

The 'dull eye' of science, in Wordsworth's passage quoted above from *The Excursion*, will be transformed. As a 'precious visitant' science will assume the qualities it does not currently possess, chief among which is the capacity to admit light to the heart. In its future role of assistance to the developing mind of man, the eye of science will no longer be 'dull and inanimate'. If chained to an object the dull and inanimate eye can never be, to use Ray's term, a flaming torch. Wordsworth's vision of what science can become also employs a metaphor of heat: the inner 'heart' of science will 'kindle'.

In *The Prelude* human sight and the inner recognition of essential truth are juxtaposed. In this passage again the word 'distinctness' appears:

> Twas only then when gross realities,
> The incarnation of the spirits that moved
> Amid the poet's beauteous world – called forth
> With that distinctness which a contrast gives,
> Or opposition![48]

Wordsworth here uses the term 'distinctness' to describe his experience as a young city-dweller awakened by Shakespeare's drama. The passage continues with a figure of seeing: 'As by a glimpse, the things which I had Shap'd / And yet not shap'd, had seen and scarcely seen'. In a passage in *The Excursion*, the Wanderer castigates the scientists whose treble handicap is first, that they cannot see, second, that they have the gift of sight but do not use it and, third and above all, their blindness is without joy:

> Shall men for whom our age
> Unbaffled powers of vision hath prepared,
> To explore the world without and world within
> Be joyless as the blind?[49]

In an earlier draft of this passage, the reference is even more specifically to the scientist who 'the optic glass of science has prepared' and those who attempt to 'weigh / The planets in the hollow of their hand'. In the same book of *The Excursion* there is another passage which might almost be a translation into Romantic terminology of Ray's duality of 'eye' and 'soul', but it has a third component. Wordsworth suggests in the following quotation a threefold division of labour between eye, heart, and soul. The Wanderer says that even the uneducated have a moral sense learned at their mother's knee:

> a Man so bred
> (Take from him what you will upon the score
> Of ignorance or illusion) lives and breathes
> For noble purposes of mind: his heart
> Beats to the heroic song of ancient days;
> His eye distinguishes, his soul creates.[50]

In such a being, the three human components act in a co-ordinated manner. The ultimate component, the soul, acts with creativity, whereas the heart's function is to feel. For its part the eye is active in its special function of distinguishing.[51]

The second meaning of 'distinctness', as defined by Johnson, 'such separation of things as makes them easy to be separately observed', also demands attention. In *The Prelude* Wordsworth deplored the process of separation either because it was a false categorization or because it broke into parts what was inherently whole. For Coleridge too there was a further inherent danger in the over-discriminating mind, that of excessive individuality. In a letter to Southey in September 1802 he makes a doctrinal statement of the opposition of wholeness and singleness and significantly it includes a figure of speech from science or chemistry in order to explain what should not be the case:

Nature has her proper interest; and he will know what it is who believes, and feels, that everything has a life of it's [*sic*] own, and that we are all *one life*. A poet's *heart* and intellect should be *intimately* combined, and unified, with the great appearances in Nature – and not merely held in solution and loose mixture with them, in the shape of former Similies.[52]

Within Coleridge's statement is both a statement of 'a life' for 'everything' and yet 'one life' for all. Similarly in the great hymn of unity in *Home at Grasmere*, composed in 1800 but used again in the 'Preface' to *The Excursion*, Wordsworth combines individuality and unity allowing both their interlinked part:

> How exquisitely the individual Mind
> (And the progressive powers perhaps no less
> Of the whole species) to the external world
> Is fitted; and how exquisitely too –
> Theme this too little heard of among men –
> The external world is fitted to the Mind.[53]

'Distinctness' in its second meaning is concerned with individuality but also with the perceptive faculty of being able to distinguish between one thing and another, which to the untrained eye appear to be the same. Again the figure of 'the eye' is a starting point. In book IIII OF *The Prelude* Wordsworth claimed that in Cambridge days he 'had an eye / which in my strongest workings evermore / Was looking for the shades of difference / As they lie hid in all exterior forms.'[54] It is the fine distinctions, the shades of difference, which occupy and refresh the maturing mind, but (and it is a major 'but') this skill to identify distinctness is directional – its ultimate aim is to reveal the elements of a fundamental union. We can look again at the lines from *The Excursion*.

> Happy is he who lives to understand,
> Not human nature only, but explores
> All natures, – to the end that he may find
> The law that governs each; and where begins
> The union, the partition where, that makes
> Kind and degree, among all visible Beings.[55]

Here is the same spirit the geologists pursued in seeking 'distinctness'. They sought to be precise about particularity within what appeared to be a mass of undifferentiated material. The geologists, like the poet, were aware of the processes of the mind that enable it to particularize and yet to comprehend how individual elements combine in a unity. An examination of the word 'distinctness' reminds us of the absorbing problems involved in distinguishing 'objective' and 'subjective' reality, a problem for the poet as it was for the geologists. George Greenough, for example, distinguishes between Nature and the mind that studies it. Science he says, in his psychological notebook, consists in making distinctions, in identifying differences whereas Nature makes none, all is unity and gradualness. Scientific activity is twofold – to see differences clearly and to see the wonder of connections. Indeed, as a geological map-maker, he demonstrates one of the major activities of 'distinctness', the analysis in pictorial form of the components of a landscape, yet the depiction of the whole unified terrain.

Greenough, Whewell, and Lyell concerned themselves with a corollary of 'distinctness', the naming of geographical and geological phenomena that have been scientifically distinguished. For the early geologists, along with the quest for 'distinctness' went the necessity to name. The 'new' identities they had abstracted from the complex mass of phenomena before them required a new vocabulary, but one which had to be internally consistent. One of the earliest committees established in 1810 by Greenough and the Geological Society was on nomenclature.[56] A consistent nomenclature was identified as a priority in the list of aims of the new Society in the first Council minutes of 1807. In chapter four, I give examples of Whewell's major influence on the new language of science. Sedgwick was also an innovator in this activity, for instance, he introduced into English from the German the word 'strike', and in a letter to Professor Jukes he claimed to have been the first to give a word for the limbs of folded strata ('synclinal').[57] To particularize and to name the components of half-distinguished folding, much of that phenomenon being out of sight, is a good instance of serving 'the cause / Of order and distinctness'.

DISTINCTNESS AND SYNTHESIS

I have already quoted a passage from *The Two Introductory Lectures* where Whewell used the word 'distinctness' as the objective of scientific activity. It should be noted, however, that he also turned to the philosophically vibrant word 'understand' in the same passage. To Whewell there are two interrelated intellectual processes which ideally should be combined in a productive mental activity. Along with the power of the human mind which progressively, rationally, and system-atically identifies 'distinctness', there must be understanding, a synthe-sizing faculty. Whewell, Sedgwick, and their contemporaries in the Geological Society began to free themselves from rigid rules of procedure or from inflexible Baconism. Laudan notes this new spirit amongst the generation younger than Greenough who assumed leading positions in the Society: 'Geology in England did not begin to flourish until a younger generation of geologists argued for a more liberal geology and put it into practice.'[58] The new geologists were conscious of the considerable power of their science and they rejoiced robustly in its achievements, but they were equally aware that this power, if exercised without a sense of the unity which it examined, was potentially destructive. When Adam Sedgwick addressed Wordsworth in his geological 'letters' accompanying *A Guide*, he reassured the poet and the reading public that science was under control. As geology advanced 'further towards exactness we shall observe only that hitherto perplexing phenomena are seen to be operating under laws'.[59] Seeking 'distinctness' by controlled methods will clarify perplexity, and in so doing will reassure those who have been confused or dismayed by the apparently disordered and chaotic.

It is in passages such as this where the geologist reassures the poet and, of course, his thousands of readers, that science leads upwards to law and not outwards in dispersion into particularities, that we can seen Romanticism and science in close harmony about their purposes and ends. Meyer Abrams (1971) in his close analysis of the features that marked Romanticism in Europe, particularly identifies the synthesis of two different directions of thought, individuation and unity, in post-Kantian European thought. Coleridge's mature philosophical works are major texts for this 'Romantic spiral' of progression from primal unity to a new, higher unity through thought. Abrams sums up the complex synthesis which Wordsworth's and Coleridge's contemporaries who studied geology would have accepted in their own language and agreed as the proper end and purpose of research: 'One must add that what was most distinctive in Romantic thought was the normative emphasis not on plenitude as such, but on an organized unity in which all individuation and diversity survive, in Coleridge's terms, as distinctions without division.'[60] The next chapter pursues the theme of 'organized unity' as a quest to which poet and geologists were dedicated and to which they openly referred within their communities of discourse.

CHAPTER 6

'The universality of Nature's kingdom'

Adam Sedgwick in his third 'letter' on the geology of the Lake District, adopts an interesting word to describe a quality which, he believes, Wordsworth's poetry encapsulates: 'no-one has put forth nobler views of the universality of nature's kingdom than yourself'. 'Universality' is defined immediately: 'All nature bears the imprint of one great Creative Mind and all parts of knowledge are, therefore of one kindred and family.'[1] Because these 'letters' were not addressed to a scientific audience, but were both personal and public, it might be assumed that Sedgwick had taken a non-scientific flight into fanciful philosophy, but his statement about universality is not peculiar to this one citation. Universality is a concept used here by one geologist, but it is also explicit in other geologists' writing, and it is a feature of Wordsworth's language devoted to the interrelationship of Nature and humanity. Levere (1990) proposed that science provided a key to intellectual and imaginative issues for Romantic writers: 'The search for interconnectedness, of reticulation, not only within a given realm of discourse, but between different realms, is surely one of the distinguishing characteristics of Romantic striving, and it informs Coleridge's life work.'[2] The belief in the universal within all nature is clearly expressed in Sedgwick's Presidential address to the Geological Society in February 1830. Admonishing, not for the last time, those who attempt to delay or even to terminate the advancement of geology on grounds that it is not reconcilable with Scripture (on this occasion in Dr Ure's *New Systems of Geology*), Sedgwick affirms that truths never war against each other. New discoveries will give us 'a larger insight into the universal harmonies of nature'.[3] Furthermore the exploration of a common truth, if pursued into its remotest consequences, will terminate 'in beauty and harmony and order'.[4] Geological investigation not only discovers what is common in all forms of nature but discovers in this association the aesthetic and the moral. Again in the third 'letter' to

Wordsworth's *A Guide*, Sedgwick uses an image of unity which is doubly revealing. The present harmony will itself disappear into a new universal: 'all bonds of matter shall be cast away and there shall begin the reign of knowledge and universal love'.[5]

The metaphor of binding or knitting together is a favourite image for Sedgwick. In his preface to a *Catalogue of Fossils* (see Burn, 1873) for use in the university, he refers to 'the wonderful manner in which the materials of the universe were knit together by laws'. Similarly in the preparatory remarks directed to Wordsworth in the first 'letter' accompanying *A Guide*, Sedgwick speaks of 'the laws by which Nature binds into union two different portions of her kingdom'.[6] As these quotations indicate, there is not one generalized law but laws in the plural which operate in various components of the natural system. In *A Discourse on the Studies of the University*, Sedgwick proposed a hierarchical and harmonious interrelationship of material laws. Every portion of matter however small is governed by its own laws. On the next, superior layer are the laws which govern the relationship between one element of nature and others. Above all there are the ultimate laws: 'all are the harmonious results of dominant laws'.[7] The assiduous student of geology will eventually discover the truth of the knitting together of this unity of operations.

There is of course, an even larger unity – that of the Divine purpose. Cannon (1978) has used the term 'the Victorian Truth Complex' for the unity between religious and scientific belief, with geology occupying a normative role in maintaining this complex, but the phenomenon is earlier than the Victorian period and for many scientists did not last long within it. Cannon again writes: 'The early Victorians denied the possibility of even two truths, but the later Victorians had to live with many as we do.'[8] Sedgwick certainly displayed a robust confidence that geology would lead to a confirmation of the Divine plan and not to the confusion of traditional belief. In the extension to his text, *A Discourse on the Studies of the University*, Sedgwick launched a formidable defence of a Divine plan which was, he asserted, discoverable at every step of geological investigation. This spirited counter-attack was mounted in response to *Vestiges of Creation*. Chambers (later discovered to be its author) had proposed a theory of development as an organic force, just as gravity is a force in the inorganic field. Creation, according to Chambers, was a single event. Species occurred by 'transmutation'. This, to Sedgwick was a process of descent, not one of ascent, and denied the benign plan. He had already marshalled his argument in the 'letters' accompanying *A Guide* in 1842. There he addressed a wider public audience than the Geological Society or the British Association, but, conscious perhaps of the poet's accompanying prose, he assumed that his readers required magisterial reassurance about the confidence derived from his studies:

We can not believe that these successive forms of animated nature were created and destroyed by the mere impulses of a capricious will: but we do believe that they were called into being, and wisely adapted to the successive conditions of our planet, during its progress from a chaotic state till it reached the perfection in which we now find it. The Author of Nature has, during all periods, formed organic beings on the same great plan.[9]

The earth, he claims, is like a great laboratory, a place for us to study processes which observe natural laws. Natural conditions may change – after all any students of the strata and the fossils within them must be aware of environmental revolutions – but 'natural laws' are unchanged. Furthermore, these major processes of nature are not permanently hidden, to be believed in as a matter of trust or faith; they are discoverable. Perplexing phenomena will become clearer as regularities under the laws' regime as scientific techniques advance towards 'exactness'.

Sedgwick's apology for geology has been used to introduce the theme of universality, but it must not be assumed that he is alone in his understanding of the universality of nature as a manifestation of the Divine plan.[10] Greenough, publicly an exponent of the Baconian spirit of judging only by observation, is equally confident expressing the theoretical statement that the world is an interrelated system closer to that of biological organisms than to that of mechanical structure. Even in his most carefully constructed geological text of 1819, which purports to avoid all speculation and urges systematic methodology for new geologists, Greenough is stimulated to tell of the connection of the parts and of the wonder of universal nature. In a phrase reminiscent of Wordsworth's 'violet by a mossy stone', he writes: 'No less true than striking is the remark of the author of a work entitled *Contemplations of Nature*, that there is no picking up a pebble by the brook-side, but we find all nature in connection with it.'[11]

The man who gave most thought to the methods of scientific enquiry, William Whewell, also endorsed both the interconnectedness of material things and the purpose of the whole. Necessarily in his *Bridgewater Treatise* he took up the argument of Divine purpose, but, because Buckland had been given geology as a subject, Whewell's material is vaster – 'Astronomy and General Physics'. Although much of his *Treatise* is Paleyian in its general thesis of Divine direction, there is an additional confidence and reassurance in it for a generation which had outlived Paley and had to learn to absorb Lyell and would eventually accommodate Darwin. Susan Gliserman says of the *Treatise*: 'I am not sure that Whewell is entirely successful in his rescues, but, more than any other science writer at this time, he gives a definite emotional hope to the negative possibility uncovered by scientific investigation.'[12] Throughout the *Treatise* there is affirmation of the hidden hand of a benign and intentional God. The word 'assent' so important for both Wordsworth and Newman in their different spheres of faith, figures in the following statement by Whewell: 'All that claims our assent on those higher grounds on which theology takes cognizance must claim such assent as is consistent with those grounds; that is it must require belief in respect of all that bears upon the highest relations of our being, those on which depend our duties and our hopes.'[13]

That quotation usefully introduces a central dilemma in a doctrine of universality linked with Directionalism. The Almighty's plan has been to create a harmonious world governed by a system of laws linking all forms of creation, but what are the roles of human will, faith, and judgement? Is there, in short, a separate set of laws for human behaviour, particularly for human moral behaviour or are we part of the same law-directed system as 'rocks, and stones, and trees'? That question raises another: is the principle of universality restricted to the middle band of a created scale, the non-human but animate world, or is it so inclusive that it includes rocks and stones at one end of the spectrum and, at the other end, the human mind? The geologists, who, it must be remembered, saw themselves as theologians and philosophers, addressed these questions. Before considering their response, and indeed to lead into a consideration of it, I wish to turn to Wordsworth's own perception of an integrated, universal world.

WORDSWORTH AND UNIVERSALITY

The identification of human attributes and feelings in Nature is a marked feature in the early poetry of Wordsworth. Rivers and mountains speak as if with a human voice. The wind and the clouds communicate with the (remembered) child and there is a 'presence' in the hills, on the mountain roads and in the waterfalls of the Wordsworthian Lake District, Salisbury Plain, or the Quantocks. The question of Pantheism in the early poetry and whether Wordsworth recanted his views of this subject have been discussed frequently. I therefore wish to turn mainly to the poems written after 1810 for evidence of the mature poet's understanding of the dual connectedness of Nature, within the non-human world and between Nature and men and women.

In *The Excursion* the Wanderer argues that the universe may appear rugged and cold, detached from human standards of caring, but it is in fact a carefully constructed system, well intentioned towards humanity. The Wanderer puts it thus:

> These craggy regions, these chaotic wilds,
> Does that benignity pervade, that warms
> The mole contented with her darksome walk
> In the cold ground; and to the emmett gives
> Her foresight and intelligence that makes
> The tiny creatures strong by social league.[14]

The interdependence of nature, even in apparently inhospitable regions, is not a mechanical, reproductive, self-sustaining cycle. It is a system which has enjoyment at its heart by a 'participation in delight':

> What other spirit can it be that prompts
> The gilded summer flies to mix and weave
> Their sports together in the solar beam,
> Or in the gloom of twilight hum their joy?[15]

The worst kinds of scientist or knowledge seeker, the archeologists, botanists, and geologists criticized by the Solitary in book III, lack the natural joy which much simpler beings possess. The sin of these narrow scientists is to divide and to partition and, worst of all, to carry out their task as dull-eyed observers rather than as participants in the universal system of nature. Their view of the world is one of naming of parts. Such scientists inhabit a broken universe which they have themselves divided by their analytical methods. The Wanderer is at pains to persuade his listeners that impressions of dispersion and separation in the physical world are misleading. The underlying unity of all life is there to be seen, if it is discerned with sensitivity, faith, and love by those who have an educated, receptive mind. In the future, scientists will be admitted to enjoy this vision, but they must approach as servants not as masters. I referred previously to the passage in *The Excursion*, book IV, about the admission of science to the highest appreciation of Nature. We should notice the religious image in the passage. Science will be a 'precious visitant', admitted to a place of worship. The language is also legal and constitutional: the scientist of the future will be allocated 'a province' which he is to hold in loyalty ('a support not treacherous'), supporting 'the mind's excursive power'.[16] Science can become enrolled as a ministering activity of the human mind, which is in the inner sanctum of the great unity of creation.

The testimony to the wholeness of Nature and of man's part in that unity is in the climax of *The Excursion*. The final book of the poem opens with a long invocation by the Wanderer, eventually leading to the closing, near-idyllic scenes of the final narrative. These episodes have, when judged in dramatic terms, the most movement of the long poem. They depict changing scenes and involve a larger cast of participants than in preceding episodes. The ideal family, including the idealized children, join the philosophizing friends walking towards the lake in a state of what can only be called transcendent peace. They row across the quiet lake, rest on an island, and then return to the hill-slopes for an evening's blessing by the Pastor. The party eventually divides and the narrative quietly concludes with a promise of the eventual completion of a longer work, *The Recluse*. Book IX is, in effect, the closing movement of a pastoral symphony. It begins with a confident theme of elaborate testimony by the Wanderer:

> 'To every Form of being is assigned.'
> Thus calmly spake the venerable Sage,
> An *active* Principle: – howe'er removed
> From sense and observation, it subsists
> In all things, in all natures; in the stars
> Of azure heaven, the unenduring clouds,
> In flower and tree, in every pebbly stone
> That paves the brooks, the stationary rocks,
> The moving waters, and the invisible air.
> Whate'er exists hath properties that spread
> Beyond itself, communicating good,
> A simple blessing, or with evil mixed;
> Spirit that knows no insulated spot,
> No chasm, no solitude; from link to link
> It circulates, the Soul of all the worlds.[17]

This highly charged testament is interesting for those tracing Words-worth's changed attitudes to childhood and maturity in his middle years. Humanity's 'active powers' continue in maturity unless they are impeded by sorrow and adverse social circumstances. They are naturally strong and, given freedom to grow, will suppress 'noxious qualities' (such as plainly have ruined the Solitary's composure). The 'active principle' will encourage overflowing gladness and a rich blessing for the mature years of a happy man. This is a vision promised for the fulfilment of all people, yet the actuality is sadly marred in modern life by social pressures and accidents. The 'active principle' is at its full in childhood (we should expect no less from this poet), but is still available for the mature and the old.

The extract above ends with the figure of a chain ('from link to link / It circulates'). A chain is a frequent enough figure of speech throughout intellectual history. 'The Great Chain of Being'[18] could be interpreted in a mechanical way as a linked set of parts, acting as a programmed set of passive components articulated into a unity. Such an image was familiar to the Associationists. Ideas, to the followers of Hartley, were chain-like. The human mind was itself a link between natural objects or events, yet essentially, despite its distinctive molecular nervous vibrations, one of those material objects in itself. The first major section of book IX of *The Excursion* contains the best examples of Wordsworth's use of the familiar image of 'The Great Chain of Being' transformed into something distinctively non-mechanical. In Wordsworth's hands the figure of speech takes on movement: 'It circulates, the soul of all the worlds.' He infuses the abstract idea of connectedness with his personal perception of energy. The images of the opening lines of book IX are about changing forms, not about stasis, they are about a variety of dynamic forms of linkage. There are links of sound as well as of vision. The experience of Nature is about 'breathing in' sensation as well as about sensations received through the five receptor senses. In short, the sensation of universality arises because the participant is an active partner in the experience. The images are of change and life. A selection from the first forty-eight lines of book IX produces the following images of movement and exchange of sensations: 'the unenduring clouds'; 'the moving waters'; 'properties that spread'; 'no insulated spot, / No chasm, no solitude; from link to link / It circulates'; '[we] breathe the sweet air of futurity'; 'their happy year spins round'; 'so moves the man'; 'the walks / of childhood'; 'the incense that ascends'; 'to breathe in such estate'; 'the stir of hopeful nature'.[19] A commentary on the language of the Wanderer in book IX would be incomplete without an acknowledgement that a powerful set of words associated with 'flowing' persists throughout the opening speech:

> What more than that the severing should confer
> Fresh power to commune with the invisible world,
> And hear the mighty stream of tendency
> Uttering, for elevation of our thought,
> A clear sonorous voice, inaudible
> To the vast multitude.[20]

Here the cataract is both the communication and the communicator, if only human beings can allow themselves to be the active receivers. Wordsworth frequently uses figures of speech deliberately close to non-figurative language. The poet's partnership with Nature is a communion with a voice which is real even though there is no immediately traceable source, like the streams which are unseen but can be heard across the mountain ranges. 'The mighty stream of tendency' refers to Nature's contribution to discourse as well as to the progress of humanity. Any other image of movement, trite or fresh, well-worn or newly minted, would not have done, for this is the language of the hills itself.[21]

The sequence of sonnets on the River Duddon, further illustrates the older Wordsworthian theme of the unity of nature both within itself and with humanity. Despite the varied scenes portrayed in individual sonnets, there is a structure to the sequence which creates a dominant impression of unity for the reader who reads the sonnets as they were intended, as one poem. There are many unities – the unity of time, the unity formed by the single stream from source to mouth, and the interwoven themes of natural and historical destiny. There is a presiding sense of reconciliation throughout the sequence. The overall pattern of the collection from 'Dedication' to 'After-thought' is, as I noted in chapter five, a framework for the theme of time, but, although time is deeper than human history, the purpose of the sequence is to reassure that there is continuity from non-human past to human present – 'The Form remains, the Function never dies'. The sonnets present a Divine contract with humanity, a reconciliation between human tradition and a law-governed physical world. In the dedicatory verses preceding the sonnets, Wordsworth celebrates a pact of concord, which includes two forms of control, tradition and law:

> Hail, ancient Manners! sure defence,
> Where they survive, of wholesome laws;
> Remnants of love whose modest sense

Thus into narrow room withdraws;
Hail, Usages of pristine mould,
And ye that guard them, Mountains old![22]

The human party to the contractual order is never absent in the sonnet sequence. It is domestically confined 'into narrow rooms': the traditional Christmas minstrels of the dedication, the children safely playing at Cockley Beck, youth and age at the Stepping Stones, the shepherds and their families, Wonderful Walker's simple place of vocation at Seathwaite Chapel, and the homely folk-tales associated with the Duddon. Nature's part in the balance is ultimately benign and reconciled, although Nature stands apart in a position of authority. The Duddon itself can be angry and violent, a force with its own, far from domestic imperatives. Sonnet xiii, 'Open Prospect', portrays 'angry Duddon Sweeping by' the hamlet where people have withdrawn to share companionship with each other 'when bleak winds roar / Through the stiff lance-like shoots of pollard ash / Dread swell of sound!' At Seathwaite, the river, to use the poet's own term, changes its 'temper' and becomes Bacchanalian in its wild excitement. Then, further downstream at that symbol of human continuity and peace, the Kirk of Ulpha, the unseen river 'gently roars'.

Within the natural non-human sphere there are agents of peace and stability. The River Duddon is both reconciled and a reconciler. The upland springs amidst the bleakest and most severe mountain passes are protected by 'thy handmaid Frost'. The 'whistling Blast' that destroyed the mighty prehistoric forest 'guards' the infant Duddon. Despite the inauspicious origins in the high fells, the river itself is a creator of harmony and a benign worshipper of Nature:

Yet thou thyself hast round thee shed a gleam
Of brilliant moss, instinct with freshness rare;
Prompt offering to thy Foster-mother, Earth![23]

By Cockley Beck there is a reciprocity of care. The alders, the ash trees, and the birches have created a shelter for the river's channel which, in its turn has tempted human dwellings to be built safely 'mid sheltering pines'. The stream progresses, contributing to the landscape, feeding the flowers (sonnet vi) which, in their turn, refresh the bees and small birds. By sonnet viii the stream's benign purpose is clearly revealed. Whatever it witnessed of pagan rites, its function 'was to heal and to restore / to soothe and cleanse, not madden and pollute'. This is no pagan stream embodying a grotesque god. Its healing function is directed towards nature itself as well as to the works and culture of humanity. Man may do the river harm – the sheep-washing in sonnet xxiii pollutes the stream and the noise destroys the peace of the valley – but 'the stains are fugitive'. When there is drought, the Duddon's function is healing. Its voice is soothing and practical:

> whose murmur musical
> Announces to the thirsty fields a boon
> Dewy and fresh, till showers again shall fall.[24]

This sonnet sequence presents a cyclic, ultimately non-catastrophic view of Nature, but not an absolute rejection of extinction or of catastrophe, for there are the far-off echoes of a time when the Deluge may have altered the whole world (and the word 'may' is important). The sequence is an affirmation that the processes of Nature are ultimately renewing and long-lasting. The doctrine of accord between Nature and the divine purpose would be sympathetically regarded by a scientific community committed to explore the great forces of nature, but equally confident that geological enquiries would lead to ultimate truth, to evidence of a Divine intention, and to confirmation of traditional religious belief.

UNIVERSALITY OF THE PAST

The connectedness of the three natural categories, the inanimate, the animate non-human, and the human, is one dimension of universality. A different dimension is temporal, the unity of the past and the present, a theme of significance in Wordsworth's later works. Charles Lamb saw this clearly when he commented on the central importance of the churchyard scenes in *The Excursion*: 'The part (or rather main body) which has left the sweetest odour on my memory (a bad term for the remains of an impression so recent) is the tales of the Churchyard.'[25] *A Guide* provides evidence of Wordsworth's awareness of a longer period of natural life than mankind's own history. References are made first to a landscape into which man the hunter makes his first appearance and second to animals that no longer exist. Wordsworth asks the reader to imagine a landscape without people, when, quoting Thomas West's *The Antiquities of Furness*, 'the *bellum inter omnia* maintained the balance of nature in the empire of the beasts'. This Edenic state was interrupted:

When the aboriginal colonists of the Celtic tribes were first driven or drawn towards it, and became joint tenants with the wolf, the boar, the wild bull, the red deer, and the Leigh, a gigantic species of deer which has been long extinct, while inaccessible crags were occupied by the falcon, the raven and the eagle. The inner parts were too secluded, and of too little value, to participate much of the benefit of Roman manners.[26]

Remoteness protected the mountains, at least from the Romans and perhaps from Celtic tribes. Nature was then in harmony, richly populated by animals and birds, some of which are no longer part of our experience. Extinction, inherently in conflict with patterns of plenitude, has been acknowledged.

The Duddon sonnets demonstrate this mature Wordsworthian theme of the universality of past and present. Even in tourist-swamped Lakeland today, there is a sense of timelessness about the Duddon Valley. Travelling from Little Langdale over Wrynose Pass by a metalled road and following the valley from the topmost point of the pass, the modern car driver cannot fail to be struck by the difference between this valley and the better-known and perhaps even more striking scenic areas of the Southern Lakes. There is an immediate sensation of remoteness at Wrynose Pass. The human scale is limited and development restricted. Whereas Grasmere, Rydal Water, and even Great Langdale are well visited and relatively populated with tourist accommodation, with many farms and, in the last-named place, remnants of quarrying, wide stretches of the col of Wrynose Pass and then the gentle slopes and open pastures around Cockley Beck before the constricted passage of the river at Seathwaite are notably short of human dwellings. If this is true today, and even taking into account post-nineteenth-century rural depopulation, it must have been especially so in Wordsworth's time. He could, as we can today, compare the well-known and the least-known areas of the Lake District. The Duddon Valley's atmosphere of an undisturbed landscape suggested to him a time before human habitation. Only the most remote regions, such as the Pass of Kirkstone, could claim the same distinction as a landscape of timelessness, yet with a reminder of what had been extinguished and lost. The vanished, natural past before human occupation, as well as the vanished Celtic and Roman worlds, is imaginatively revived in the collection of poems and sonnets of 1820. Myth and classical legend introduced into a number of the sonnets also act as points of historical reference.

The dimension of history is enlarged by Wordsworth's knowledge of Natural History and archeology. The uppermost levels of peaty, wild

grassland and exposed rocks where the Duddon's many springs arise
are depicted in sonnet ii as once the habitat for:

> Those mighty forests, once the bison's screen,
> Where stalked the huge deer to his shaggy lair
> Through paths and alleys roofed with darkest green;
> Thousands of years before the silent air
> Was pierced by whizzing shaft of hunter keen![27]

Wordsworth's own note of 1820 explains that the deer 'is the Leigh, a
gigantic species long since extinct'. Canon Rawnsley in the late nineteenth century, the indefatigable researcher into the locations of
Wordsworth's poems, observed in the upper Duddon valley fragments
of birch trees exposed by the stream, giving evidence of former forests.[28]
After five sonnets describing the blissful harmony of wind, trees, bees,
and small birds, with children at play at Cockley Beck, the peaceful
scene is again disturbed by a world at the moment of the first human
occupation: 'What aspect bore the Man who roved or fled, / First of his
tribe, to this dark dell.' A little further in 'Open Prospect', sonnet xiii, the
undisturbed pre-human landscape appears again, but in another place
at another time: 'loud as the gusts that lash / The matted forests of
Ontario's shore / By wasteful steel unsmitten.' This non-human distant
landscape is immediately balanced in the final lines of the sonnet by the
actuality of the human scene in England, with the laughing 'generous
household' of Donnerdale people gathering around 'the warm hearth'.
Closely following those lines is the most primitive reference of all, to the
Flood, in sonnet xv, which I have previously noted.

The sonnet sequence's final poem is concerned with the present and
future as well as the distant past:

> I see what was, and is, and will abide;
> Still glides the Stream, and shall for every glide;
> The Form remains, the Function never dies;
> While we, the brave, the mighty, and the wise,
> We Men, who in our morn of youth defied
> The elements, must vanish; – be it so![29]

In one sense the sonnet sequence and 'Ode: The Pass of Kirkstone',
published with the sonnets, is about an historic time, the world of
triumphant Roman armies or of the arrogant warriors of remote
castles, but it also celebrates an ever-present natural world, depleted
though it is by extinction. There is universality of time, a continuity
with the past, filtered through the poet's memory. The 'Ode: Com-

posed upon an Evening of Extraordinary Splendour and Beauty',
written in the summer of 1817 and perhaps completed at the end of
that year, also unites the remote Edenic past, the poet's youth, and the
present. The extraordinarily beautiful evening is not a transitory
moment's glimpse of beauty – 'But 'tis endued with power to stay'. It
originates in a blissful time when angels sang in perfect harmony
linking earth and heaven. Their perfect song could not be more
moving in its effect on the poet than the present evening scene: 'This
silent spectacle – the gleam –/The Shadow – and the peace supreme'.
The theme in the second verse paragraph is again that of linking past
and present, heaven and earth within a patriotic context, a typical
notion in Wordsworth's later poetry:

> From worlds not quickened by the sun
> A portion of the gift is won;
> An intermingling of Heaven's pomp is spread
> On ground which British shepherds tread![30]

If we omit the third verse printed in the 1820 (River Duddon edition)
and read the next verse of the ode as it appeared, according to
Ketcham, in the Dove Cottage manuscript of 1817, the time linkages
are more striking. These visions 'from some celestial urn' were the
colour of the poet's own morning, of his 'blissful infancy'. They restore
him, at least temporarily, rejoicing in a 'second birth', then the 'Night
approaches with her shades'. A powerful association for any reader of
Wordsworth must be the echoes of the 'Ode: Intimations of Immortality' completed in 1804. For a student of the later poems, the interest
of this ode of 1817 is in its published association with the River Duddon
sequence of 1820 and with *A Guide*, depicting the permanence of the
landscape. It is a new Romantic interpretation of immortality overriding extinction and change.

UNIVERSALITY AND THE FUTURE: IMMORTALITY FOR HUMANS OR FOR ALL?

Immortality was in the poet's mind in a companion ode in the Duddon
sonnets in the 1820 publication, sometimes called 'The Vernal Ode'.
Wordsworth himself directed the reader to its theme in a dictated note
to Isabella Fenwick: 'Composed to place in view the immortality of
succession where immortality is denied as far as we know, to the
individual creature'.[31] This was clearly a topic of some importance to

those beginning to feel anxiety about the evidence of extinction in palaeontological studies, but we should concentrate here on what the poet selects in order to convey immortality. The first images are again classical and religious. Like the previously considered ode in the 1820 collection, the angelic is evoked. A landscape of perfection is praised, it is the perfect abode for angels, one of whom has descended to earth. The poem is in fact the song of this imagined figure, appearing not in reality, but 'in presence of that spiritual eye / That aids or supersedes our grosser sight'. This is a country of the eternal and the inextinguishable. In the 1819 text, the stars are 'free from semblance of decline'. However, in a much later emendation (1832–1836) even the galaxies may be subject to decay. In the later version, the stars may fade and be extinguished, as contemporary astronomy tells, but the Divine intention is to send out through their successors tokens and images of perpetual peace:

> What if those bright fires
> Shine subject to decay
> Sons haply of extinguished sires,
> Themselves to lose their light or pass away
> Like clouds before the wind
> Be thanks poured out to Him whose hand bestows,
> Nightly, on human kind
> That image of endurance and repose.[32]

Eternity is now internalized, through the eye of the beholder. This amended poem, from Wordsworth's old age, had a long time-span in mind, as long as the death and renewal of stars, but the Almighty's benevolence to humanity makes use of natural symbols, even of these, the oldest vestiges of extinction.

As the ode proceeds, the theme moves from greater to smaller things. Survival is the eventual theme of this ode, in the humble shape of the bee. The bee's murmur to the drowsy ear of the poet-angel

> A slender sound, yet hoary time
> Doth, to the *Soul* exalt it with the chime
> Of all his years; – a company
> Of ages coming, ages gone;
> Nations from before them sweeping
> Regions in destruction sleeping.[33]

The humming bee and its primitive origins complete the ode. The bee's ancestry is traced to a time of earthly bliss, perhaps even, 'Thy sting was needless then, perchance unknown'. Angels and men mixed familiarly and there was a 'universal heaven' combining earth and stars in a pre-lapsarian serenity. This idyllic scene may be of a long-lost Eden, but the present-day bee is in England and the angel of the opening lines has descended to play his golden harp in a very earthly spot, within an English landscape. The angel himself is compared to a firm, old, British castle tower. The reality of the English landscape on an April evening provides the setting for the play of fancy on the 'spiritual eye' of the poet. Immortality as a theme returns in the final lines: 'Though yet confined to earth', the poet's soul 'Rejoices in a second birth'. Although the final line threatens extinction ('And night approaches with her shades'), the poet has been reborn in this very present world. Extinction and decline are not ignored, but the living present triumphs because it has two vital sources for survival: the actual English landscape and the receptive and creative soul of the poet. The connection between the spiritually timeless and the present actuality, which may be extinguished in one form but returns in another, elaborates the idea of immortality. Whereas in 1804, Wordsworth's great ode was about human immortality and the origins of human feeling, there is in the later poems an extension of this theme into the other forms of the natural world. As usual there is no easy, unqualified connection. Perhaps because of a self-imposed discipline to avoid Pantheism, or perhaps because Wordsworth is a poet who inevitably qualifies and controls his expression of beliefs, the notion of universality and of its association with immortality is not straightforward. Are animals or plants guaranteed immortality? Are stones a different order of perpetuity, but within the same scale of universality? These were two questions which disturbed the new generation of biologists and geologists as they encountered the phenomena of extinction and the vestiges of long departed life in the fossil record.

In a relatively short collection of late poems, *Yarrow Revisited, and Other Poems* published in 1835, there is one sonnet which typifies Wordsworth's conception of the universality of animate and inanimate nature. The fifth poem in the sequence, entitled 'Composed in Roslin Chapel, During a Storm' depicts the poet sheltering in an ancient chapel listening to the sound of the wind. His eyes are attracted by some weeds growing between the building stones, the animate and the inanimate combined in a place set apart for faith:

From what Bank
Came those live herbs? by what hand were they sown
Where dew falls not, where rain-drops seem unknown?
Yet in the Temple they a friendly niche
Share with their sculptured fellows, that, green-grown,
Copy their beauty more and more, and preach,
Though mute, of all things blending into one.[34]

The source of the incident was, as so often, Dorothy Wordsworth's journal, on this occasion from long ago, the Scottish tour of 1803. The particular setting of this poem in a religious, historical building is indicative of the issues entwined around the older Wordsworth's idea of the universal. First, is the sheltering poet whose imagination is stirred, and next is the uniting, cohesive power of an ancient religion. 'All things blending into one' is a sermon of the stones of history, of the living plant and the poetic observer – past and present, animate and inanimate – indeed 'all things'!

The later poems, although they have a literary consistency with the poems of the middle years, have as stronger, persistent themes, religious belief and its roots in English history. If *The Excursion* proposes that the answer to the doubter's depression lies in accepting the benign nature of the caring Almighty, the later poems do more than propose, they insist on that view. God is a far-seeing, kind deity who protects all His creation and that creation is not restricted to human or even to living things, though He makes distinctions between them. The unity of the inanimate and the living, which the early poems tentatively explored, is in the later poems confidently asserted because of the assurance of God's overarching care. In this respect Wordsworth makes an important philosophical statement about the extent of the Creator's beneficence, in contrast to persuasive and popular writings of Christian apologists such as Paley. Wordsworth endorses the unity of the inanimate and animate, yet distances both from the human condition. As Fitzgerald has noted: 'by degrees, and certainly by 1805, the perceiving mind and the object it contemplated separated into a dualism, whereby the human mind appears ontologically different from and superior to nature'.[35]

One theological difficulty which obstructs a belief in the total unity of all nature, human, animate, and inanimate, is the doctrine of immortality. Immortality in traditional Christian doctrine has been promised to human beings. The inanimate world of mountains, oceans, and valleys has been regarded as long-lasting but temporary

remaining until the will of God closes the account and ends his
creation. An apocalypse was the dramatic closing scene for the created
world, except for the human element of creation which was guaranteed
immortality in another world. There is scattered evidence in the later
poems of Wordsworth's vision of the ending of our world. An explicitly
didactic example, introduced by a prose 'argument', is 'On the Power
of Sound' (composed 1828 and published in 1835):

> A Voice to Light gave Being;
> To Time, and Man his earth-born chronicler;
> A Voice shall finish doubt and dim forseeing,
> And sweep away life's visionary stir;
> The trumpet (we, intoxicate with pride,
> Arm at its blast for deadly wars)
> To archangelic lips applied,
> The grave shall open, quench the stars.[36]

How far an apocalypse was a confidently held article of faith for
intellectuals in 1830 is difficult to say. For geologists who accepted
Playfair's summary of Huttonian theory or Lyell's Actualism there
appeared to be a truce in the debate on the finitude of the physical
world ('No vestige of a beginning, no prospect of an end'). Sedgwick
confidently asserted the unity of Nature in the Divine plan but also
held a vision of a heaven which left behind material creation. In his
later poetry, Wordsworth is careful to state a conventional religious
case, when he has to do so, about the end of the world. He is clearly
orthodox, in defining the difference between individual immortality
promised to humans and that denied to other animate beings. This
definition, however, kept open the possibility of a form of eternity,
although perhaps not an individual one, for the non-human. In sonnet
xxiv of *Memorials of a Tour in Italy*, 1837, 'In Lombardy', there is an
affecting scene depicting a labourer in a mulberry garden. The old
man bends under his load of mulberry leaves. The silk worm spins at
her ease, the old man serving 'as her slave'. Both will 'pass into new
being' but the old man can have hopes of endless bliss and glory,
whereas the worm 'Transfigured, sinks into a hopeless grave'. Proffitt
(1982) has argued that Wordsworth in the later poems has turned away
from 'redemptive' views of immortality to more generalized statements
of universal rather than individual immortality. This is an interesting
point of view, but I have some reservations about its overall applic-
ability. In the first place, I have not found any abandonment of a belief
in individual human immortality in the later poems. Wordsworth's

statement to Isabella Fenwick about 'The Vernal Ode' of 1817 that the poem was 'to place in view the immortality of succession where immortality is denied as far as we know, to the individual creature',[37] suggests to me a position recognizing two classes of immortality – individual for humanity and a different, perhaps generalized future for the non-human world. It is illuminating to consider how his close friends were able to discuss individual loss with the poet. On 10 August 1847 Adam Sedgwick wrote to Wordsworth after the death of Dora Wordsworth: 'I know there is one topic of consolation, and one only, I dare to touch upon – your daughter is now an Angel in Heaven – no man who has the hopes of a Christian can doubt this for a single moment.'[38] The sympathy might appear to us to be conventional, but we have no reason to believe that Wordsworth, in his seventy-seventh year found it unacceptable theologically.

Wordsworth's earlier unorthodox understanding of death with its theory of ever-present continuity, conveyed most clearly in 'We are Seven', was many years in the past. The strange child of that early poem displayed a confidence in continuing individuality, surviving death. In Wordsworth's later years, something of that faith in a kind of eternity persisted, but extended to the non-human world. A poem of 1835, 'The primrose of the rock', celebrates the blessing of a Divine providence applied to all non-human nature, animate, and inanimate, despite the annual repetition of death:

> Close clings to earth the living rock,
> Though threatening still to fall;
> The earth is constant to her sphere;
> And God upholds them all:
> So blooms this lonely Plant, nor dreads
> Her annual funeral.[39]

The 'living rock', the primrose and the constant earth belong to an economy of a natural system established to interconnect the non-human elements of the world under Divine protection. Geologists, exploring the animate turned into inanimate, plant and creature into hard fossil, found reassurance in this kind of verse.

Despite their frequent assertion of God's Divine plan, the British geologists of the first forty years of the nineteenth century faced intellectual problems about the idea of immortality. Their private, theological language may have been about Eternity, but their public dialogue was about extinction or about the progressive appearance of species. The two worlds were reconcilable if a long view was taken of a process of equilibrium guided by a Divine hand. Some forms of nature may have become extinct, but, argued Sedgwick in his determined attack on Chamber's *Vestiges of Creation*, palaeontology shows no evidence to conflict with the 'balance of nature'. Chambers had proposed major rifts in nature by 'transmutations' of species. Sedgwick robustly maintained that there was a 'balance of nature' and a continuity of species. His argument could be summarized by Wordsworth's own phrase about 'The Vernal Ode', 'an immortality of succession.'

Many sources sustained the enthusiasm of the students of rocks and stones, of strata, folds, and angles of strike and dip, but one important spring maintaining commitment for their subject was the quest for confirmation of links between their hard, ancient subjects of study and the softer less durable parts of the natural system. Levere (1981) shows Coleridge in his later years elaborating a complex thread of unity between the geological and biological worlds. Coleridge invokes the vegetable origins of marble, coal, coral, and peat to support the theory that Levere claims he acquired from the German philosopher, Steffens and from 'Naturphilosophie': 'Chemical substances were transmitted through nature into the substance of living organisms. Geology thus drew on and led into chemistry, biology and the life sciences.'[40] Coleridge's later philosophical weavings from the German threads of post-Kantian nature theory may never have entered into Wordsworth's reading. In a sense, they would have been superfluous for he had already appreciated, striven for, and tried to express in his poetry a world where the stone and the flower have a unity of immortality.

Earlier in this chapter I quoted from the passage in *The Excursion* where the Wanderer explains that there is a reassuring gift of abundant happiness in the natural world, a world where the mole is content with 'her darksome walk in the cold ground', where gregarious animals live together for 'participation of delight' as much as for protection. The joy amongst the living animals, birds, and insects is celebrated, but the Wanderer's hymn of praise continues into the non-biological sectors of nature:

> 'And, over all, in that ethereal vault,
> Is the mute company of changeful clouds;
> Bright apparition, suddenly put forth,
> The rainbow smiling on the faded storm;
> The mild assemblage of the starry heavens;
> And the great sun, earth's universal lord!'[41]

The vast, inanimate world of nature is also graced by God's plenitude of joy; it is of no lower rank than other components of the non-human world, but it is part of a universal and interrelated creation. The poet's elevation of the material world, of mountain, clouds, rivers and lakes, was profoundly satisfying to men who devoted their intellect to rocks, strata, and the shape of hills and valleys. Always sensitive to the charge of aridity, the geologists found a poet who wrote about the very places where they did their field-work and, more important, admitted that actual landscape into the hierarchy of created phenomena, which found its highest, most complex expression in the human form and mind. Whereas for a long period 'landscape' had been the property of the sophisticated and aesthetic, now it ceased to be exclusive. Here was a cultural shift from mental subjective 'pictures' of landscape to objective 'realities', measurable, orderly and describable. Landscape became the province of the natural philosophers, as indeed shortly it became everyone's property and inspiration. For the many who engaged in scientific pursuits in that landscape, Wordsworth was their laureate.

THE UNIVERSALITY OF LAW: MORAL LAW AND THE LAWS OF NATURE

The geologists themselves were professionally absorbed in a search for universal laws and they met a poet who was equally absorbed. *The Excursion* was a key work for them, because of their diligent attention to philosophy and particularly to moral philosophy. *The Excursion* provided them with a text saturated with the themes of conscience and inner laws. A typical example of the poet's reliance on law and duty to act in a 'comprehensive' way, that is to say arming the good man for all eventualities, is the following passage:

> O blest seclusion! When the mind admits
> The law of duty; and can therefore move,
> Through each vicissitude of loss and gain.[42]

To Whewell such moral laws are ultimately of the same divine origin as physical laws. At an early point in *The Philosophy of the Inductive Sciences* (and repeated in *The History of the Inductive Sciences* and in *The Elements of Morality Volume I*) he insists that the process of creating 'general truths' from 'particular facts' is not limited to the world which is external to human beings. Since truth is a unity in all subjects and between all subjects we may find it if 'we contemplate the world within as well as the world without'.[43] He is not foolish enough, however, to simplify the problem of how morality can be studied. *The Philosophy of Inductive Sciences* in fact may begin with a confident statement that the inductive process can be applied to the 'world within' as well as to the 'world without', but it ends with the more tentative prediction that 'the principles of truth which we are now laboriously culling among the results of the physical sciences, may possibly find some application in those parts of knowledge towards which men most naturally look with deeper interest and more serious reverence'.[44] In the event, when in the next five years he began to survey moral sciences, he did not attempt a transference to the realm of human behaviour of what he had discovered in scientific geological research. *The Elements of Morality* is not about generating laws by inductive processes; it is a book about how human societies make law and it is an argument that human law has a pragmatic basis. In one important respect, however, both fields of study, geology, and moral 'science', observe the same procedural principle. They do not explore their respective first origins. In Whewell's geology there is an assumption of a First, mysterious Cause but by its nature it is unexaminable and therefore it is left in place. Similarly, in his study of moral law, the First Cause is unquestioned; it is accepted that morality is part of man's nature.

Whewell's idea or conception of moral nature is most clearly expressed in a letter of 1846 to Sir John Herschel. This is a classic statement of opposition to Utilitarianism, with its doctrine of the pursuit of happiness:

I found my Morality, not upon something which man is to get, but on something which he is to be. He is to be truly a man: he is to conform to Rules; to Rules which recognise a common Humanity in himself and others...We must conceive that man is a moral being, and then try to see how he can be so.[45]

Here is the moral categorical imperative absorbed into the confidence of early Victorian England. Human nature is distinct from brute Nature. It is distinguished because it is at one and the same time 'intellectual, moral, religious and spiritual'. This uniquely 'comprehensive' moral nature has its origins in something other than external circumstances. The evidence provided from fossils about the extinct species of plant and animal life may appear to demonstrate that environment determines the nature of the living being and may appear to endorse the adaptation of species to changed conditions, but an essential difference is built into the human species. Men possess 'a special and indestructible germ in human nature'. There is, for this if for no other reason, no 'gradation' between the animal and the human kingdom. They were created as separate entities. With this argument Whewell confirmed for himself and others the essential dignity of humanity. It was still possible, in the years before the issues raised by Darwin and later by Huxley were fully discussed, for a leader of the scientific world to reiterate a confident affirmation of the essential difference between two natures, human and non-human, and yet to continue to find the non-human a source of wonder. One source of confidence for men like Whewell came from a poet who also presented the mind and the moral nature of man as superior to the natural world, yet also respected that other sphere. The final lines of *The Prelude* also express this distinction between the much valued, persisting, and exalted beauty of the earth, and the superior 'mind of man':

> we may teach them how,
> Instruct them how the mind of man becomes
> A thousand times more beautiful than the earth
> On which he dwells, above this frame of things
> (Which, 'mid all revolutions in the hopes
> And fears of all men, doth still remain unchanged)
>
> In beauty exalted, as it is itself
> Of substance and of fabric more divine.[46]

Whewell may have known very little or nothing at all of *The Prelude*, but the early poems and *The Excursion* contributed to his construction of values. Wordsworth's 'universality', so much appreciated by Sedgwick, was generous and inclusive of the natural world, even of the rocks and stones, the raw material of geologists. Concurrently the poet's conception of 'universality' included an elevation of the principal component of that natural world, 'the mind of man'.

CHAPTER 7

Duration and decay: the abyss of time

Two passages, one from a geologist the other from Wordsworth, resonate on the subject of time. The first is by John Playfair in his *Biographical Account of the Late Doctor James Hutton* of 1803. Accompanying Hutton on a geographical excursion, he looked down into a quarry and recorded: 'The mind seemed to grow giddy by looking so far into the abyss of time.'[1] In his unfinished account of travelling in the north of England, written in 1811 or 1812 and called by his modern editors *An Unpublished Tour*, Wordsworth also writes about the sensation of looking down into the unmeasured depth of a quarry, at Tilberthwaite:

the curious Stranger will be brought to the brink of a steep, from which he will have an opportunity of looking down and he will not look down without emotion into the cleft thro' which this brook flows. Among sensations of sublimity, there is one class produced by images of durate, [or] impassiveness by the sight of rocks of ever-lasting granite, or basaltic columns, a barrier upon which the furious winds or the devouring sea are without injury resisted. In the chasm above which we are now standing, Nature has employed contrary means to seize upon the imagination: the predominating impression being of decay and change, and danger and irregular power, and havoc and insecurity. Permanence is indeed seated here but it is upon a shattered and unquiet Throne.[2]

The contrast between the two 'classes' of sublimity, enduring time and its opposite, 'decay and change, and danger and irregular power, and havoc and insecurity', is increasingly a theme of Wordsworth's poetry after 1810. Stephen Gill comments on 'The Vernal Ode', 1817 and 'Ode: Composed upon an Evening of Extraordinary Splendour and Beauty': 'they actually invite the reader to consider the passing of time embodied in the poet's evolving canon...But all of the poems dwell on the human being as a creature of time, on experience placed in the context of the aeons of the past and the unimaginable timelessness of the future.'[3]

An image from a prose work first published in 1810, *Essays upon Epitaphs*, serves to start the search for the older poet's years of interest in the complexities of time which cannot be measured by the human span. Wordsworth prepared his reader for the discursive exercise on the nature of epitaphs by imagining a child playing by the banks of a stream. There is an important difference between this child and the central image of a child in 'Ode: Intimations of Immortality', with its evocation of a distant, receding past. The child in the essay ruminates on the future, the unlimited sea to which the river is flowing:

Towards what abyss is it in progress? what receptacle can contain the mighty influx? And the spirit of the answer must have been, though the word might be sea or ocean, accompanied perhaps with an image gathered from a map, or from the real object in nature – these might have been the *letter*, but the *spirit* of the answer must have been as inevitably, – a receptacle without bounds or dimensions; nothing less than infinity.[4]

Both past and future are conceivable and can be given names, but they are equally incomprehensible. Wordsworth conveyed here the shock of contemplating limitless time, or, to use the spatial metaphor, 'deep time', which disturbed many people of his generation. In this chapter I shall examine the way in which contemporary geologists conceptualized time, then return to Wordsworth's concern with the related twin themes of duration and decay.

TIME AND THE GEOLOGISTS

There are two persistent geological issues, according to Rachael Laudan (1987); one is historical (the development of the earth from its earliest beginnings to its present form), the other causal (the distinctive processes that produced the surface of the earth): 'But many of the basic issues that were debated in the classic period are still debated today, and many of the agreements that were reached about the aim and methods of the discipline (though not about its specific theories) continue to be accepted.'[5] The theories of the 'classical age' of geology, as Laudan describes it, were posited in order to account for the processes that produced the present surface of the earth as well as to give a 'history' of the earth and a forecast of the future, hence the historical and the causal are frequently combined. Theories that accounted for the 'what' (the present condition of the world) were often answering different questions, 'why' the earth is as it is and what it will be. Not only were theoreticians of Laudan's classical period of geology concerned with hypothetical explanations of origins and futures, they were 'directionalist', sustained by a belief that what had been planned was driven by Divine will. Having said that, it is wise, as I stressed in chapter two, not to over-simplify the history of geology by labelling all geologists as members of one 'camp' or school of orthodoxy. The English and Scottish geologists of the eighteenth century who prepared the way for the early members of the Geological Society, though they had much in common in their inheritance from Burnet, differed considerably from him and from each other in explanations of the origin of the earth and of its subsequent changes of form. By the second decade of the nineteenth century, there was in England apparent unanimity about a Deluge or a sequence of Deluges, but, as Rudwick (1971) and other modern historians of geology have demonstrated, what the geologists of the 1830s had in common was 'Directionalism' rather than a solidarity about the way one or more catastrophic phases of the world's history had occurred. It is unsafe to assume that each student of a 'geological school' even in the relatively unified 1820s was insulated from an opposing theoretical position. To do so is to accept at face value categorizing by the geologists themselves, with labels such as Wernerian, Vulcanist, Huttonian, Plutonist, Catastrophist, and, eventually, Uniformitarian. Such rigid divisions not only obscure more complex groupings of geologists, they encourage in studies of non-geological literature and of disciplines interacting with geology, the enrolment of men of letters into supporters' organizations for scientific 'teams'.

The subjects of the origin of the earth and of its related topic, the length of time during which the present landscape developed, are cases in point for exercising caution in assessing the allegiances of individual geologists. It is common to simplify the situation into two broad spheres of belief: the biblical, with a religiously fundamental belief in the Genesis story, specifically the story of the Flood; and the scientific explanation which interpreted the age of the earth as considerably longer than biblical time, for instance as worked out by Archbishop Ussher. Roy Porter's study (1977) of eighteenth-century natural philosophers and theologians demonstrates that a generous interpretation of the biblical account of the Flood had begun long before Hutton spoke to the Edinburgh Royal Society in 1785. In many ways, the Society was well prepared for a revision of the traditionally understood age of the earth.[6] John Woodward (1665–1728) for instance, interpreted the

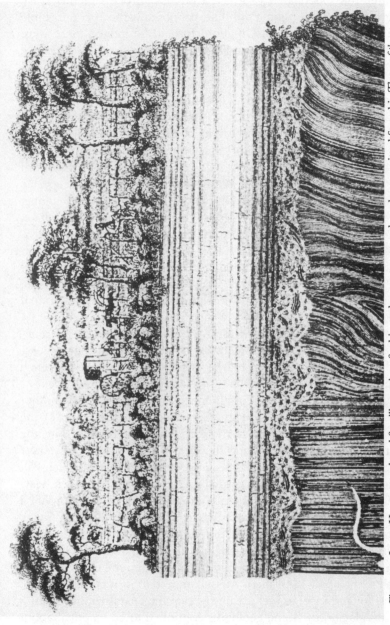

Figure 5. James Hutton produced few illustrations for his works; most seem to have been omitted from his *Theory of the Earth* (1795) (see Dean, D. R., 1992). The cross-section shown here is a sketch of an unconformity, probably at Jedburgh. The sense of 'deep time' is appreciated best by glancing at the peaceful rural surface of late eighteenth-century life, and then looking down at the message of long-term change in the two main sections of unconformed strata below.

period after the Flood as a protracted physical process of successive sedimentations. Buffon (1707–1788) had proposed a more comfortable time span than seven days of Creation. Instead he judged there were six epochs of time. It is understandable that non-specialist writers like Wordsworth could at one and the same time use a fixed point, 'the Flood', as a commonly understood term for a first cause of present landforms and yet show some understanding of processes that continued for thousands of years with no clear evidence of a beginning.

The Wernerian theory of the origin of the earth was based on a hypothesis of the precipitation of matter held in suspension in vast oceans and a subsequent elevation of continents and mountains out of the seas. It is often suggested, that Wernerism was peculiarly acceptable to men who were professional churchmen as well as professional geologists, because the theory seemed to support the Noachian Deluge. In fact Werner's geology equally sustained religious belief for individuals as diverse as Buckland, Davy, Greenough, Sedgwick, and Whewell not because of approximations to the words of Scripture, but because Wernerism confirmed the intentionality and directionalism of the Divine plan. Furthermore, Werner's mineralogy and his seminal work on stratigraphy were valued in their own right and established a framework and a nomenclature used by a first generation of nineteenth-century geologists and mineralogists, at least until that generation modernized his findings in the light of English and French stratigraphical studies.

I commented in chapter two on the need for caution about another large label in the history of geology, Catastrophism. In respect of the concept of 'deep time', it is particularly wise to realize that the geologists we identify as espousing theories of Catastrophe may have had much in common with 'Actualists' or Uniformitarians, at least in acknowledging the long periods of our earth's story. To take the view that Lyell converted the geologists to Uniformitarianism is to simplify a more complicated history of change in scientific ideas. Gillispie (1951), one of the strongest exponents of the view that belief in a modified form of the biblical Catastrophe, the Flood, dominated the 1820s and 1830s,[7] considered that Catastrophism did not disappear on the day that Lyell's book was published. An accommodation was made in the late 1830s, for instance, to include newly identified catastrophes such as continental glaciation. Some geologists continued to be sceptical about Actualism or Uniformitarianism on the grounds of the limited range of observations possible to a human being. Here are two careful statements from Whewell about the controversy. The first argues that catastrophes may well have occurred, although the data that geologists normally consider lead to opposite conclusions: 'The limit of intensity being really unknown, catastrophes are just as probable as uniformity: If a volcano may repose for a thousand years, and then break out and destroy a city; why may not another volcano repose for ten thousand years, and then destroy a continent; or if not a continent, why not the whole habitable surface of the earth?' Only a page further on, Whewell adopts a less extreme view related to the position of the observer: 'The course of things is *uniform* to an Intelligence which can embrace the succession of several cycles, but it is *catastrophic* to the contemplation of man whose survey can only grasp a part only of one cycle.'[8] The vital point of Whewell's cautious critique of Lyellian Actualism is that it was as possible to conjecture a major span of time in a doctrine of Catastrophe as it was in the unlimited time horizons of Lyell's theory.

Whewell is a sceptic on theories which seem to wrap up all opposition and close down debate and enquiry. In the 1830s and 1840s he assumed the mantle of the authoritative leader of the scientific establishment, capable of standing back from joining the extremes of one camp or the other of this current controversy. Ruse (1991) clearly classifies him as a Catastrophist, but Whewell's views on Actualism, in the review he wrote on Lyell's *Principles of Geology* in *The British Critic*, are a good example of a reserved position.[9] His review was clearly respectful to Lyell, but ultimately found his long time-embracing scheme unacceptable as an explanation for all phenomena at all periods of the earth's history. More important than Whewell's detailed destruction of Lyell's argument is the fact that it was Lyell himself who had asked Whewell to be the reviewer of *Principles of Geology*. This is yet another mark, not only of Whewell's stature, but of the fact that the geological establishment, though devoted to controversy, enjoyed debate and kept open certain positions.

All the above reservations about 'schools' of geology are relevant to the geological concept of time. Biblical time assumes a first cause and an unwinding process leading directly to an Apocalypse, but Catastrophism takes various forms. Repeated catastrophes may be part of a series of steps towards the break-up of the world, but equally well may indicate items in a series of destruction which do not terminate the world's history. A phase of large-scale destruction provides material for another landscape. To some Catastrophists this sequence of alternating decay and rebuilding presumed long ages of time. Obviously members of schools of Actualism (Hutton, Playfair, and Lyell) also believed that building and destruction have occurred and will occur in a virtually unmeasurable time span.

S. J. Gould has conceptualized two kinds of explanation of the formation of the earth's surface which help us to understand the questions raised by geologists in the period from 1810 to 1850. First, he uses the metaphor of the arrow; a bow shot has a beginning and pursues a trajectory, leading directly to an end. Thomas Burnet's theory would be an 'arrow' explanation, with its description of a path from a perfect world through the Catastrophe of the Fall and the consequent break up of the smooth surface of the sphere. The resulting ruined world will only disappear when 'the arrow's' journey reaches its destination of the Apocalypse. Gould's second metaphor is the cycle, a sequence where what is destroyed forms the material for a new formation, which in turn is destroyed and so on. Hutton and eventually Lyell are theorists who propose this self-renewing system.

There are a number of perspectives on this simple categorization. A cyclic system of destruction and renewal might to some be purposeful and arrow-like in the sense of achieving gradual, planned perfection. An attractive alternative – attractive at least to those who see the world as a waiting-room for God's planned Apocalypse – is a theory of balance.[10] A balanced world may imply a static position achieved by natural process, but awaiting a supernatural, disturbing finality. Whatever form of explanation satisfied the Catastrophist or the Uniformitarian, the two great forces, decay and renewal, were accepted as being in some form of interaction. Both Hutton and Lyell extended the geologists' scale of time by turning attention away from First Cause and Apocalypse in order to attend to the vast spans of time in which actual processes of destruction and renewal operate, but the geologists who had espoused Werner's polar division of primary and secondary phases of the building of the earth were already committed to a concept of deep time. Lyell did not 'discover' the formidable age of the earth! The Diluvialists and the Catastrophists were prepared for an understanding of an earth which in the past had experienced the effects of vast surges of energy and even in the present suffered localized destructive forces.

It is perhaps Hutton's major contribution to the development of geology that he encouraged a debate about the interrelated energies of decay and renewal. While his painstaking *Theory of the Earth*, whether in the original forms or in Playfair's more reader-friendly version, may have been dismissed by the first members of the Geological Society,[11] Hutton and Playfair produced two concepts which, although they were published to support and exemplify the larger theory of the earth, were acceptable to younger geologists who espoused a different overall scheme of thought. The two concepts were the principle of unconformity and the phenomenon of igneous intrusion. Both imply deep time. There is a diagram in Hutton's *Theory of the Earth* showing a peaceful rural landscape with a country gentleman out on his business. Beneath his feet are two planes of structure, the uppermost, younger rocks are lying over an older, different structure of strata and the difference between the two formations is clearly marked by a 'plane of unconformity'. Although unconformity became a more complicated concept than Hutton first imagined, even in its simplified form it signifies a protracted time span with a separation of two different periods of the earth's history, one sequence of processes completed (if that is a word which can be applied in Huttonian theory) and a new sequence taking its place long afterwards. The second concept, the idea of the intrusion of molten material into a mass of already existing rock, earned Hutton the title of 'Plutonist'. Such large intrusions represented, as did unconformity, massive processes occurring over vast stretches of time. Hutton verifies theory by quoting observations in named cuttings, quarries, and exposed rock faces.[12] Deep time became visible even to the casual geologist. Gould draws our attention to the philosophical implications of these two seminal concepts. The principle of unconformity supports Hutton's view that the earth did not decline into ruin on one primitive occasion. On the contrary the record reveals a sequence of former surfaces each with a long history of reduction and ruin, followed by rebuilding. The intrusive granitic and doleritic masses confirmed to Hutton that nature had been rebuilt – the concept of repair has been added to the doctrine of ruin.[13]

Lyell's doctrine of repair and renewal, when it appeared in a full-blown, more persuasive scheme than Hutton ever produced, proclaimed an obvious and reassuring sermon in stone – the world is a well-regulated system. It was not, however, a world of eighteenth-century 'plenitude', that most comforting conception of God's best of all possible worlds. 'Plenitude' had been reinterpreted in dynamic terms. Movement and change might give a surface impression of destruction, but comfort was at hand because destruction was part of the grand plan. Repair could not take place without new materials from the processes of erosion. Geologists and astronomers reassured

their readers because they took their long view of the balance of
nature. Not all scientists were finally satisfied even by a long-term view
of the perfection of the system. Within the sphere of biology there was
increasing evidence of extinction of species rather than of cyclic
renewal. The fossil record and the discoveries of mastodons and
monsters, whether from the Liassic of Lyme Regis, or from the newly
explored Ohio River Basin, or from the Urals, made it difficult to
maintain a belief in a benignly finalized balance of nature with everything present and correct from the beginning of time. As Greenough
commented in his notebook on Lyellian assurances: 'Change is as
constant as uniformity itself. The caprice of nature is quite as remarkable as her steadiness.'[14]

Geologists and general theoreticians of science like Greenough,
Sedgwick, and Whewell reserved judgement about the permanence of
the present processes which Uniformitarians considered as eternal. The
first and greatest catastrophe, the First Cause, was something which
they did not wish to abandon, though, like Hutton and Lyell, they
thought it was fruitless to use geological methods to confirm or deny its
occurrence. Whewell particularly recognized that the partial position
of the human observer was inevitable. In *The Novum Organon Renovatum*
Whewell compares Uniformitarians to people who live in a city and see
old houses demolished and replaced. They believe the streets are
continuously changing and therefore may never question how the first
city came to be established. His argument supports the possibility of
periods of Catastrophe beyond our comprehension, yet containable
within the vaster canvas of uniformitarian gradation. It is also a
statement about our lack of ability to perceive the original foundation
of the earth, and therefore the worthlessness of expressing views about
ultimate events. We may, in short, writes Whewell, 'apply the Method
of Gradation in the investigation of geological causes, provided we
leave the limits of the Gradation undefined'.[15] Even in the late 1830s,
when Lyellian Actualism appeared to cover all possibilities and when
leaders of the geological community like Sedgwick made public
recantation of Wernerism, there was no closing of discussion; on the
contrary there was a new depth of time to investigate.

WORDSWORTH'S THEMES OF DURATION AND DECAY

The continuing debate in geological circles about the economy of the
world is reflected in some fundamental questions asked by Romantic

artists. Is the world a place of benevolence in equilibrium for the human journey or is it a battleground for mankind, opposing living spirit against decaying, and at times, inimical matter? Is Nature ultimately tragic or, to take a further extreme, is the present age a witness to the last act of a tragedy with a stage littered with destruction? Is there, more optimistically, a transcendent spirit behind all matter, which, if we could only shed our presuppositions about subject and object, we could recognize as having affinity with ourselves, dying, but blest with immortality. At another level, the geologists like the poets dealt with grand themes of destruction and rebirth. For writers who found creativity in tensions and contradictions there was rich material in evidences of opposition of huge forces. Wordsworth's themes on decay and renewal are of this nature, opposing one experience against another and finding sublimity in that opposition. The tradition in which Wordsworth played his own part has a long history in Romanticism.[16] Young Werther, in Goethe's story of stricken Romantic youth, compares in one passage the two impressions of the universe, one benign and protected, the other destructive and voracious, eating itself:

Immense mountains surrounded me, chasms yawned at my feet, streams swollen by rain tumbled headlong, rivers flowed below me and the forests and mountains resounded; and I could see those immeasurable and incomprehensible powers at work in the depths of the earth, and above the earth's surface, there seemed all the infinite species of creation [And then the opposite sensation after his wounding by an impossible love:] It is not the major but rare catastrophes of the world, the floods that wash away your villages, the earthquakes that swallow up your cities, that move me; what wastes my heart away is the corrosive power that lies concealed in the natural universe – in Nature, which has brought forth nothing that does not destroy both its neighbour and itself. And so I go my fearful way betwixt heaven and earth and all their active forces; and all I can see is a monster, forever devouring, regurgitating, chewing and gorging.[17]

To travel in a literary journey from the sensibility of the young Goethe in 1774 and the young Wordsworth of 1800 to the later Romanticism of the older Wordsworth is to see a shift from the perception of the world as a system in decline to a system in dynamic balance. The same shift of view is to be perceived in reading the history of geology from Burnet to Hutton and Lyell.

Dorothy Wordsworth touches the heart of the tension of duration and decay in her journal of their European Tour of 1820. The Alps, in all their grandeur, stimulate her to write: 'No spectacle that I ever beheld – not even the ocean itself – has had an equal power over my mind in bringing together thoughts connected with duration and decay – eternity and perpetual wasting – the visible and invisible power of God and nature.'[18] The same phrase occurs to her in the Rigi Valley, where she is conscious not of sudden catastrophe but of gradations: 'In passing through the Rigi Valley, perpetual works of falling range or decay of mountains are visible, yet no fearful devastations; scars gradually wasting – and fragments tumbled down. Threads and ribbands of cataracts were now gently performing their work; but there paths and declivities told a plain tale both of perpetual and fitful wasting.'[19]

Over and above their physical impact, the high Alpine passes were rich in sensations for Dorothy Wordsworth because of her brother's youthful journey there. It is no surprise therefore to find a correspondence between Dorothy's visions of the Alps and Wordsworth's own record in poetry which his sister must have seen first in *Descriptive Sketches* of 1793 and then in *The Prelude* in its various forms between 1798 and 1805. In a passage in book VI of *The Prelude*, which has attracted critical attention in respect of Wordsworth's understanding of contemporary geological theory, there is a richly romantic sequence of the opposition of permanence and destruction, rather more important an issue than the meagre evidence it gives of specific knowledge of mineralogy:

> The immeasurable height
> Of woods decaying, never to be decayed,
> The stationary blast of waterfalls,
> And everywhere along the hollow rent
> Winds thwarting winds, bewildered and forlorn,
> The torrents shooting from the clear blue sky,
> The rocks that muttered close upon our ears –
> Black drizzling crags that spake by the wayside
> . . .
> Were all like workings of one mind, the features
> Of the same face, blossoms upon one tree,
> Characters of the great apocalypse,
> The types and symbols of eternity,
> Of first, and last, and midst, and without end.[20]

Jonathan Wordsworth suggests that this passage and a manuscript draft of *The Ruined Cottage* provide evidence of the influence of Milton and of Thomas Burnet.[21] After reading Wordsworth's passage alongside that of geologists I am also inclined to hear echoes of a geological theory which is cyclical and renewing. *The Prelude*, a document of a relation-ship between the developing inner life of a man and the 'active universe' of the earth's various forms, presents here a world in torment, expressing itself in human terms. The ever-changing, but persisting universe is thwarted, bewildered, forlorn. The very rocks 'mutter' and speak. What they pronounce is about first and last and 'midst' but also about the never ending.

In *A Guide* Wordsworth attends to both processes which alter the landscape, decay and repair. The deposits of rapid mountain streams, the formation of alluvial deltas, and the deposition of silt forming the gentle curves of the larger lakes, these are the shaping, positive forma-tions of renewal. But *A Guide* is also a record of destruction. Jonathan Bate has drawn our attention in *Romantic Ecology* to Wordsworth's consciousness of the destruction of the Lake District by tourism, by careless planting, or by large-scale agriculture. The destruction that Wordsworth records goes back much earlier than the newly-found popularity of the Lakes. In the second section of *A Guide*, there is the first note of total extinction of the Leigh deer.[22] By the third edition, there were further extinctions to record: the wild swine which were once common in Boardale (a tributary valley of Martindale) and the red deer of Martindale, said in that edition to be 'the descendants of the aboriginal herds'. The old forests have long gone and the desolation of pastures by ploughing (as in the poem, 'Michael') continues. The contrast between loss and continuity is not emotionally neutral. Even in locations where Nature appears at its most remote from humanity, there is an emotional tension between lifelessness and a strange natural will, which is almost human. Taking the description of the tarns in *A Guide*, Byatt (1970) notes the melancholic sensations produced by the scenes of the high mountain patches of water and their association with an atmosphere of decay. The passage Byatt refers to is about the high fells with rocks and boulders strewn around these lonely small lakes:

The contribution of ages! A not unpleasing sadness is induced by this perplexity, and these images of decay; while the prospect of a body of pure water unattended with groves and other cheerful rural images by which fresh water is usually accompanied and unable to give furtherance to the meagre vegetation around it – excites a sense of some repulsive power strongly put forth, and thus deepens the melancholy natural to such scenes.[23]

The imagination of the visitor is 'tempted to attribute a voluntary power' to the changes produced by wind and sunlight. The landscape engenders melancholy because it appears decayed and deserted, yet it appears on the contrary to energize itself with a life and a spirit of its own. Byatt sees in passages such as this an essential unity: 'It is an image again of eternity in change and decay.'[24]

Duration and decay, threat and reconciliation, are the essence of Wordsworth's landscapes of his middle and later years. The writer of *A Guide* and the poems published with it, such as 'Ode: The Pass of Kirkstone', is conscious that he is inhabiting a solid, material world. He knew that his task as a poet–guide was to control, to explain, and to describe that world which appears to be complex, chaotic, and ultimately indescribable. He knew too that former interpretations of this landscape, picturesque visions and carefully constructed views glimpsed through a Claude glass from selected stations, produced a distorted and untrue picture – an illusion. Yet the hard reality of mountains, lakes, tarns, and vales is itself a kind of illusion, a living, interacting entity which is perpetually changing and reshaping. What endures is both the original 'primary' earth and the everlasting forces that erode that old form.

One aspect of the theme of duration is continuity. The Lake District is a continuous landscape from prehuman times through the histories of the ancient people who erected Long Meg and its companion stones on into the present day. Sunlight, moonlight, wind, frost, rain, the changing seasons, and the responding grass and bracken interact with a landscape which is only superficially inactive and dead. A territory has been created which is permanent and can transcend human history; yet human history is included within it, as 'Ode: The Pass of Kirkstone' declares:

> Here, 'mid his own unvexed domains,
> A Genius dwells, that can subdue
> At once all memory of You, –
> Most potent when mists veil the sky,
> Mists that distort and magnify:
> While the coarse rushes, to the sweeping breeze,
> Sigh forth their ancient melodies![25]

The Excursion presents in a dramatic form the same tensions between duration and decay. While the Wanderer attempts consistently to oppose the Solitary's despondent materialism by uplifting messages of permanence and Divine beneficence, there is a second participant, the upland peaks and hanging valleys playing variations on the theme. In book III, the elevated valley, where the three human protagonists are about to engage in debate, appears to the narrator–poet as a symbol of all that is permanent. It is like another Eden:

> Far and near
> We have an image of the pristine earth,
> The planet in its nakedness: were this
> Man's only dwelling, sole appointed seat,
> First, last, and single, in the breathing world,
> It could not be more quiet.[26]

Duration stretches before the Wanderer and his companion. Then, in one of those cruxes of sound used with effect in this long poem (others are the bleating of a lamb and the crying of a raven), the serenity is shattered by a reminder of decay. The funeral dirge is heard, eerie and disembodied at first, approaching from below. The shock is doubled by the Wanderer's immediate presumption that it is his friend, the Solitary, who has died. Locations of retreat and withdrawal, even the blessed urn-like valleys, are never totally apart from the realities of the world. They are only moments of stasis in a moving narrative.

Another similar moment is located in what I take to be the same geological feature:[27]

> Upon a semicirque of turf-clad ground,
> The hidden nook discovered to our view
> A mass of rock, resembling, as it lay
> Right at the foot of that moist precipice,
> A stranded ship, with keel upturned, that rests
> Fearless of winds and waves.[28]

In this small, completely hidden area to which the Solitary leads the friends are two more material features, each a visual metaphor of the issues they are to discuss. There are standing stones, here conveying their message of the destruction of past civilizations. The image of the upturned boat reinforces the sensation of wreck and ruin. A different power is the movement (but apparently no movement) in the fall of water over the steep cliff at the back of the cirque:

> And softly creeping, like a breath of air,
> Such as is sometimes seen, and hardly seen
> To brush the still breast of a crystal lake.[29]

These are the emblems of eternity and change, of duration and decay. To the Wanderer they are a 'wealth'; to the Solitary, who reluctantly values them, they might well be 'the sport of Nature, aided by blind chance'. One image however confirms the Wanderer's hopeful message, the almost impossible survival of a holly bush growing out of the barren tablet, one of the standing stones. Life continues. Frail though it may seem, it can be interpreted as relative to human life: 'in these shows a chronicle survives / Of purposes akin to those of Man'.[30]

This passage has richness in it for the readers seeking to understand the choice of location for the debate that follows. Like Blea Tarn and its upland valley, this smaller patch of rest in the high fells contains an element of paradox. A lowland physical feature, a valley, has been transported to higher regions. Nature has been reversed. The Wanderer continues in the spirit of paradox to describe the peculiar nature of their hidden arena. It is a 'strait', but not between rocks in an ocean. The sky above is reversed into a 'chasm', an 'abyss / In which the everlasting stars abide'. This descriptive passage is not an original conceit. It has important literary connections. De Selincourt and Darbishire note the term 'lapse' describing the fall of the stream (it is also used in the River Duddon sonnet sequence as well as in book VIII of *The Excursion*). The editors draw the reader's attention to an inheritance from Milton. Similarly at the end of the verse paragraph, Wordsworth's own note on the line 'lost in unsearchable eternity' reminds the reader of the poet's recent study of Thomas Burnet's Latin text of the theory of the earth. This is a carefully constructed passage of verse description where the scene is realistic enough to satisfy a geologist's description of highland landforms and yet of profound importance as a figure for the illusory nature of a material world, and, at another level, as a stage for a debate on the mental and moral state of humanity.

I have already indicated enough from the River Duddon sonnet sequence to demonstrate the theme of continuity of the river and its accommodation with history as it flows from Wrynose Pass to the Duddon Sands. As a commentary on the idea of permanence, there is the anecdote I quoted in chapter two from Wordsworth's own notes to the poems about the stranger who thought that the Seathwaite ravine was unfinished. This minor instance is as revealing about Wordsworth as it is about the effect of a catastrophic landscape. It is the poet not the stranger who is a sophisticate about the process of geological decay. The location is the narrow channel of rapids and white water above Seathwaite, flanked by the high precipice of Wallowbarrow Crag and, further off on the opposite bank, the mound of the Pen. To Wordsworth in 1820 this is clearly not a landscape half created, nor is it a ruin of what was once perfect. It is a section of the mountains shaped by continuous forces which put human history in the shade.

In the later poems, the continuity of history dominates sequence after sequence of poems. The directional drive of human destiny leads so often to the England of Milton and from time to time to Wordsworth's own day (on the occasions when its standards conform to Miltonic excellence). Sometimes, as in the sequence devoted to the story of St Bees Head, its monastery and school, permanence is rock like. At others, duration is in the falling stream that seems to pause, but in fact is changing as it falls, as in 'Musings near Aquapendente'. One particular sequence of poems illustrates the basic opposition in the material world between duration and decay. *The Itinerary Poems* of 1833 include episodes of visits to Staffa and to Iona. They record a theme of disturbance in the poet's mind. In the last poem of the four Staffa Cave sonnets, Wordsworth contrasts persistence and loss. The flowers growing above the cave mouth have survived the storms that have carved the caves, yet the people of the past, who constructed heroic myths to explain the origin of the rocks, have long since gone. This Wordsworthian tension between duration and decay is immediately followed more explicitly in the three following sonnets about Iona.

> On to Iona! – What can she afford
> To us save matter for a thoughtful sigh,
> Heaved over ruin with stability
> In urgent contrast?[31]

In the Staffa and Iona sequence once more legend appears in close association with a dramatic geological feature, as was the case in the River Duddon sonnet sequence. Wordsworth uses myth and legend, not as a fanciful explanation of phenomena for the amusement of the educated, but to contrast with 'mechanic laws', as if to illustrate that the power of human imagination still has room to play alongside more scientific and, in their own sphere, admissible explanations:

> Thanks for the lessons of this Spot – fit school
> For the presumptuous thoughts that would assign
> Mechanic laws to agency divine;
> And, measuring heaven by earth, would overrule
> Infinite Power.[32]

A religious geologist such as Sedgwick would have recognized the distinction between mechanic laws (which geology and the sciences could generate from their observations) and divine agencies working by other means. The poet avoids the 'presumptuous thoughts' that merge these two worlds and the sonnet ends with an octet praising the powerful material force of the ocean that created the majestic pillars and sculpted roof. Wordsworth here recognizes the destructive power of nature, but also concedes that the ocean builds as well as destroys, creating natural monuments such as Fingal's Cave, the rocks of Iona, or the mysteriously isolated Ailsa Craig. These monuments of durability can serve as allies to human endeavour, as in the case of the cliffs of St Bees Head and its attendant sea fogs that confuse invaders, or as awe-inspiring structures which generate a sense of worship. What is in no doubt is the active involvement of the poet-observer in the interpretation of an ever-changing landscape. Seeing 'into the life of things', the poet-seer reflects on change but also on permanence. De Man (1993) in a study of the 'Winander Boy' sequence in *The Prelude* and the two final poems of the Duddon sonnets makes this telling statement: 'The key to an understanding of Wordsworth lies in the relationship between imagination and time not in the relationship between imagination and nature.'[33] The same might well be made of his contemporaries, the geologists.

THE ECONOMY OF NATURE

At the beginning of the nineteenth century, the phrase 'economy of nature' was used, by Wordsworth and by geologists alike, to summarize the directional outcome of the tension of decay and renewal. It is tempting to condense the years between the middle of the seventeenth century, when 'the economy of nature' was first used through 1750 to 1850 and to assume that there was a continuity of meaning in the term. What distinguishes eighteenth-century natural philosophers, who conceived a natural economic system of balanced forces, from the early nineteenth-century geologists is that the latter were convinced that the universe was active, but not so obviously 'in balance'. To Catastrophists and Uniformitarians alike the world was only superficially stable. Their grasp of 'deep time' gave them a different perspective on the magnitude of the changes that they assumed had occurred in the world's history, together with a scepticism about an easy assumption of the ordinary human being's power to comprehend that change. Temporary stasis was a product of dynamic change. An eighteenth-century writer on Nature, such as Lord Shaftesbury, saw order and balance and was cheered by it, whereas a nineteenth-century geologist saw apparent disorder and conflict, but was reassured because his skills enabled him to discover hidden laws which were ultimately in control. The following passage from Shaftesbury's *The Moralists: A Rhapsody* is about an essentially static and hierarchical nature which is a carefully calculated balance of forces: 'It is on the contrary, from this order of inferior and superior things, that we admire the world's beauty, founded thus on Contrarities: whilst from such various and disagreeing principles, a universal concord is established.'[34] Contrast this with Hutton's phrase, full of the continuously changing movement of nature: 'this active scene of life, death and circulation'.[35] Like Shaftesbury the nineteenth-century geologists looked at nature and found nothing to damage their faith in Divine goodness and universal goodwill, but what they perceived in nature was change and restlessness. The geologists were not dismayed. Challenge and reassurance could be sought in flux. Humphry Davy in his Royal Institution lectures on geology in 1811 was as aware as anyone of the appearance of disorder, but he was buoyed up in his confidence as much by the activity of scientific study as by what it discovered:

By wise and beautiful laws the equilibrium of things is constant. Life is preserved by operations which appear destructive, order and harmony arise from what at first view seems derangement and confusion, the perfection of the work is perceived the more it is studied, and it declares, in distinct language, the power and wisdom of the author.[36]

Shaftesbury in *The Moralists: A Rhapsody* was also aware that the human observer cannot be fully appraised of the Divine plan by surface observation, and so must be content with a passive role in the plan. He compared the human condition to the case of a traveller on a ship for the first time who is unaware of the overall layout of the vessel. He is ignorant of the importance of the independent functioning of the parts: 'In this dark Case of Flesh (he is) confined even to the Hold and meanest station of the Vessel.'[37] For Shaftesbury, trust in the Divine plan and confidence in the longer view would help to resolve apparent anomalies; but writers like Davy, and later Sedgwick and Whewell, did not wait in anticipation. They engaged as participants in the quest for a sense of order, actively prising out of their object of study anomalies and mysteries (such as the origin of fossils, the explanation of faulting and discontinuities in bedding planes, or the deeply hidden story of the oldest 'primitive' formations), equally confident, as their predecessors had been, that there was one conclusion, one truth, and one plan. The early nineteenth century in coping with a dynamic geology had to take on board the two issues which have occupied this chapter, the sense of deep time (aeons may be necessary to complete a process) and the problem of discontinuity (major changes must have occurred in climatic conditions, species may have been extinguished by change). Duration and decay preoccupied but did not overwhelm them. Part of the explanation for their buoyancy was the confidence created by their own calling and by its methodology. The joy of geologizing provided the student with an incentive to pursue his task. The next chapter turns to that activity and the geologists' assessment of the virtues of their vocation.

CHAPTER 8

Geology, the poetic discipline

In 1842, when Adam Sedgwick was writing his introductory remarks to the 'letters' to accompany Wordsworth's *A Guide*, he apologized to his friend that his material might appear to be dry, although, on the contrary, his purpose was lofty, to 'open the mind to the nature of the subject, and to point out the right way towards a comprehension of some of its general truths'.[1] This apology was more than a polite literary convention. Sedgwick was particularly anxious to avoid the charge of aridity. Like many of his contemporaries, he did not remain long on the defensive. From the founding of the Geological Society in London, geologists delivered equal quantities of self-assertion and of self-consciousness. Because their materials for study, rocks and stones, strata and fossils, were so solidly inanimate, the geologists sought to counteract the allegation of dullness with vigour.

If their raw material was superficially stolid, the issues the geologists engaged in were volatile. Geologists engaged in debates about theology, philosophy, the psychology of learning, and, though they would not have used the word, the sociology of their own profession and its relation to other scientific institutions. Above all, they interacted with each other vigorously, whether in London clubs or in regional meetings. 'Victorian geologists took pride in their communality and were indeed one of the most visible scientific communities in Britain at this time.'[2] Oldroyd's remark is equally applicable to the geologists of the pre-Victorian decades of the century. The subject certainly attracted some very visible figures. There are many stories of Buckland's lecturing techniques and his robust jokes and eccentricities while on field excursions. Sedgwick lecturing to thousands on the beach at the Newcastle meeting of the British Association was a formidably popular figure, who attracted envious comments from scientists working in less popular disciplines.[3] In short, the story of the ascendency of geology over mineralogy and, in the first fifty years of the nineteenth century, over other emerging disciplines such as biology and botany, is one of considerable success in gaining public as well as specialist scientific attention. Many writers have identified the potent benefits of geologizing for early nineteenth-century leisured people.[4] Fieldwork was healthy exercise and it satisfied a collector's and categorizer's instinct, which, Dean (1968) suggests, was brought into action in the early Romantic period. Geologists engaged at close quarters with Nature, chiming with the literary and artistic developments of the time. One aspect has been less touched upon, geology as a poetic discipline and why it was judged to be so. How those pursuing the subject viewed it as poetic is worth examination because it gives a clue to the nature of the attraction of Wordsworth to his contemporaries after 1810 and also explains the verve with which the new science was followed.

When the word 'poetic' is examined in context, it can be seen to have a range of meanings. Here, for instance, is Sedgwick in his Presidential address to the Geological Society in 1831, using the term to describe the sense of excitement, mystery, and speculation about the unknown outcome of future empirical research, which is more exciting than old-fashioned theories spun from unsupported conjecture:

They require a moral elevation; and a dignified forbearance, to free the mind from those attractive visions of ancient cosmogony, and the seductions of fanciful hypotheses, by which the history of geology has often been degraded...That which is exact in science must be circumscribed and defined; but of our labours we have not power to foresee the limits, and there is an intense and poetic interest in the very uncertainty and boundlessness of our speculations.[5]

Thirty-eight years later, the Scottish geologist, Hugh Miller, compares the scientist with the poet. In *The Testimony of the Rocks* Miller refers to a piece from Coleridge's *Aids to Reflection* where the poet says that the bee and the swallow were overshadowed by the advance of humanity:

There is fancy here; but it is that sagacious fancy; vouchsafed to only the true poet, which has so often proved the pioneer of scientific discovery and which is in reality more sober and truthful, in the midst of its apparent extravagance, than the gravest cogitations of ordinary men.[6]

Here the scientific discovery itself rather than the activity of discovering belongs to the realm of the poetic. Whewell, describing in 1821 the pleasures he will gain from a scientific journey to the Lake District, in a passage quoted in chapter four, sees himself first sketching the outline of a mountain, then measuring its barometric pressure, taking a geological sample and then quoting Wordsworth.[7] In the field, the geologist is accessible for the Muse.

Greenough clearly associated place and poetry. In his travel note-books of 1802 he writes that he read Virgil's *Georgics*, as he walked along the promontory of Posillipo: 'The perusal of them can never give me so much pleasure elsewhere as in the country where they were written.'[8] Similarly his description of Etna as a mysterious distant presence is that of a poet traveller not that of a geologist collecting examples of vulcanicity. This description incidentally was read by Davy to Coleridge and encouraged him to undertake the journey of 1805 to Malta via Italy. 'Poetic', however, meant much more than the interaction between landscape and a poet *manqué*. I shall examine three senses by which the geologists felt their discipline earned the title 'poetic' and 'sublime'. One is the most obvious, that the material they investigated was beautiful and therefore created sensations of appreciation of beauty in the observer. The second sense was the nobility and high moral tone of their studies of nature matching in prestige the poet's creation. The third was the geologists' claim that they made use of imagination.

EDUCATION IN BEAUTY

The aesthetic appreciation of the natural world was enhanced for the geologists by the specialist activity in which they engaged. They approached the mountains with awe but never without an acknowl-edgement of the part played by the human mind in the perception of the natural world. James Hutton's literary style does not at first sight lead to an association with the aesthetic, but his faithful biographer, Playfair, wrote that Hutton possessed 'an exquisite relish for whatever is beautiful and sublime in science'.[9] Hutton's *An Investigation* links intellectual activity in its highest forms with the aesthetic; the natural world is not merely the source of a beautiful sensation passively received. In the following quotation, very close in spirit to Wordsworth's closing lines of *The Prelude*,[10] there is an ascending aesthetic order for the natural world ('the order, the beauty, the magnificence'), but also an elevated priority for the human mind interacting with nature:

In how much then as we admire the order, the beauty, the magnificence of the material universe, which we perceive, or which we truly know in having it revealed to us, so much more we must admire the mind of man, a being that is made to know, that is made to act in consequence of that knowledge, that is made to reason in order that it may become wise, and is made to become wise, in order that it may become happy.[11]

Greenough, like many of his contemporaries in the Geological Society, is stirred by the world of his studies, the wonders of the natural world, and also by the activity of studying nature. Writing in 1819, his language is selected from the vocabulary of aesthetics:

It is always useful to enlarge our ideas of nature by reflecting on the comparative littleness of those objects which we are accustomed to consider the most sublime. The interest, however, which mountains and valleys are calculated to excite in us, depending not upon their relation to our planet, but upon their relations to our species, is little affected by any comparison that may be instituted between their magnitude and that of the world at large.[12]

This is from the pen of one of the most pragmatic geologists of the time, more given to methodology than to mythology, to process than to poetry. Greenough, though rarely showing it, is capable of the flights that we see in more excited colleagues such as Whewell and Sedgwick when they extol their scholarly pursuit. It is in Greenough's younger effusions on the picturesque scenery of the Alps in 1802 that we can see the education in appreciation of the aesthetic that continued, though changed, from the eighteenth century into the new age of Romanticism.

   Greenough's travel notebooks from 1802 are particularly interesting because for part of the journey he followed the same route that Wordsworth had taken twelve years earlier and which the poet described in *Descriptive Sketches* and then in *The Prelude*. Greenough's companion, Underwood, was a landscape painter, obviously trained to compose a picturesque representation of mountain scenes by reassembling the constituent parts. His geologist companion, after quoting Gilpin on the problem of accurately representing Alpine scenery, paints a word picture by a similar process of redeployment of the Romantic components. Significantly this passage in the diary is unusual in that there are many emendations. The language had to be right:

the tranquillity of the Evening, the beautiful tints of the setting sun, the grandeur of the Mountains had thrown me into a mood which it is impossible to describe and rendered me in the highest degree susceptible of pleasure. A rudely sculptured cross let into the hollow stump of an old tree long since cut down and placed in a most romantic situation burst suddenly on my sight – a little further lay in the midst of a field of exquisite verdure large misshapen

Figure 6. Portrait of George Bellas Greenough.

blocks of granite partially overgrown with mosses and covered with the broad lengthened shadows of several venerable oaks among whose twisted branches many a huge craggy peak of naked rock became faintly discernible. Beneath me the rapid Arve winding among the mountains foamed and roared along its rocky channel. Close upon its banks the ruins of some proud edifice, the works of many hands which in the days of its prosperity must have appeared immortal seemed to teach the everlasting works of nature that the time would come when even they would be dissolved.[13]

The sound of the village church bell reminds him of thanksgiving. He offers up a prayer of gratitude not from duty, but (a poet's phrase this) 'relieving himself from the overflowing of his heart'.

Particularly in Whewell's writing, but also, though to a lesser extent, in the later notebooks of both Greenough and Sedgwick, there is an influence of literary and artistic models of the 'poetic', 'sublime', or beautiful. Greenough was not just stirred by classical material as he travelled through Italy. He noted mediaeval building styles and the fine art of the Renaissance. In Sedgwick's workaday field notebooks of the 1820s there is an occasional interruption of lists of angles of strike and records of rock specimens to record a visit to a mediaeval abbey or an attractive ruin. Whewell published books about the history of architecture and engaged in correspondence with Wordsworth amongst others on aesthetic issues. Sometimes the aesthetic influence is directly Wordsworthian as in Sedgwick's description of the Fens in winter:

Wordsworth told me he considered a dead interminable plain a sublime object. The eye of the body finds nothing to stop it, and has nothing to rest on and therefore it is that the mind's eye is upon conjuring tricks, and easily finds a beast for the poet's soul to stride over. I don't think I express the thought in his exact words, but I trust you understand all about it without any more words. One day the vision of Peterborough Cathedral seen across the hazy fen was very sublime. It seemed of supernatural magnitude, and its clustering forms were very majestic.[14]

This brief evocation of a winter landscape with its intriguing image of the conjuring trick is recognizably Burkean in its definition of sublimity and grandeur. Similarly the distinction between the bodily eye and the mind's eye is a common line of argument of earlier writers such as John Ray.[15]

The Romantic geologists' appreciation of natural beauty was not only an exercise in aesthetic judgements, it was an emotional experience. Theirs was not only an intellectual appreciation or a perception of good taste. The geologists freely used words like 'joy', 'pleasure', and 'delight' in describing natural scenery, but even more in considering the attraction of being a geologist. Whewell, who, more than any of the geologists, had substantial expertise in other disciplines, selected geology as a specially rewarding study and refers personally to 'the delighted discoveries of our geological teachers'.[16] Hutton associated order with pleasure and used the same term as Whewell's, 'delight', for the geologist's emotional reward in communicating his findings to others.[17] There is, in many of the geologists from Hutton onwards, a level of pleasure above the satisfaction of discovery. It is a pleasure akin to Wordsworthian 'joy'. Indeed in one early passage from Hutton's medical dissertation for the University of Leiden, he describes joy as being felt in every 'component part' of a natural system:

Nature, everywhere the most amazingly and outstandingly remarkable producer of living bodies, being most carefully arranged according to physical, mechanical, and chemical laws, does not given even the smallest hint of its extraordinary and tireless workings and quite clearly points to its worth as being alone worthy of a benign and omnipotent God: and carries this bright quality in all of its traces, in that, just as all of its general mechanisms rejoice, so also do all of their various smallest component parts rejoice in the depth of wisdom, in the height of perfection, which lie far beyond every investigation of the human mind.[18]

Throughout the first half of the nineteenth century this enthusiasm for the effects of discovery continues. Lyell's style can swell to the rhapsodic. Here is a passage from *Principles of Geology* of 1832 which links Lyell's own science with history, quoting the bright, contemporary star of history, Niebuhr, in the process: 'Meanwhile the charm of first discovery is our own; and as we explore this magnificent field of enquiry, the sentiment of a great historian of our times may continually be present to our minds that "he who calls what has vanished back again into being enjoys a bliss like that of creativity".'[19] Geology could be tackled with zest, as when Lyell describes his undiminished vigour working on a cliff face in 1852: 'But I never enjoyed the reading of a marvellous chapter of the big volume more.'[20]

Roy Porter comments about the age: 'The Enlightenment ideal of cosmopolitan stoicism gave way to passionate Romantic engagement.' Porter continues with the words of the geologist, the Reverend W. D. Conybeare in 1811: 'I partake more largely of the spirit of the knight of La Mancha than of his craven squire and prefer the enterprise and adventures of geological errantry to rich castles and luxurious entertainments.'[21] Because Romanticism encouraged the love of the natural rather than the urban environment, of hills and rock faces rather than the satisfaction of fossil collections in cabinets, the geologists were in tune with a vast contemporary public interest. Geology provided for the public the possibility of excitement, albeit an innocent excitement, of making discoveries which might turn out to be as amazing as Mary Anning's fantastic fossil monsters, yet did not appear to disturb the religious faith of most of the countless amateurs who became keen collectors. It was not only amateurs who experienced a thrilling sensation in their search for specimens. Charles Darwin, trained as a geologist by Adam Sedgwick, expresses the 'professional's' enthusiasm using both terms, 'poetical' and 'imagination': 'I a geologist, have ill-defined notions of land covered with ocean, former animals, slow force cracking surface, etc. truly poetical...There is much imagination in every view.'[22]

Distinguishing between the sensations derived directly from Nature, from great mountains, deep valleys, and cascading waterfalls and the intellectual delight of scientific enquiry into why and how these phenomena occurred might, at first sight, conceptualize the essential difference between the poet's realm and that of the man of science. A Romantic poet, it might be thought, was a medium for the unimpeded effect of Nature, of childhood memories stored and recalled in later life. The division between the poetic in the true realm of the poet and the poetic in the second kingdom of geology is, however, artificial. In the first place it is a gross oversimplification to suggest that Wordsworth records immediate sensations. He is the essential poet of preparedness for Nature's impact, of rumination on the sensations of the past, of the education of the mind to receive the experiences which eventually are incorporated into the heart and along the veins. Fitzgerald (1984), approaching the study of the younger Wordsworth through the contacts he had made with the sciences of physical chemistry and physiology, has recorded the poet's philosophical journey out of necessitarianism into the principle of 'elective imagination' in correspondence with Nature. The geologists and the poet alike were clear that the human mind was not a passive receiver of sensation. The beneficial effects of studying were both emotional and moral. The geologists, like Wordsworth, accepted that Nature's hand was hidden, but they knew that Nature's benefits could be realized in adult life by diligent application and careful understanding.

I have already instanced Whewell quoting the 'Ode: Intimations of Immortality' and reflecting in a highly Wordsworthian manner on his childhood experiences: 'We owe to the early years of our boyhood, influences which remain with us through all the years of succeeding life.'[23] Sedgwick in his unpublished autobiographical notes written in old age offers up a prayer of thanks, which combines not only the testament of a geologist who sought in Nature more than facts, but also the witness of a man who wished it to be known that he was sensitive to

Nature's influence on all people. This summary of his life's work celebrates a link with humanity in a way which echoes the Wanderer's positive statements in *The Excursion* and the definition of the Poet's task described in the 'Preface' to *Lyrical Ballads*:

And here I am still – in my easy chair; thankfully and hopeful. Thankful for an active and I would fain hope an useful life – thankful that I was taught early to love the face of nature – sky, sea, stars, mountains, valleys, brooks, and trees: that I have spent so much of my life in direct communion with nature, which is the reflection of the power, wisdom and goodness of God – that I have thus been enabled to draw strength for the battle of life, and a deeper sympathy with my fellow creatures of every grade.[24]

Both Whewell and Sedgwick display a receptive attitude to the unbidden influences of Nature, but both men acknowledge that such a gift has to be nurtured and developed. Sedgwick advised his audience at the Geological Society in 1831 that their discipline required 'more than common powers'.[25] Wordsworth too as the years passed adopted a more cautious tone about the inevitability of the direct influence of Nature. In *The Excursion* the Solitary is exposed to the hills and the winds of the Lake District, but they have not mellowed his cynicism. In book II, although he had experienced one of the most vivid of cloud-created visions, the Solitary is moved to prayer, but in the end is left defeated:

> I have been dead, I cried,
> And now I live! Oh! wherefore *do* I live?
> And with that pang I prayed to be no more![26]

The Wanderer's task is to make the Solitary see with new eyes the message of the mountains and the rivers. He has to be educated to see reality again. The 'poetic' process is not a passive experience for the geologists, whose task is to enable others to see Nature in new form, like the characters in *The Excursion* who are given the task of opening the inner eye of the Solitary, blind in his despair.

THE NOBLE SCIENCE OF GEOLOGY

The 'poetic' was pleasurable yet serious. An important word in the context of both the poet's mission and the geologist's task was 'nobility'. Neither geology nor poetry were trivial pursuits. Dean summarizes the position: 'Geology for them [the Romantics] was not an idle diversion, interesting, but remote. It was fundamental and connative for them, and interesting because of its immense significance.'[27] Humphry Davy in 1811 made an important distinction between the common enjoyment of the great outdoors and the higher level that is reached by the serious student of geology: 'mountain country which is the very theatre of science is always impressive and delightful', but 'a new and nobler species of enjoyment arises in the mind, when the arrangement of it, its uses, and its subserviency to life are considered'.[28] Geology is noble for a number of reasons, the lowest being the sheer scale and difficulty of the geological enterprise. Greenough took on in the decade of 1810 to 1820 (at the same time as William Smith) the publication of a geological map of the British Isles, assimilating knowledge from hundreds of collectors of specimens and recorders of local detail. Later he organized and achieved the geological mapping of the Indian subcontinent. Sedgwick and Murchison explored what were then regarded as the oldest rocks of the earth's history. This was exploration in depth in a double sense – the deepest layers in a stratigraphical column and the most ancient stretches of created time. Sedgwick robustly dealt with ancient rocks, despite their obscured story and without fear of the far-reaching theological implications which might ensue. He concluded his Presidential lecture in 1831 by saying that his task was to 'comprehend the more intricate phenomena of still older periods, and to connect them with the great physical laws by which all matter is governed'.[29] Whewell similarly engaged with large-scale issues, becoming a one man collection centre for knowledge of tides from around the world and systematizing tidal information, literally on a global scale.

It is not difficulty alone that raised geology to the level of status. The character of the geologist is elevated by his studies. According to Whewell, members of the Geological Society of London 'have shown that there are no talents and no endowments which may not find their fitting employment in this science'. Their labours have been pursued with the great character-forming qualities of zeal, knowledge, and philosophical eloquence. One of geology's great advantages, as seen by the early nineteenth-century members of the Geological Society, was that it enabled its students to travel and to mix with different classes of society. Just as Whewell in his letters recommended to his sisters the pursuit of literature, because it widened social experience, so he commends geology's virtue of broadening the mind. It is hard not to be amazed at the improvements that are claimed: geology has given its acolytes 'that prompt and liberal spirit, and that open and cordial bearing, which results from intercourse with the world on a large and unfettered scale. It is not too much to say that, in our time, Practical Geology has been one of the best schools of philosophical and general culture of the mind.'[30]

Greenough is in some ways a test case for judging Romantic and Victorian enthusiasm for geology. Outwardly preferring a strict Baconian methodology and always on guard against fanciful conjectures not based on experience and systematic collection, in his notebooks and in his more prestigious public addresses, he is as much concerned to demonstrate the nobility of his subject as to recommend control and hard facts. Greenough's Presidential address to the Royal Geographical Society in 1840 was an emotional occasion. He described the pursuit of seeking causes for phenomena as occasioning 'delight, not to say the glory'. Such a quest he regards as 'the noblest part' of a geographer's craft, although (here the practical man speaks out) not that part which is most useful to the world and which will encourage worldly success. Whether it is his own original idea or someone else's we shall never know, but on a slip of paper in the unpublished notebook entitled *Philosophical Dictionary* is found an elevated mission for science. It reads: 'Science is the attribute of the most high – and every addition to our knowledge brings us so much nearer to the condition of the Godhead.'[31] Rudwick in his study of the foundation of the Geological Society provides a revealing quotation from its anonymous publication, *Geological Enquiries*, which is now attributable to Greenough: 'Geology in its comprehensive sense is consequently a sublime and difficult science, but fortunately for its progress it is susceptible of divisions into many different departments, several of which are capable of being extended by mere observation.'[32] Sublimity is the garland of those who are fortunate to be full-time priests of the study, attended by well-trained, part-time observers.

It is Sedgwick more than any of his contemporaries, until the younger Hugh Miller took over the mantle, who most represents the ennobling quality of geology. From the point of view of the modern interpretation of the relationship between science, technology, and the industrial revolution, there is strikingly little economic or instrumental argument in Sedgwick's writings to justify the study of geology. The function of science is not to aid the economy but to elevate the human spirit. His justification uses a significant metaphor from the human family: 'She is a handmaid of those toiling for the good of fellow man...claims kindred with offspring of exact knowledge and lends no vulgar help to loftiest investigations of human thought.'[33] Readers of the 'Preface' to the second edition of *Lyrical Ballads* will recall the metaphor used by Wordsworth when he looked forward to the remote possibility of science becoming 'a genuine inmate of the household of man', giving man a higher conception of his capacities and duties, and a better power in following them 'to their proper end'.[34] When, in 1819, Sedgwick established with other Cambridge tutors a 'Society for Scientific Communication' it was not to encourage the growth of the national economy. Its very title, the Cambridge Philosophical Society, indicates its roots in an older tradition of learning. The first rule of the Society was 'That this Society be instituted for the purpose of promoting Scientific Enquiries, and of facilitating the communication of facts connected with the advancement of Philosophy.' At its first meeting the words 'and Natural History' were appended further endorsing an English tradition of learning, largely for its own sake, related to the enlargement of the human mind and to its improvement.[35] Geology was at a relatively early stage in its institutionalization in the university but clearly admitted to this liberal house of intellect. Indeed, in 1823 the subject for the Chancellor's Prize for Poetry was 'Ars Geologica' (Rupke, 1983).

ADDRESSING THE IMAGINATION AND INFORMING THE REASON

Sedgwick was as careful as any of his contemporaries to separate moral matters from scientific exploration of material facts and to make clear in which domain he was writing; nevertheless, he felt that the scientific and the moral met at the frontiers of science. With his usual, vigorous spirit, Sedgwick frequently entered into controversy with those who feared the most from geologizing. In these pugnacious arguments, and in other more serene contexts, such as the geological 'letters' printed with Wordsworth's *A Guide*, he always demonstrated a passionate interest in the human condition and a conviction that scientific enquiry was conducive to the elevation of human life in both a moral and a spiritual sense. In the 'Preface' to the second edition of *Lyrical Ballads*, Wordsworth also foresaw a type of science which could become a noble adjunct to human progress. He could find no more convinced discipline for this doctrine than Adam Sedgwick. Many passages of Sedgwick's writing justify geology as a way of extending the consciousness of mankind and awakening it to the mind of the Creator. *A Discourse on the Studies of the University* is a key document for the understanding of the interpretation of Romanticism and its connection with the sciences and theology. In a passionate justification, which has within it the Romantic image of Prometheus, Sedgwick returns again to the allegation of aridity in his discipline: 'To many minds, the forms of natural knowledge presented in the abstractions of severe science, are cold and uninviting: but, if we follow them with the light of other kindred studies, such as those I have endeavoured faintly to shadow out; we bring down the fire from heaven which at once gives them movement and animation.'[36]

Sedgwick was the geologist who claimed geology as the territory of imagination. We may not presume that his enthusiasm was always uncritically received. Sedgwick's Commemoration Sermon of 1832 from the pulpit of Trinity College Chapel, for instance, provides Greenough with a target: 'He advocates the imagination in lieu of reason, of feelings in opposition to reflexion – he prescribes in moral philos the language of demonstration and of inductive proof in politics, as mischievous and impracticable, he finds fault with Locke for discarding from his system of metaphysics the power of the imagination.'[37] Greenough continued in a similar, stern vein to castigate Sedgwick, as a few pages previously in the notebook he had chided Whewell, for suggesting that moral ideas were innate. However, Greenough was himself interested in trying to define the imagination and to make it more precise. His attempt to do so has literary echoes. In the unpublished, half-developed notes for the *Philosophical Dictionary* a fruitful reference occurs: 'Imagination or fancy is wilful delirium under control. With the growth of judgement it declines, as the fruit ripens the blossom falls. Delirium is nearly related to chance; it is a state of mind in which ideas follow each other in an order that could not have been anticipated and without any apparent connexion.'[38] The words 'under control' are written slightly above the line of handwriting as if they are an emendation. At one level, particularly by a Wordsworthian, this definition of imagination or fancy could be understood as the falling away of childhood's vision. At a more philosophical level it is an instance of Greenough's scientific doctrine of controlled experience and empirically derived truth in the ascendant over feeling and immature spontaneity. Behind this statement, however, is a literary ancestry. Greenough's classical education would make him aware of Plato's use of 'mania' to describe the artistic excitement of possession by the Muses. The words 'delirium' and 'control', however, make a more contemporary connection. They strikingly echo the passage in *Biographia Literaria*, where Coleridge contrasts fancy and imagination:

To the faculty by which I had characterized Milton, we should confine the term *imagination*; while the other would be contra-distinguished as *fancy*. Now were it once fully ascertained, that this division is no less grounded in nature, than that of delirium from mania, or Otway's

Lutes , lobsters, seas of milk and ships of amber,
from Shakespeare's.
What! Have his daughters brought him to this pass?
or from the preceding apostrophe to the elements; the theory of the fine arts, and of poetry in particular, could not, I thought, but derive some additional and important light.[39]

There are also similar echoes of Wordsworth's association of fancy with mania (for example, 'Mad Fancy' in *The Excursion*, book IV). Like Greenough, the poet uses the epithet 'wilful': in book VIII of *The Prelude*, Wordsworth writes of 'wilful Fancy grafted upon feelings / Of the imagination',[40] whereas Greenough writes of 'wilful delirium under control'. Not surprisingly, for a dedicated apostle of rational methodology, Greenough in this passage emphasizes the word 'control', but the idea of control is not absent from Wordsworth's complex notion of the dedicated, prepared imagination of the poet.

This combination of reason, doubly controlled by the prepared mind and by the power of educated imagination, was how the geologists articulated their methodology. Sedgwick's apologia for geology is also a statement of different ways of being a scientist. In *A Discourse*, Sedgwick argues that the investigation of the external world, through the new sciences, leads a student to acknowledge 'the being of God'. How does this revelation by science occur? In a dual form: Nature is made available to the young student 'by addressing the imagination and by informing the reason'.[41] Sedgwick confidently asserted in his Presidential address in 1831 that the geologist is no longer kept at the door of 'Nature's temple'[42] but 'allowed to pass within and to be so far a partaker of her mysteries, as to see with his intellectual eye both the past and the future'.[43] He is clear that, wherever it enquired, geology would discover material which would foster the imagination. The secrets of the temple would not shrivel in the light of science, but instead they would be enhanced by the scientist who enters the sanctum in the spirit of communion.

Sedgwick's consideration of the faculty of imagination is worked out in hierarchical fashion in *A Discourse*. In the third part of that text he criticizes both Locke and Paley for an inadequate theory of mental powers. Here Sedgwick is referring to Paley's *Principles of Moral and Political Philosophy*,[44] in a phrase which might have come from either Coleridge's or Wordsworth's pen, he writes that Locke and Paley neglected the fact that the external word is 'fitted to our imaginative powers'. The phrase is reminiscent of Wordsworth's lines from the 'Preface' to *The Excursion*.

> How exquisitely the individual Mind
> (And the progressive powers perhaps no less
> of the whole species) to the external World
> Is fitted: – and how exquisitely too –
>
> Theme this but little heard of among men –
> The external World is fitted to the Mind.[45]

Sedgwick continues, 'It is by the imagination more perhaps than by any other faculty of the soul, that man is raised above the conditions of a beast.' These powers are the 'high attributes of the soul'. They operate in three ways. First, imagination applies 'creative energy' to the soul; second, it helps the soul to generalize by pure reason; and third, it enables the soul to link material and immaterial things so the soul mounts 'up from earth to heaven'. 'All that is refined in civilized life, all that is lofty in poetry or ennobling in art, flows chiefly from this one fountain.'[46] It is important to identify the seat of the activity from the last-quoted passage. It is the soul, for Sedgwick is in fact dealing with three human faculties and attributes: reason, imagination, and, above them all, faith. Reason, he argues, in *A Discourse* is 'purged, expanded and sanctified by the influence of Faith'. By participating in the rational process of understanding Nature, we are taken beyond the evidence conveyed by ordinary human senses. This journey of the mind has one purpose only, to understand 'the great scheme of Providence'.

THE HIGHER STRATA ABOVE REASON

The intellectual roots of the idea of the hierarchy of human perception from the simple sensory up to higher states of perception and on to the moral order are in a strong English tradition at least as old as Locke. Contemporarily with Wordsworth, this hierarchy is found, differently expressed, in the psychological writings of Hutton and Greenough and, of course, in Whewell's studies of inductive reason. Much of this ladder of human perception (the senses, the power of reason, combined with imagination and processed through faith) is close to Wordsworth's doctrinal expression in *The Excursion* of the assenting, excursive power of the human mind.[47] Sedgwick was not alone among his own contemporaries and among younger men in acknowledging a higher level of human thought than the rational. Both Wordsworth and Sedgwick, the latter in a much less powerful way, shared with a new generation of early Victorian intellectuals a faith which progressed above and beyond material, rational argument. Their powerful notion of faithful assent emerged in its most articulated form in John Henry Newman's later studies, drawn together in 1870 in *A Grammar of Assent*. Sedgwick is fully theological and yet scientific in the terms of his times.

Sedgwick's highly charged statements about the place of geology in the schema of faith are not, however, restricted to a popular non-scientific readership such as those who read *A Discourse* or the 'letters' accompanying *A Guide*. In one of his most important papers to the Geological Society of London in 1831, at the conclusion of a long disquisition on the structure of the Lake District, Sedgwick reiterates his reassurances about the higher mental powers made accessible by a geologist's methodology. This science may be new, but it 'has supplied materials of thought for intellects the most robust, and results to satisfy imagination the most ardent'. Unlike other 'exact sciences', geology is unlikely to lead to precision because it is so complex in its enquiries. In this dilemma lies one of its most attractive features and a further illustration of its imaginative powers: 'That which is exact in science, must be circumscribed and defined, but of our labours we have no power to foresee the limits and there is an intense and poetic interest in the very uncertainty and boundlessness of our speculation.'[48] Reason takes the ardent student of geology to the boundaries of experience. There are, beyond those frontiers, areas that are properly the domain of religious belief but not of empirical study. Sedgwick appears to have been able to live comfortably with this division of experience in a way which later Victorian scientists would not. He was not alone amongst contemporary geologists in believing in a Divine order of circumstances, but, more confidently and robustly than Lyell for instance, he was able to accept, and indeed to state with conviction and authority, that there were areas of human experience approachable only by faith enriched by imagination.

William Whewell's considerable studies on the nature of scientific thought provide a vast source for understanding a scientific culture which rose above the level of technique and mechanical materialism. One of the chief interests for anyone seeking out Whewell's approximation to or sympathy with the thinking of Wordsworth must be the place Whewell gave to imagination in his scheme of inductive thinking. Whewell's work was devoted to erecting a secure framework for a scientific establishment that had to avoid two intellectually disastrous traps, disastrous that is for British intellectuals. On the one hand, there was the spectre of cold reason, particularly of French materialism and, at home, of Utilitarianism. On the other hand there was fundamentalism – revealed religion rejecting the rational power of the human mind. Another aspect of the same force of irrationalism on which science might founder was the spinning of unsupported theories (for instance about the origin of the earth), unrelated to empirical observation and verification. Avoiding this pair of disasters, unredeemed reason and irrational fundamentalism, Whewell and his contemporaries had to steer a path which retained the values of objectivity and which created hypotheses in a disciplined, orderly way by inductive processes. To Whewell there is no doubt that reason must be deployed in the investigation of the world of objective phenomena. However, he was always sharply aware of the need to avoid a mechanical methodology. Yeo comments on Whewell's wish to avoid too great an emphasis on empiricism: 'His subsequent major works on this history and philosophy of science were a continuation of his earlier defence of the claims of theory, and can be read as an extended indication of the role of hypotheses and imagination in scientific thought.'[49] In an earlier article, Yeo wrote succinctly that 'Whewell attempted to repudiate empiricist philosophy without sacrificing the empirical dimension of physical science.'[50] It is in this careful steering between the two whirlpools of materialism and irrationalism that Whewell achieved considerable success and admiration in his own lifetime. Significantly, for the purposes of this study, the same judgement was exercised by his close friend, Wordsworth, in his mature years.

Science may rely upon experience but that experience is never only of the present. To Whewell, scientific discovery is a continuous process, it is the 'heir of a vast patrimony...Our species from the time of its creation has been travelling onwards in the pursuit of truth...'[51] Previous ages may have made errors in their explanations, but nothing which was done then is now useless or inessential, although a former theory will be less likely to attract the attention of modern scientists, because they are so close to making new discoveries. Whewell is keen to avoid a scientific habit of mind which assumes the repeated, rapid overthrow of previous scientific beliefs. Whereas, in the twentieth century, we are comfortable with titles such as *The Structure of Scientific Revolutions* (Kuhn, 1970), Whewell, perhaps fully aware of painful political implications, is at pains to argue that 'what might appear as a succession of revolutions' is in reality 'a series of developments'.[52] Even the language of past science becomes part of the continuous development of truths and, like a medal of gold, is 'a treasure as well as a token'. However, there are undoubtedly moments of great change in the development of each science. To Fisch (1991), Whewell's *The History of the Inductive Sciences* was fundamentally Catastrophic. Scientific progress is achieved in unanticipated creative leaps – a far cry from the piecemeal uniformitarianism of Lyell and Darwin.[53] Whewell designated the phases through which scientific progress occurs. The preliminary period before a moment of change he calls a 'Prelude'. The moment of rapid expansion or even reversal of old truths is an 'Epoch', after which there is always a 'Sequel'. There were periods when the Sequel lasted so long as to seem almost stationary. At such times, and the mediaeval period was one, men proceeded to state truths from accepted principles rather than by observing facts from which followed general principles. Deduction, not induction, is the mark of such an age and its progress in scientific endeavour is negligible.

To Whewell the primary scientific process of his own time was induction. By 'induction', he meant the process of generating statements of truth from observed experience: the doctrines of the sciences 'are obtained by a common process of collecting general truths from particular observed facts, which process is termed *Induction*'.[54] From the start of the major work, *The Philosophy of the Inductive Sciences*, Whewell opines that there are truths which we can find by contemplating the world within as well as the world without. Experience is not limited to what we can see or hear or feel. However, in this text he established limits, confining his analysis to the study of the external, material world, reserving for a later, perhaps ultimate, study, a science of morality. By 'experience' of the material world Whewell means much more than Locke intended. Indeed, he specifically rejects the limitation of what we can know from our five senses. Like Coleridge, Whewell respects the complexity of the mind: 'The mind is in some ways passive as well as active.'[55] Such a statement reminds the reader of the excitement of a Romantic poet at the moment of perception of Nature, when there is an energetic involvement of both subject and object. It is therefore interesting to note that in the opening pages of *The Philosophy of the Inductive Sciences*, where Whewell elaborates on the theme of ideas being 'moulded, combined, and interpreted by mental acts', he quotes 'a philosophical poet'. The philosophical poet is Wordsworth; the poem is 'Lines written a few miles above Tintern Abbey'.[56]

At an early point in the major work on induction Whewell introduces the word 'Idea' to 'express that element supplied by the mind itself, which must be combined with Sensation in order to produce knowledge'.[57] Ideas are not Platonic, waiting passively behind substance; they are created by human mental action: 'For us, ideas are not objects of thought but laws of thought.' Ideas are progressive, for, just as the general may be produced from particular experience, so there can be a movement onwards from general to more general. It can be readily appreciated that, with the benefit of this expanding facility, the human mind is admirably adapted to scientific activity. In the *Bridgewater Treatise*, where his task was to construct an argument justifying a belief in the power and wisdom of the Almighty, Whewell endorses the essential rightness of scientific activity. Exact and profound study of Nature confirms for the student of science the vague, unformed, but natural impression that there is a 'creating and presiding Intelligence'. However, Whewell steps back from Paleyean Natural Theology: 'It is far from our purpose to represent natural religion as of itself sufficient for our support and guidance; or to underrate the manner in which our views of the Lord of the Universe have been much more, perhaps, than we are sometimes aware, illustrated and confirmed by lights drawn from revelation.'[58]

Whewell is no eighteenth-century deist, with an orderly world-in-waiting, ready to be opened up for discovery solely by the application of human reason. Belief rests on guidance both by reason and by revelation. However, there is a further elaboration to be made. The notion of the 'Idea' which involved the human mind in the act of recognition of a Divine law was an important addition to discussions of the nature of the advancement of knowledge, for it introduced the self-conscious activity of 'understanding'. 'Laws of thought' are different from mechanical laws, but just as discoverable. Science is thus not a cold, procedural activity, but a way of life which involves faith and imaginative interpretation of observed experience. Whewell seems to propose two related intellectual processes, which when working together are most productive. One is the realization of thoughts which generate ideas and the other is human, active will. I referred in chapter five to *Two Introductory Lectures to Two Courses of Lectures on Moral Philosophy*, where Whewell describes the act of will which a thinker must exercise as the 'constant effort' which he makes to realize his thoughts and to understand his actions. Commitment and application will bring the idea before him, 'in the perfect clearness and distinctness which constitute science'.[59] Calculating, recording, and willing are all essential. There is a reminder here of Coleridge's distinction in 'The essays on the principles of method' in *The Friend* between the 'contemplation of reason, namely, that intuition of things which arises when we possess ourselves, as one with the whole, which is substantial knowledge' and 'abstract knowledge or the science of the mere understanding'.[60] Both Coleridge and Whewell have passed beyond the stage of distinguishing the simple collection of data about phenomena which the ignorant might call knowledge or which Wordsworth in *The Prelude* castigated as 'the monster birth / Engendered by these too industrious times'.[61] Wordsworth similarly makes a simple distinction between two ways of knowing, the accumulation of 'knowledge' and the wider 'knowledge' derived from a richer experience.

The influence of Kant and German idealist philosophy on Whewell and his contemporaries has been carefully explored.[62] Certainly, Whewell, Sedgwick, and their Cambridge colleagues, if not all the members of the Geological Society, were as aware of German 'Naturphilosophie' by the 1830s, just as Greenough and a generation including Wordsworth and Coleridge had gained a first inkling of German and French scientific and philosophical studies in the 1790s and in the first decade of the nineteenth century. By the time that Whewell came to publish his history of scientific method, at least for those who were not declared materialists or Benthamite Utilitarians, it had become possible to adopt what Laudan calls a 'more liberal methodology' in their geological enquiries.[63] The recognition of the combining, synthesizing power of imagination was a major step in the acceptance of 'Understanding' (as distinct from Coleridge's 'mere understanding') as a more inclusive approach to interpreting nature. 'Understanding' with its sense of the engagement of an active, cultivated scientific mind admitted the scientist to fields of activity which could not be entered by those who merely pursued the collection of facts or who held rigidly to empiricism. To the geologists of the 1820s and 1830s the mind was as much an area of interest as the material with which the mind engaged. Geology in short became a very human science. Before proceeding in the next chapter to that theme, I shall briefly consider Wordsworth's mature attitude to what science could become.

WORDSWORTH AND A NOBLE VISION OF SCIENCE

The most famous passage where Wordsworth laid down a possibility for science to engage in the sublime task of serving humanity is in the 'Preface' to the second edition of *Lyrical Ballads*. As noted earlier, Sharrock's study has shown that Wordsworth enlarged his original draft of the 'Preface' in order to respond to Humphry Davy's argument (or rather to Coleridge's report of it) that science had a distinguished role to play in the future of mankind. The well-known analysis of the distinction between the Poet and the Man of Science stems from this argument. The future prospect as seen by Wordsworth is not exclusively dominated by the Poet. A glimmer of hope is held out that eventually a day will dawn when there will be a union profitable to humanity and joyously accepted by 'the most philosophic of writing'. By the time that *The Excursion* was written, there is a more optimistic agenda for the role of science, although there is no diminution in the castigation of lifeless science, of prying and poring. In book IV of *The Excursion*, 'Despondency Corrected', the Wanderer depicts a new future for humanity, a change of heart which will 'clothe / The naked spirit, ceasing to deplore / The burden of existence'. I have already quoted the lines which foresee science as a 'precious visitant' and noted its religious tone. What follows immediately from that passage is the commissioning of science in the order of nobility:

> not for this
> Shall it forget that its most noble use,
> Its most illustrious province, must be found
> In furnishing clear guidance, a support
> Not treacherous, to the mind's *excursive* power.[64]

Like the geologists, Wordsworth's vision of science is elevated. The function of science for both poet and geologist is to be a kind of energy that releases ever higher powers of the mind, expanding its excursive capacity.

The theme of the elevation and ennobling of scientific activity is pursued years later in *Memorials of a Tour in Italy, 1837*. There is still a scepticism about the outcome of science in the present generation:

> The Stream
> Has to our generation brought and brings
> Innumerable gains, yet we, who now
> Walk in the light of day, pertain full surely
> To a chilled age, most pitiably shut out
> From that which *is* and actuates, by forms,
> Abstractions, and by lifeless fact to fact
> Minutely linked with diligence uninspired,
> Unrectified, unguided, unsustained,
> By godlike insight. To this fate is doomed
> Science, wide-spread and spreading still as be
> Her conquests, in the world of sense made known.[65]

What is necessary for modern man to redress the lost balance? The poet
seeks an answer a few lines further on. His response to the question is
important because in one brief phrase, Wordsworth explains so much –
about the inadequacy of dull and lifeless sciences, about 'prying and
probing', but even more about the insistent historical quest:

> By gross Utilities enslaved we need
> More of ennobling impulse from the past,
> If to the future aught of good must come
> Sounder and therefore holier than the ends
> Which, in the giddiness of self-applause,
> We covet as supreme.[66]

The key phrase 'ennobling impulse from the past' has memories of the
young Wordsworth ('one impulse from a vernal wood') but 'ennobling'
and 'from the past' marks this as a poem of his later years. Into place
for the reader falls the long section from what is effectively three books
of *The Excursion* devoted to the mountain graveyard. There the friends
devoted themselves to ghostly impulses, the voices of the churchyard
past. We can now also understand the urgency in *The Ecclesiastical
Sonnets*, published in 1822, to seek for a pattern in Christian history.
The iteration of historical and prehistorical references in other sonnet
sequences also becomes more than a conventional historical decora-
tion. Many of the long historical poems of the later years (such as 'The
White Doe of Rylstone' composed from 1807 to 1808 but not published
until 1815, 'The Egyptian Maid' composed in 1828, and 'The Russian
Fugitive' also composed in 1828) may be understandable at a superficial
level in the context of the age's absorption with mediaeval trappings.
They make, however, even more sense in the light of the older poet's

elevation of an 'ennobling impulse' derived from an unbroken historical tradition in opposition to mechanical utility.

Whewell's history of science shares the same set of values about a
living tradition. There is an 'advance and progress in the main' in the
story of scientific progress, but Whewell's account of science and its
history is a cumulative one rather than a sequence of error remedied
by new 'correct' discoveries. The potential of their science as well as
the privileged glimpses it had already given excited those who began at
first warily, then with total confidence, to call themselves geologists.
Wordsworth, to whom they publicly acknowledged a debt, was at one
with them in approving the potential of their discipline, but like any
good mentor, he was unsparing in his condemnation of their failings.
Like them he had no patience with those who did not reach for the
highest rewards. Look again at the famous passage which appeared to
dismiss archeologists, botanists, and geologists in book III of *The
Excursion*:

> Nor is that Fellow-wanderer, so deem I
> Less to be envied, (you may trace him oft
> By scars which his activity has left
> Beside our roads and pathways, though, thank Heaven!
> This covert nook reports not of his hand)
> He who with pocket hammer smites the edge
> Of luckless rock or prominent stone, disguised
> In weather stains or crusted o'er by Nature
> With her first growths, detaching by the stroke
> A chip or splinter – to resolve his doubts;
> And, with that ready answer satisfied,
> The substance classes by some barbarous name,
> And hurries on; or from the fragments picks
> His specimen, if but haply interveined
> With sparkling mineral, or should crystal cube
> Lurk in its cells – and thinks himself enriched,
> Wealthier, and doubtless wiser, than before![67]

Wordsworth's own disarming apology to Sedgwick about this passage
(it is a character's voice not the poet's and it is about mineralogists not
geologists) side-steps the truly critical note, which is twofold: first, the
level of joy is low – the collector has only the satisfaction of a collector;
second the mineral collector is a poor achiever – he has no ennobling
experience from his collecting. Indeed his situation is even more
doleful, because he believes himself to be richer and wiser, when all he
has achieved is a 'ready answer' and a new 'barbarous name' for the

mineral. A new ranking order for science was beginning to emerge – the lowest mundane, arid, object-related, the highest character forming, socially purposeful, ennobling – in short the 'poetic'.

One episode recorded at second-hand sums up Wordsworth's mature position on 'the proper sense of the word Science'. It is an incident which reinforces the poet's prediction for science in the 'Preface' to the *Lyrical Ballads* of 1802, although it is from a much later period in Wordsworth's life when geologists had become his friends. When he was visiting his friend, the mathematician, William Rowan Hamilton, in 1829, Wordsworth read aloud from *The Excursion* and then defended 'its slight reverence for science'. Eliza May Hamilton, the scientist's sister, recorded the occasion:

Science in the proper sense of the word Science, that raised the mind to the contemplation of God in works, and which was pursued with that end as its primary and great object; but as for all other science, all science which put this end out of view, all science which was a bare collection of facts for their own sake, or to be applied merely to the material uses of life, he thought it degraded instead of raising the species. All science which waged war with and wished to extinguish Imagination and the mind of man, and to leave it nothing of any kind but the naked knowledge of facts, was he thought much worse than useless. . .and of dangerous and debasing tendency.[68]

William Hamilton ventured to suggest that the intellectual faculties held equal rank with imagination. William Wordsworth 'smiled kindly' at Hamilton's remark which, after all, to him, was neither more penetrating nor more advanced than the arguments made by Humphry Davy twenty-seven years previously. This small incident reveals that, for men like Hamilton, Whewell, and Sedgwick, Wordsworth had become the sage to whom the scientists turned, not he to them.

CHAPTER 9

Geologists and humanity

Descriptive terms, however broad (such as man of science or natural philosopher) or however specific (such as geologist or biologist) require definition according to the historical context in which they were used. It can not be assumed that the early nineteenth-century use of an intellectual 'class name' signified what we mean by the categorization almost two hundred years later. There is in any case a risk of exclusivity in categorization. A geologist, for instance, 'must' be one type of intellectual, but by definition not another. Research into the lives of early nineteenth-century British and Continental scientists (again, a modern terminology) demonstrates that the intellectual range of these men, and a small and largely hidden group of women, was very wide and, furthermore, they were conscious that connections could and should be made between their disparate intellectual pursuits.[1] This study of a selected small group of geologists attempts to demonstrate what those interests were. These geologists were confident that there was a relationship between geology and human studies, particularly the moral, the political, the social, and, above all, the historical. This chapter aims to consider the intellectual routes followed by geologists who related their scientific studies to human history and to moral philosophy.

THE REFLEXIVE SCIENTIFIC MIND

A distinctive feature of both Continental and British Romanticism, varying in form from writer to writer, but emerging in some guise in all, was an intense interest in the reflexive activity of the human mind. Whereas eighteenth-century writers (in Britain, particularly those who followed Locke) considered in detail the processes by which the mind processed experience, at the end of that century and the beginning of the next, thinkers turned their attention from the process to an intense interest in how and what the subject knew about the processes of his own mental activity. It was, in short, an age with a passion for introspective psychology. In their collection of articles on European Romanticism and the sciences, Cunningham and Jardine head their first chapter, 'The Age of Reflexion' and quote from Heinrich Steffen's *Alt und Neue* of 1821: 'Do you want to know nature? Turn your glance inwards and you will be granted the privilege of beholding nature's stages of development in the stages of your spiritual education. Do you want to know yourself? Seek in nature: her works are those of the self-same spirit.'[2] Statements of this kind could equally well reappear in a geologist's autobiography as in a poet's. The interactions of inner and outer Nature act as clear markers for the ending of a Descartian division of mind and matter, with its distinction between alert observer and the inert observed. The mind engaged in interaction with Nature becomes a legitimate topic for both philosophers and poets.

George Bellas Greenough can be produced in evidence as a reflexive scientist. His notebooks and private papers, in contradiction to his external image as a Baconian with a rationalist methodology, reveal a continuous process of self-examination and an intensive interest in the human mind in action. Indeed, the preparation of a *Philosophical Dictionary*, though it never saw the light of publication, was an act of reflexion in itself. In religious matters, Greenough's scepticism is concentrated on the destruction of myths and of irrational doctrines such as the Trinity and the Atonement[3] but, unshaken by the power of reason, his fundamental faith stands firm. 'Atheism', he remarks in the *Philosophical Dictionary*, 'is the creed of thinkers, Christianity of Believers', and then continues, 'Belief is an act of mind after considering a proposition, as seeing is an act of the eye after looking at an object.'[4] He robustly confessed in the same jottings, 'I have the same reason to believe in God as in Gravitation – neither of which I understand.' Understanding was an act of assent, an activity of the human mind. There was, he wrote, 'a great difference' between knowing something and being aware that you knew it.

Greenough's psychological musings place him firmly in the tradition which Cunningham and Jardine have identified in Continental scientists and philosophers. Greenough read German and particularly engaged with Kantian thought. He could not accept Locke's dismissal of innate ideas. In the *Philosophical Dictionary* he notes that not only does the evidence from biology and from human beings confirm that there are instincts built into each individual from birth, but there is a strange intermixture of matter and mind: 'Both matter and mind may be imperishable tho' entering continually into new combination.'[5] Perhaps, after death, mind and matter may separately enter into new forms so that neither actually 'dies'. Genius plainly has to be accounted for (another sign of Greenough's Romanticism) and it is obviously associated with extreme forms of variety of the human mind, although (here the rationalist–materialist intervenes) great men usually have good constitutions, and minds weaken as ageing occurs. For procedural, orderly reasons, the mind, whatever strength it may have, whether it is a mind of genius or that of a normal human being, must be studied separately from physical phenomena, despite its link with matter.

Above all, Greenough's theory of mental processes is one of activity: 'There is a power existing in the brain of receiving, retaining and combining with ideas, sensations communicated to it by the outward sense.'[6] Here there are three interacting components: sensations, 'ideas', and the power that actively operates with them. The period of our study is notable for its attention to the mind which is active in reflexion and self-examination. The geologists and the poets were at one in their different spheres in the intense interest they gave to this aspect of being human. Both poets and geologists expressed consciously how they felt about their own activity of interacting with Nature.

Greenough's private excursions into the theme of the active mind are far from unique, nor are they innovative. The overall idea of an 'active universe' has been documented by Piper (1962). He traces the revival of the conception of a living universe to Priestley, Erasmus Darwin, and Hartley. For the historian of geology, it is interesting to note that Piper acknowledged the role of James Hutton's *An Investigation* in extending Priestley's notion that inert matter is a living force. The importance of this last work of Hutton's, has, I believe, been underestimated. It gives an early instance, not only of the active universe, but of the self-reflecting powers of the mind. Probably the most significant contributor in the British Isles to the theme of the human mind in action, reflecting on its own processes was David Hume, whose influence can be perceived in *An Investigation*. Hutton extends the idea of activity to all natural processes and forces. He writes in volume III of *An Investigation* that all external things have power, energy, and force. Nothing is really passive. It is, he writes, 'vulgar prejudice' to regard all external matter as permanent. Those who had attended his geological lectures at the Royal Society of Edinburgh would make the necessary connection between this philosophical doctrine of constant change and a theory of geology declaring perpetual destruction and renewal through vast but slow processes of mountain building and mountain destruction.

Not only has the human mind, to use Greenough's simple terms, 'power existing in the brain of receiving, retaining and combining', in Hutton's conception and in Whewell's explanation of scientific activity, there is a cumulative development, a compound interest of scientific thought. Earlier than the period on which I concentrate in this thesis, Wordsworth had expressed in *The Pedlar* (then reworked into a personal form in *The Prelude* in 1805 – and later through the figure of the Wanderer in *The Excursion*) a statement of the human mind growing and developing, reinforced by its own success. The process of pursuing what may be unattainable but what becomes more desirable by the development of creative faculties is expressed in *The Prelude* thus:

> but that the soul –
> Remembering how she felt, but what she felt
> Remembering not – retains an obscure sense
> Of possible sublimity, to which
> With growing faculties she does aspire
> With faculties still growing, feeling still
> That whatsoever point they gain they still
> Have something to pursue.[7]

Abrams (1973) defines one of the features of Romanticism, particularly imbibed from 'Naturphilosophie', as a 'Romantic spiral' – 'a self-moving circle' of ascending powers.[8] Greenough and Whewell in their different ways are within this tradition. They are not concerned with a mind like a machine ready to receive images, but with one which enhances 'forms'. As the mind works on the forms, it develops a readiness to receive new sensations. Wordsworth's passages on the ascending mind in *The Pedlar*, in excerpts from *The Prelude*, and in the later poems illustrate a doctrine of growth of human power by active thinking – a concept of growth and development not so distant from the theories of philosopher–geologists. Wordsworth's Pedlar is a man whose own thoughts enhance his stock of 'forms' or, as Whewell would express them, of ideas.

> A precious gift, for as he grew in years
> With these impressions would he still compare
> All his ideal stores, his shapes and forms

And, being still unsatisfied with aught
Of dimmer character, he thence attain'd
An *active* power to fasten images
Upon his brain.[9]

Enough has been said in earlier chapters about Sedgwick's rationale for the study of geology, particularly in *A Discourse*, to associate him with these concepts of the ascending powers. It is Whewell, more than any other scientist, who produced for his colleagues a manifesto-like statement of the active mind enhanced by scientific endeavour. His major work, *The Philosophy of the Inductive Sciences* is the key text, but it is significant that his *The History of the Inductive Sciences* was published first, for he presents a thesis of human ability which is essentially developmental and cumulative. Whewell argued that the great names of the past contributed the essential steps in the process; without their work the brilliant perceptions of the present would never have been attained. For Whewell however, there was a special problem about the reflexive power of the mind. By which laws do these subtle powers operate? If the scientific spirit had cumulatively achieved so much in physics, astronomy, and geology, could its power be applied to the human mind itself? Is there a science of psychology with the same laws as the science of physics or of geology?

Throughout the years when he was writing his major works about the nature of inductive science in the material world, Whewell prepared his readers for a parallel work on the laws that operate in the inner world of human beings. Always involved in practical matters relating to scholarship, he was foremost in establishing the study of moral philosophy in Cambridge. The time had arrived to replace Paley's work as a basic undergraduate text, although Becker (1991) points out that it was in fact retained in the Cambridge syllabus at this point and for many years afterwards. Whewell had a larger vision than merely updating an undergraduate's reading. The major publication that he eventually produced, to be read in parallel with the intellectual maps of the history and principles of induction, was *The Elements of Morality Including Polity* (Whewell, 1845). An equally good title might well have been 'The Philosophy of Law', because it is in fact a sustained argument about the way that men are controlled by conscience and also by government. Good government, he argues, produces the appropriate laws for the support of individual conscience. Significantly the dedication of this work is to Wordsworth. It opens with an expression of thanks to him for 'the general privilege of his friendship'.

It is not, however, friendship alone which stimulated the author to justify human morality: 'And there is no one to whom I could with more propriety dedicate such a work: since in your Poems, at the season of life when the mind and the heart are most wrought on by poetry, I along with many others, found a spirit of pure and comprehensive morality, operating to raise your readers above the moral temper of these times.'[10] That dedication in 1845 was a public statement of indebtedness to the, by then, grand old man of poetry.

There is a personal letter of 1841 from Whewell to Wordsworth which gives a more extensive interpretation of Wordsworth's influences. Whewell did not only thank the poet for strengthening moral sense, he also recorded that Wordsworth played a part in his intellectual development:

One of the main objects in the remainder of my life will be to pursue such moral speculations as I have already entered upon, and in these, if there has been anything really good, I am persuaded that I have been led to it in no small degree by the lessons which in former times I learnt from your writing to which I always ascribe a considerable portion of the formation or information of my intellectual character.[11]

Systematic, scientific thought in a subject like geology could take the intellect to the borders of the country that was ruled by special 'laws'. Wordsworth received the credit from scientists like Whewell for interpreting this culture of human behaviour. He was not assumed to be a stranger because he was a poet from the neighbouring domain of intellect.

THE GEOLOGIST: THE ANTIQUARY OF A NEW ORDER

The placing of geology in the parade of the sciences – its ranking in a table of intellectual prestige – gives an indication of its position relative to the study of humanity. In Whewell's table of sciences published in *The Novum Organon Renovatum*, geology is categorized in the group next to the highest subject. Natural theology holds the supreme position. Geology is indeed honoured, but the reasons for its elevation are strange to modern minds used to classifying the sciences separately into the 'earth sciences' and the 'life sciences'. Geology, the study of inanimate phenomena, in Whewell's scheme is also closest to the most animate human sciences, those concerned with language and the study of cultures. Raub (1988) in his examination of Whewell's part in the debate on Chambers's *Vestiges*, suggests why the same intellectual territory was shared by geologists and students of the history of language – they both had to grapple with the mystery of First Causes. The myths of Noah and of Babel, both biblical explanations, had to be replaced. I believe there was in addition an identifiable European influence on Whewell's taxonomy. We may start to explain why geology and the study of cultural history were related by considering the phrase of Cuvier that Whewell quotes on at least four different occasions: 'the geologist is an antiquary of a new order'.[12] The analogy with the activities of the antiquary, who researches human life through human artefacts, is pressed home in *The History of the Inductive Sciences*: 'The organic fossils which occur in the rock, and the medals which we find in the rivers of ancient cities, are to be studied in a similar spirit and for a similar purpose. Indeed it is not always easy to know where the task of the geologist ends and that of the antiquary begins.'[13] There is an even more vivid analogy between geology and the human sciences a little later in the same text when Whewell judges that geology is similar to the history of language: 'English is a conglomerate of Latin words, bound together in a Saxon cement.' Latin words came partly from a 'parent quarry' with all their edges sharp, but they became like pebbles 'obscured and shaped by rolling in a Norman or some other channel'.[14] It is much easier to appreciate, after reading passages of this kind, how guidebooks like Wordsworth's can smoothly move from describing natural landscape, in terms close to those of the geologist, to describing the man-made features which we now classify as belonging to the historian's realm. It is also relevant to note that the well-known passage in book III of *The Excursion*, where the Solitary deems the work of the botanist and the geologist to be so trivial, is preceded by lines denigrating the endeavours of archeologists.[15]

Lest it be thought that William Whewell interpreted in an individualistic way the link between geology and human history, it is useful to remember that William Buckland took the same view of what Rupke (1983) calls 'progressive earth history'. Buckland writing at a time of increasing European interest in the nature of historical method wrote:

If it be interesting to trace the history of our century during the Norman, or Saxon, or Roman, or Celtic periods of its history, it is not less interesting to extend our investigations still further backwards into yet more distant periods of entirely different operations at the bottom of the sea when the strata of our present land were themselves receiving their formulations.[16]

Buckland, like Sedgwick and Whewell, appreciated that the researches of antiquaries and archeologists were closely allied to the way geological evidence was being accumulated. Also like them he freely used the metaphors of 'medals of nature', medals, coins, and inscriptions in writing about geology.[17]

The bridge between geology and the human realm is more than a mere methodological similarity between research methods and reliance on resurrected data. The argument that the 'world of matter' is closer at this point to 'the world of thought and feelings' is based on what, to Whewell, was the fundamental idea underpinning geology. That idea is one of historical change which includes 'the productions of Man as well as of Nature'. For this scientific activity which embraces human as well as natural phenomena, Whewell invents a term of classification, Palaetiology, which fortunately has not survived his own lifetime of enthusiasm for its value: 'While *Palaeontology* describes the beings which have lived in former ages without investigating their causes, and *Aetiology* treats of causes without distinguishing historical from mechanical causation, *Palaetiology* is a combination of the two sciences; exploring by means of the second, the phenomena presented by the first.'[18]

The practice of tracing historical causes by studying present evidence sits reasonably comfortably of course for any geologist whose work was published after 1832, when Lyellian Actualism began to be dominant. For Playfair, thirty years earlier, the teaching of Hutton had provided the same stimulus. In the years after Lyell, Whewell can look to geology with confidence for confirmation of a doctrine of the Creator's uninterrupted sequence: 'The Past has been a series of events connected by this historical causation, and the Present is the last term of this series.' However, the apparently unquestioning acceptance in this quotation by Whewell of an orthodoxy of smooth progression throughout geological time remains consistent with the wary line between Catastrophism and Actualism which he walked during discussions in the Geological Society.

Whewell writes both of science in the singular and the sciences in the plural, but by the time of the publication of *The Philosophy of the Inductive Sciences*, distinctive scientific disciplines had evolved as diverse professional academic activities in European intellectual institutions. The dispersion of knowledge (or 'explosion', as we would now say) is not Whewell's chief thread in his survey of the history of science. He admits that there had been a centrifugal movement of new sciences but regards his own mission as one of unification, seeking out what is common between them. To achieve this task he must group the apparently individual fields of study into clusters of like activity. In *The Novum Organon Renovatum* and in book II of *The Philosophy of the Inductive Sciences* he presents an interesting table of classification. One column lists the 'Fundamental Ideas' or conceptions of scientific activity, the next names the sciences that rely upon those fundamental ideas, and the final column proposes a group name for the collection of cognate sciences. Thus the fundamental ideas of space, time, and number underlie the sciences of geometry and arithmetic, which in turn are grouped as the 'pure mathematical sciences'. The fundamental idea of 'Historical Causation' provides the common group for geology, the distribution of plants and animals, for glossology (or philology), and for ethnography. These are the 'Palaetiological Sciences'. According to Hodge (1991) Whewell's positioning of geology is unique to his methodology, not supported by prior intellectual or institutional precedents. Mineralogy, the subject in which Whewell held the Chair at Cambridge in his younger years, is classified with crystallography, botany, zoology, and comparative anatomy. Unlike geology, mineralogy was one of the 'Classificatory Sciences'. Whewell compares the mineralogist in relation to the geologist with the antiquary who provides medals on which the philosophical historian can base his theories. Mineralogy provides: 'a classification of a large proportion of the objects which Geology employs as the evidence of its statements'.[19]

The principles of 'Historical Causation' and the advance of human life raise a problem of some significance to thinkers in the 1840s and 1850s. The question went like this: if the progress of science continued steadily to clear away superstition and mystery, and at the same time made the scientists themselves more moral and more intelligent people, does that presage a golden age for humanity or even a race beyond the human? To George Greenough, this was at least a proposition to be considered, but note in the following passage the word 'possibly': 'That there exists a mysterious connection throughout the whole of nature that we need not seek in the third heavens another and better world, but that in strict conformity with what we know of the archiology [*sic*] of our globe that the earth itself may survive and furnish an abode to other beings possibly more noble and intelligent.'[20] Greenough's reference to seeking another world was an echo of a more extreme hypothesis of progressivism, the widely discussed theory of life, and successful human life at that, on other planets. Whewell was disturbed

enough to enter into the debate with vigour. One of his last works was
a long essay, *On the Plurality of Worlds*. It is a detailed argument executed
in order to test, and largely to reject, notions about human life on other
planets. Whewell's argument depends upon a special relationship
between God and humanity. Crowe (1986) suggests that Whewell's
antipathy to extraterrestrial life depended upon his grasp of the
theology of Incarnation. The contrast is drawn between the noble
purpose of man and his physically puny state. Astronomical and
geological research supported by new biological and evolutionary
hypotheses could lead to a loss of morale amongst believers about the
special nature of human beings. If the fossil record shows a gradual
improvement in the species, could humanity be superseded by an
improved species? On all these speculations Whewell comes down
hard. His defence is similar to that of the Wanderer in *The Excursion*
who begs the Solitary to consider the merits of the present world rather
than those of a theoretical Utopia. Whewell affirms that God 'has
found it worthy of Him to bestow upon Man his special care, though
he occupies so small a portion of time, and. . .although he occupies so
small a part of space'.[21] There is no need for new species. Although
modern inventions seem amazingly rich and full of great promise, they
are phenomena appropriate for man's already existing powers and
talents. Technical innovations astound the age, but they are not
harbingers of a new form of life.

In book VIII of *The Prelude* Wordsworth also contrasts the apparent
weakness of human beings compared with the massive, elemental
forces of Nature. The following description is of a country fair on the
slopes of Helvellyn:

> Immense
> Is the recess, the circumambient world
> Magnificent, by which they are embraced.
> They move about upon that soft green field;
> How little they, they and their doings seem,
> Their herds and flocks about them, they themselves,
> And all which they can further or obstruct –
> Through utter weakness pitiably dear,
> As tender infants are – and yet how great,
> For all things serve them: them the morning light
> Loves as it glistens on the silent rocks,
> And them the silent rocks, which now from high
> Look down upon them, the reposing clouds,
> The lurking brooks from their invisible haunts,

> And old Helvellyn, conscious of the stir,
> And the blue sky that roofs their calm abode.[22]

The servant of humanity is Nature, but not only animate Nature ('herds and flocks'). 'Nature' means also the rocks, the rivers, the clouds, the dome of sky, and the light of the sun itself, massive entities, and, as geology was demonstrating, massive forces, yet all subservient to humanity.

NATURE AND MAN: THE RELIGIOUS DIMENSION

The elevation of humanity above non-human Nature, the specification of the god-like, rational creature above all other created beings, has the reassuring sound of the Enlightenment, with its confident manifesto of the education of the human mind and its progressive elevation through practising science. Butler (1981) reminds us that Wordsworth 'stubbornly retained so much of the Enlightenment spirit, especially its simplicity, its universality, and its validation of essential human experience'.[23] Accepting the continuity between eighteenth-century ideas and the new wave of nineteenth-century science, it is important not to underestimate the differences that the varied expressions of Romanticism were articulating. First, there was the belief in a partnership between the human mind and Nature, which I have indicated emerged in both Greenough's uncertain soundings and Sedgwick's confident, Wordsworthian assertions of the influence of nature on his youthful, mental, and spiritual formation. In Wordsworth's own case there is a complex change of emphasis from 1798 to 1807 (the first drafts of *Home at Grasmere, The Prelude* of 1805, the 'Ode: Intimations of Immortality') to the period after 1810. 'The individual Mind' is 'fitted' to nature and nature is 'fitted to the Mind' in the 'Preface' to the 1814 edition. When they join together they can accomplish a creation by their 'blended might'.[24] 'Blending' is one expression of this union. The other is religious and sacramental. These images of religious ceremony, first found in the drafts of 1798 or 1800, were restated in 1814:

> For the discerning intellect of Man
> When wedded to this goodly universe
> In love and holy passion shall find these
> A simple produce of the common day.
> I, long before the blissful hour arrives,
> Would chant, in lonely peace, the spousal verse
> Of this great consummation. . .[25]

Wordsworth in his anxiety to avoid the charge of equating Nature with God, imputed to him because of readings of the *Lyrical Ballads,* did not make a merely theoretical, finicky defence against being categorized as a Pantheist. By 1814, Wordsworth's personal religious journey had arrived at a more orthodox resting place than in 1807. Sedgwick stoutly defends both his friend and his own position. Pantheism is too rarified for him: 'I never could be content while thinking of these things to feel myself dangling in mid-air without a resting point for the sole of my foot.'[26] In the 1853 edition of *A Guide* Sedgwick added a supplementary (fourth) 'letter' to his geological information on the Lake District, in which he noted that some people have become 'idolaters of Nature to the verge of Pantheism'. In contrast, his friend Wordsworth was 'pure from habit and self-control; but he was pure from the influence of a principle that soared above any motives which he drew from his communion with Nature'.[27] Sedgwick affirms that Wordsworth's affiliation was to the supernatural realm; he was a man of sincere religious convictions like himself and like the circle of friends in the geological establishment.

The faith of Sedgwick, Whewell, and Wordsworth was socially and theologically different from Deism. All three shared an orthodoxy of early nineteenth-century Anglican belief. Greenough, the Nonconformist, was a geologist who moved only part of the way from rational, Unitarian beliefs towards an assenting faith and a controlled acknowledgement of a sphere for the irrational. Some of the quotations from Greenough's notebooks already produced in earlier chapters have demonstrated his philosophical and theological stance. He does not take on board all the orthodox doctrines; for instance his rational mind does not admit the possibility of miracles. In his notebooks on religion there are scientific explanations of biblical events, such as the occurrence of very large tidal waves which enabled the crossing of the Red Sea. His wide reading of travel literature satisfied him that there were world-wide stories similar to the events recorded in the Old Testament. In true Enlightenment spirit, he is keen to see superstitions evaporate with the help of scientific exploration. Similarly, he forecasts that old forms of religious behaviour, such as sabbath observance, are likely to disappear as a more democratic, less priest-ridden culture takes precedence in society. Despite Greenough's cool observation of religious tradition, he still espouses Christianity, albeit a Christianity divested of worn-out forms: 'Christianity is a religion without priests, sacrifices or ceremonies.'[28] He may say, 'The force of revealed religion must become less and less as time advances because the chances of its adulteration become greater', but he does not assert that all religion will disappear. 'The force of natural religion on the contrary must always be on the increase, because as knowledge advances man becomes more and more qualified to interpret nature correctly.'[29] Sedgwick, Whewell, Wordsworth, and certainly Coleridge would not have shared this revisionist attitude to the traditional basis of belief, but Greenough illustrates a border position between the older rationalism and the new seriousness of the evangelical commitment to organized religion.

Greenough is thoroughly a part of his generation's movement towards intensity in moral theology. He is a 'humanized' Utilitarian displaying more of the attitudes of John Stuart Mill than of Bentham. People do seek pleasure, do avoid pain, but overriding these simple forces, people have an in-built desire to be active. Greenough is of his period in his strong assertion of a moral philosophy which makes self-control vital for the attainment of a morally lofty human stature. Human beings are not naturally good, nor are they naturally noble. They achieve greatness through the controlled strength of their character. A good starting point in seeking to understand any thinker is to consider the nature of his or her concept of the ideal human being. One example, from Greenough's Presidential address to The Royal Geographical Society in 1840, tells the reader much about what a later generation would call his 'values'. Major Henry Creswicke Robinson, the explorer of Susiana (now South West Iran or Khuzistan) and Kurdistan was awarded the prestigious Founders' Medal. Greenough praised him thus:

In the person of this gallant officer we find united to the sterner qualification of a geographer the accomplishments of the scholar, the antiquarian and the man of taste. Familiar with all the accounts that had appeared either in ancient or modern times in regard to the region which he was about to explore, equally conversant with the dead and with living language, observation and erudition acted reciprocally upon his mind, sometimes exciting, sometimes restraining the speed with which he pressed onwards to his conclusions. To form a just estimate of his merit we must look not only to the termination of his labours, but to the severe self-discipline he underwent lest he might not feel qualified to commence them.[30]

The description of this paragon, it will be noticed, conveys to the distinguished gathering that science, exemplified here by geography, was a stern mistress, demanding more than a narrow technical ability.

A nation's heroes say much about its dreams. An individual's heroes perhaps tell us also what he has read. Just as Greenough himself, and, as we shall see, other geologists of his time, were educated in a classical tradition, so was Robinson, but this example also shows the effect of education acting upon an active, receptive mind. Excitement has its turn 'sometimes' but there is the restraining influence of the disciplined mind. Like Wordsworth's figure of The Happy Warrior this exemplary character suffers the harsh call of duty and the demand to undertake more than adequate preparation for a difficult task.[31] Over all hovers the severe hand of control.

Greenough's moral seriousness and the intensity of his commitment to his political as well as to his scientific activities were widely accepted in his own day as appropriate for scientific leaders.[32] The reputation of early geologists as interpreted in the twentieth century appears to rest either on their rumbustious eccentricity or on their scientific subservience to social and religious conformity. In fact their religious conformity was no mere social convention. It was deeper than a convenient membership of a social club, which comfortably supported them in their accustomed standards of living. They belonged, as David Allen has commented, to an age of religious enthusiasm and their geology matched it:

we own the massive strength of Victorian Natural History largely to a cultural accident. The Natural History that now emerged was in its whole essence an Evangelical creation, and like every other aspect of life lucky enough to be assimilatable to the new preponderant mental type it swept in with an overflowing pervasiveness...In their study of nature, the Victorian middle-classes gazed out on their own image.[33]

There are a number of strands within the general scope of evangelical enthusiasm. One is qualified hope, qualified because fear and failure were acknowledged as unavoidable states of life which have to be sturdily recognized. In religious terms sin has to be recognized but triumph over sin justifies religious optimism. *The Excursion* is dedicated to hope on theological grounds, but also as a social necessity. The opening lines express the poet's intention:

> Of Truth, of Grandeur, Beauty, Love, and Hope,
> And melancholy Fear subdued by Faith,
> Of blessed consolations in distress;
> Of moral strength and intellectual Power
> Of joy in widest commonalty spread;[34]

The Wanderer's main mission is to triumph by argument over despondency, but he gives no false reassurance: mankind will not necessarily triumph over oppression. Crude necessitarianism had been abandoned along with Hartley's and Godwin's social philosophy. The reader of *The Excursion* is conscious of the forces that drag people down: the mills, those who 'sorrow barricaded evermore / Within the walls of cities' and the solitary anguish of rural poverty and abandonment like Margaret's in 'The Ruined Cottage'. It is a text with a substantial reference to hope in heaven but also to the fallen world we inhabit. The final prayer by the Priest in book IX with its references to 'the frail earth', 'cleansed from mortal stain', 'Time's weary course', 'the sting of human nature', resonates with the tone of religious orthodoxy in an age of serious enthusiasm.

Cannon somewhat exasperatingly questions, 'Why young Englishmen like Sedgwick, Darwin and Ruskin were impressed by *The Excursion* is still a mystery to me but they were.'[35] The reason why *The Excursion* was such an important text for the geologists was that, unlike their doubting successors after 1850, they held a genuine, optimistic religious belief and an orthodox acceptance of doctrines which the deistic philosophers fifty years earlier, and the agnostic or atheistic thinkers fifty years later, found burdensome and either rejected or revised. Furthermore, *The Excursion* presented the virtues of privacy, domesticity, and a gentle conservatism which Marilyn Butler (1981) reminds us were Wordsworth's reactions to the times of the Age of Revolutions.

Sedgwick is a good example of the man of science who is confident in religious faith. Marston's study (1984) of Sedgwick's Anglicanism shows that his tenure of the cathedral office at Norwich was no sinecure, nor was his belief a 'front' to enable him to be unencumbered in his passionate teaching of geology. These two commitments were one. He, above all the geologists, expressed what was for many geologists the unified nature of truth: 'All nature bears the imprint of one great Creative Mind and all parts of knowledge are, therefore, of one kindred and family.'[36] The pursuit of truth was not only intellectually satisfying. Truth was also concerned with morality, and Sedgwick, for all his tough, hard-bitten leadership of the Geological Society and his vigorous engagement in university politics, was in many ways a simple, straightforward man seeped in traditional virtues. In old age Sedgwick's greatest fear, generated by the scientific world's growing support for Darwin, was that science was being diverted from supporting the providential in the world. Geology must be linked with morality: 'Tis the crown and glory of inorganic science that it *does* through *final causes*, link material to moral.' The breaking of this link, by theories such as Darwin's, would not be regrettable solely for epistemological reasons, it would damage the nature of humanity 'and sink the human race into a lower grade of degradation than any into which it has fallen since its written records tell us of its history'.[37] Geology does not produce moral laws, but it leads to the point where moral laws can be perceived and studied by philosophers. This circumscription of the sphere of geological methods of observation, confining the scientist to generating material laws was no second best vocation, for Sedgwick felt that the area granted to geology was wide and deep enough to occupy geologists with the solving of mysteries for generations to come.

There are clear instances in public and in private correspondence of Sedgwick's belief in a kind of Platonic, ideal form for the world. In 1850 he returned to public debate this time to take on the Dean of York, reiterating the value of a scientific approach to issues where geology and theology met. In an expanded preface to a further edition of *A Discourse*, which by this time had swollen from a sermon to a textbook apologia for science, he writes, 'before the creation of all worlds, there was an archetype of nature (dead as well as living, past as well as present) in the prescient mind of God'.[38] This outright commitment to a trust in the non-material, eternal forms was not a phenomenon of his old age. In the first edition of *A Discourse*, he takes a similar position on the philosophical notion of the *tabula rasa* of the human mind and in so doing, adopts the style of Wordsworth's 'Ode: The Intimations of Immortality'.

Naked he comes from his mother's womb, endowed with limbs and senses indeed, well fitted to the material world, yet powerless from want of use; and as far as knowledge, his soul is one unvaried blank, yet has this blank been already touched by a celestial hand, and when plunged in the colours which surround it, it takes not its tinge from accident but design, and comes forth covered with a glorious pattern.[39]

Sedgwick held comfortably both to the truth revealed by geology and the truth revealed in biblical sources. I have referred in chapter six to Sedgwick's pastoral reassurances to Wordsworth on the occasion of Dora Wordsworth's death. If poet and geologist exchanged the consolations of religion, equally they shared the same world of moral values. In the same letter Sedgwick states that the poet and his poetry have established a standard which the theologian and geologist can but admire: 'how happy must you be in having your poetical memory unsullied by the recollection of one single line written by yourself, which ministers to evil, or was fit to raise a blush on a modest woman's cheek'.[40]

GEOLOGY: A SUBJECT FOR HEROIC INDIVIDUALS

Another strand in the practical theology of orthodox believers like Whewell, Buckland, Sedgwick, and the ordained men who played a prominent part in the foundation of the Geological Society was a conviction that the individual has the power to make a mark on history. Such a view of history is an aspect of the Romantic belief in 'genius' and its powers to change the world. Individualism and individual responsibility for events correspond closely to the geologists' moral theory. Men like Greenough, who came from non-Anglican, Nonconformist backgrounds (and there were many in the Society and in the British Association for the Advancement of Science) endorsed the seriousness of the duties of the individual to his neighbours. Each individual had a hefty conscience with which to struggle, each person faced decision, and must exercise personal self-control. The same spirit of doughty individualism coloured the developing years of the new science. Team work in anything like the sense of the modern geological research laboratory was unknown. Although geologists (equals such as Buckland and Greenough or apprentice and master such as Darwin and Sedgwick) travelled together, surveyed together, and collaboratively mapped, the age was marked by the names of individual giants of geological discovery. There is a special meaning in the term 'the heroic age of geology'; it encompassed geologist 'heroes'. These were men who completed very demanding, physically exhausting journeys. Sedgwick and Buckland are perhaps the most characteristic of this group. They returned laden with specimens from some of the toughest transects across the highlands and moors of the British Isles. The journals and transactions of the Geological Society are records of achievers. A discovery was personalized, a fossil or a section attributed to a discoverer, a theory acquired a name, a human label. A highly individualized history of science is written. This was a period when there was still room for a single geologist to make a unique interpretation of geological history.

In our own generation, we are apt to reduce the significance of individuals in the march of history, but in the early nineteenth century the individual hero of science could be fulsomely praised for changing the course of a discipline. The early founders of the Geological Society and those who succeeded them in the 1820s and 1830s were unsparing in the verbal duels in which they gleefully engaged and in the debating blows that they administered to those with whom they disagreed. The other side of the coin was warm and uninhibited praise for the geologist who had made expeditions to uncover new areas of study or had returned from a field-trip laden with evidence that filled a gap in the record. There was no doubt in the minds of these scientists that the word 'influence' was properly applied to great names. This picture of the strength of individualism must have light and shade added by the support given to each giant of geology by a close personal associate or by a small peer group of great figures. Warm friendships are recorded: Hutton and Black in Edinburgh, Sedgwick and Whewell, Greenough and Buckland. Sometimes partnerships such as Sedgwick's and Murchison's swing to opposite temperatures when in dispute, but always there were networks of friendships that supported innovation and helped geologists to test their ideas on each other.

Greenough was anxious about the ending of this passionately involved age of geology:

When the Society was founded novelty presented itself to us in every direction – whatever part of the Kingdom our investigations were carried on, we were sure to be rewarded by making discoveries and the English geologist was tempted to explore the strata of his own country by many of the same motives which in the 14th century operated so powerfully in urging on to the coasts of the new world the adventurers of Portugal and Spain. These motives have now ceased to act: there is not longer any portion of England, Scotland or Ireland of which the principal features are not known to us, and tho' perhaps there is scarcely a square mile in which slight discoveries may not still be made, yet these in general must be so slight, so little calculated to affect the imagination, that we must be prepared to expect a considerable and rapid falling off of that interest which the public has taken of late in geological researches unless we continue by some means or other to support the flame with fresh fuel.[41]

Shades of the prison house may be observed closing in on the growing science as it moves away from its early freshness, but there were still years when great names would step forward with great discoveries to their individual credit.

Greenough's personal jotting, quoted above, is not only interesting because of its reference to imagination, but also because of the analogy he chose: the early voyages of discovery motivated by high endeavour. The comparison is over-ambitious to modern ears, but it usefully relates to one other aspect of individualism, the history of great names. The published surveys of current geological knowlege for the general reader from the *Encyclopaedia Britannica* of 1797, with its long section on 'the Earth', through to Lyell's major work, adopt a convention of opening with an historical survey of the science linking names with discoveries or more often with new theories. The ancestry of the science was honourable; the first pioneers were distinguished men, if unenlightened. It is significantly a mark of Wordsworth's later poetry, particularly those poems which in a sequence plot the development of Christianity, the growth of liberty, or the events of European history, that key players in the long journey to the present are identified. Like the scientists, Wordsworth was convinced of the power of individuals to change the course of events. Mohamet, Wordsworth says in *The Convention of Cintra* of 1808, swept history forward like a transitory wind! The later works of Wordsworth are dominated by a concern to praise the general forward movement of England and, to an extent Europe, energized by key figures of history. If we are to look for examples of the *Zeitgeist* as it was interpreted in England in the early part of the nineteenth century, Wordsworth's *Ecclesiastical Sonnets*, books VI and VII of *The Excursion, Sonnets Dedicated to Liberty and Order*, or *The Essays upon Epitaphs* will provide vital source material. They are in essence a record of the continuity of history with decisive moments created by outstanding individuals. We should be reminded again that the notion of the individual in history held a strong place in philosophy. Herder's seminal work was to give the first inspiration to German poets and, in turn, to fire a long line of artists to explore the significance of great and often tragic figures of the past from Schiller's *Maria Stuart*, through to Southey's poem *Joan of Arc*.[42]

An important text for Wordsworth studies is Hazlitt's collection of essays called *The Spirit of the Age*. As McFarland's study of Hazlitt, Lamb, and de Quincey (1987) shows, these essays were not alone in creating a literary mode, one in which there is constructed a belief that ideas are generated by individual genius. Wordsworth's own work includes a substantial record of heroic figures. In the collection which Wordsworth himself grouped in 1845 as 'Poems Dedicated to Independence and Liberty' the list of great men includes Napoleon, William Tell, and Hofer of Switzerland, the King of Sweden, Toussaint l'Ouverture, Shakespeare, Milton and his parliamentary friends, Falkland, Montrose, Arminius, Palafox, and John Sobieski. Earlier *The Ecclesiastical Sketches* of 1820 traced a line of failure and success linked with the great names in the history of the Church of England. Earlier still in 1802, Wordsworth explained the weakness of France in the sonnet, 'Great Men have been among us'.[43] France unlike England has a dearth of books and men. England can trace an unbroken line of heroes some of whom are stamped with the ultimate mark of liberal approval – they knew John Milton!

The individualistic interpretation of history was set within a broad theory of historical development and change. There is a fascination at this time with, to use Wordsworth's own phrases, 'the mighty stream of tendency' and 'an ascent and progress in the main'. The early nineteenth century gives us examples of both modes of interpretation of change and decisive moments in history, the individual and the general. Kant proposed as early as 1784 that man's unsteady but inexorable progress into building a civil order was driven by a 'secret plan'. Later Hegel was to propose that the philosopher's task was to explain this plan: 'the natural conclusion to draw is that the philosopher is concerned with making explicit what we may call the operative idea of the culture or nation to which he belongs. He is an interpreter of the spirit of his time (die Zeitgeist).'[44]

For my purpose, three comments may be made on this manifesto. First, that Wordsworth became increasingly clear that, if there was a 'secret plan' of history, it was closely associated with the history of England which offered example and leadership to the world. Second, like the philosopher, Wordsworth saw his own task, the task of the poet, as that of explaining and making explicit what was happening in his nation. Perhaps there are tones of German idealism as early as the ambitious claims of the 'Preface' to the *Lyrical Ballads* of 1802.

Aristotle, I have been told, has said, that Poetry is the most philosophic of all writing: it is so: its object is truth, not individual and local, but general, and operative; not standing upon external testimony, but carried alive into the heart by passion, truth which is its own testimony, which gives competence and confidence to the tribunal to which it appeals, and receives them from the same tribunal.[45]

A third point is that the geologists had this in common with Wordsworth: they too had a sense of duty – to their science. The acceptance of the idea of 'an operative idea of the culture' (Hegel) or 'truth. . .general and operative' (Wordsworth) called for more than a passive absorption of an intellectual theory of history. To the geologists a progressive theory of the spirit of change demanded personal, practical support and involvement. They viewed their geological investigation as a quest for truth which was far from 'individual and local' but 'general and operative' through the action and the improvement of the mind. Like Wordsworth, and perhaps more generally like their intellectual colleagues in European literature, science, and natural philosophy, they regarded their scientific calling as a vocation. The record of the rocks was important not for its own sake, nor instrumentally for improvement of commerce or industry, but because it provided an opportunity for scientist-captains to conquer another stage in the march of the progress of humanity. The secret advance of Divine creation not only waited to be unveiled; it was the geologist's duty to unveil it. In summary, Wordsworth and the geologists occupied a world that responded to action. They were, as poet and geologists, not passive travellers on a fast-flowing stream of time, but active participants who, through dedication, unsparing efforts, and occasionally with a dash of heroism, were commissioned to make the most of their times.

CHAPTER 10

Conclusion

There are procedural difficulties in attempting summaries of early nineteenth-century 'high' culture, sometimes because of the volume of studies that have been produced to encapsulate the nature of the Romantic territory.

Modern studies of Romanticism struggle to avoid simple diagrams or route maps to explain the very complex topography of their subject. We can, if we wish, take at face value the judgements of their own times made by Romantic writers who had an interest in presenting to history a simplification which hides negative or contradictory phenomena. Alternatively, we can present our own twentieth-century conceptions of Romanticism, coloured by our contemporary preoccupations such as the quest for the origin of our own current cultural crisis. One such quest for an historical root of present-day dilemmas is the search for the origin of the division between science and literature. There are two simplifications in this pursuit. One is to find the bifurcated root of the 'two cultures' planted by the activities of the scientists and poets in the first decades of the nineteenth century. I believe this study of one major poet and a group of philosophers (as they commonly called themselves) has demonstrated not two distinct cultures, but considerable communality and shared attention to the way in which human beings interpret Nature. A growing self-consciousness about becoming Men of Science did not seal the geologists off from literary, theological, and more general philosophic enterprises. On the contrary, the geologists were proud of being all-round figures of literature, theology, and philosophy.

The second, simplistic reinterpretation of the early nineteenth-century intellectual ferment is to jump to the other extreme and to deny that there was any division at all between literature and science. Valiant attempts have been made, for instance, to suggest that Wordsworth and other writers such as Shelley, Byron, and Keats were thoroughly versed in the discoveries of their scientific contemporaries. Too much is claimed for the poets' knowledge of geology, without considering what was actually being produced by the geologists' detailed studies of stratigraphy and palaeontology and in philosophical work. Chapters two and three have shown that by patient reading and a sharp eye for small pieces of evidence, there are to be found in Wordsworth's poetry and particularly in *A Guide* traces of acquired geological knowledge which a previous writer would not have possessed, such as the names of rocks or theoretical notions of Diluvialism or Catastrophism. The subsequent chapters have argued, however, that on the whole the major appropriation by Wordsworth from his geological acquaintances (and theirs from him) was at a different, more general, philosophical level. Poet and geologists alike struggled with changes of perspective on philosophical and theological issues, such as the depth of time, the excitement of intellectual, excursive mental activity, and the shifting issues of decay and duration. The human being stood disturbed at the centre of the imaginative storms that geological enquiries had provoked. At this point, it is worth considering briefly how Wordsworth compares with two other major poets who have also been studied for their knowledge of science in general and of geology in particular.

Both Shelley and Byron give evidence of their reading in geology. Shelley's Alp in 'Mont Blanc', published in 1816, is comparable to Wordsworth's high Alps. This is a landscape of ruins and destruction, of restless winds and a perpetually threatening noise. The storm-broken trees, for instance, intrigue both poets. Shelley's poem turns to two particular physical aspects of the Alps, both with some geological significance. One is the interest in caves, ice, and the mountain itself. It is as if Mont Blanc is hollow and the echoes of destruction reverberate in its interior. The hollowness of the high Alps was indeed a theory of the early eighteenth-century travellers and, for some, accounted for the perpetual flow of glaciers. The ice-rivers of the Chamonix Valley also intrigue Shelley and he observes the wreckage of rock scattered on the 'river of ice'. There is, moreover, a direct reference to the origins of the Alps, a reference which has convinced many readers that there is a Catastrophist within the poet:

> How hideously
> Its shapes are heaped around rude, bare, and high,
> Ghastly, and scarred, and riven! – Is this the scene
> Where the old Earthquake – daemon taught her young
> Ruin? Were these their toys? or did a sea
> Of fire envelop once this silent snow?[1]

Other poems may be produced to confirm an eye for ruin and large-scale Catastrophe, for example Panthea's speech in act IV of 'Prometheus Unbound' or 'Ozymandias' (1817). An aspect of Catastrophism which had special appeal to artists and early palaeontologists was the notion of a prehuman state where beast fought beast in a struggle, ending for the losing species in extinction. The opening stanzas of Shelley's 'Ode to Liberty' (1820) portray a vicious state of Nature before the dawn of human history. Shelley's vision of 'the dædal Earth', is also found in 'The Hymn of Pan', also published in 1820. The story emerging from Cuvier's studies of fossils, quickly absorbed by English geologists, such as Buckland, provided for many of Shelley's contemporaries a rich source of excitement coinciding with Gothic imaginings (see Gaull, M. (1988)).

Byron's longer narrative poems can also be explored for evidence of the excitement of Catastrophism. *Cain – A Mystery* published in 1821, is often quoted in this context, and correctly so, because in the preface there is a direct acknowledgement of Cuvier's theories about the repeated destruction of the world before the creation of man. Cuvier's research on fossils of Mastodon provided Byron's Lucifer with a vision of a world peopled by giants who matched in stature the mammoths studied by early palaeontologists. In the period when these poems were published the theme of a violent preAdamic world occupied the writers of popular literature. A typical example is James Montgomery's *The World Before the Flood* of 1813.[2] The themes of Deluge and of violent destruction attracted painters and engravers too. The most famous and now the most quoted artist of Catastrophe was John Martin, whose paintings were exhibited to an admiring audience in the 1820s and 1830s.

Wordsworth's comment on an exhibition of Martin's paintings gives us a lead in attempting to draw some conclusions on the difference between the use by Shelley and Byron of geological material and Wordsworth's own use of his scientific sources. Writing to Charles Lamb in May 1833, Wordsworth agreed with him that Martin's artistic endeavours were a sign of barrenness of imagination. Indeed, the remarkable feature of Wordsworth's writing in the period after 1810 (and therefore contemporary with the newly-emerging generation of poets) was that he did not introduce Catastrophism in the form chosen by his younger contemporaries. My study leads to a proposal that writers like Shelley and Byron (and to a much lesser extent John Keats in his occasional reference to the origins of natural features) sought their inspiration from a different social and scientific group than those with whom Wordsworth found compatibility and intellectual comfort. Chapter four elaborated the 'triangle of intellect' of Cambridge, London, and the Lake District. I suggest that Wordsworth's social network and its cultural manifestation in geological ideas and the different social groups in which Shelley and Byron circulated are instances of the complex pattern of Romanticism in the early nineteenth century. Many different streams of alliance flowed, sometimes in opposition.

It is also worth stating a more obvious differentiation of the age in order to redress a possible impression left by this study of uniformity about Wordsworth's stature. My attention has necessarily been drawn to the admiration and near-reverence of the poet by Whewell and Sedgwick. Further instances of Wordsworth's prestigious position will be mentioned in paragraphs which follow. It is, of course, an illusion of the narratives which I have selected to suggest that Wordsworth was the universally admired and uncriticized poet of the period from 1810 to his death. He certainly occupied a major position in the 1820s, in the 1830s, and then on the Victorian Parnassus, but the previous mention of the 'new men' – Shelley, Byron, and Keats – will remind most readers that Wordsworth was regarded at least with reservation and by many with outright hostility. He was condemned by some contemporaries on two counts. He had committed the ultimate betrayal of abandoning the leadership of reform. As Shelley's sonnet published in 1816 alleged, Wordsworth had obliterated himself: 'Deserting these, thou leavest me to grieve, / Thus, having been, that thou shoulds't cease to be.'[3] For some reviewers of his poetry, he had composed works of unacceptable dullness conveying sentiments inappropriate for intellectually demanding literature. Whewell's comments on Wordsworth's poetry referred to in chapter four (both in his subjects, such as rabbits and Waggoners, and in his tone, the 'solemn bleat' of *The Excursion*) may have been overridden by the personal experience of the poet, but they were not unusual sentiments of the times. Indeed Whewell's changing attitude may be the best indicator of the period's attitudes to Wordsworth. I have already indicated in chapter four that Whewell disagreed with Julius Hare on the importance of Wordsworth's poetry. The biography of Whewell by Mrs Stair Douglas is at pains to show, as I have done, that there was a change of view when Whewell aged. Some substantial criticisms remain in Whewell's letters. It was the poet, rather than the poetry that eventually impressed

Whewell. The early poetry in which Whewell had found a prosaic style and an attachment to pedlars, a 'deification of children', was succeeded by loftier language and loftier schemes. If we remember the characteristics which Whewell praised in Wordsworth, we can understand some of the values of the time and particularly the values behind geological thought. It is Wordsworth's robustness, his appetite for climbing the high fells, and indeed the very opposite of the expected appearance of the author of *Lyrical Ballads* which Whewell admired.

A good image of these manly qualities is conveyed by the portrait of Whewell as a young don. He sits boldly facing the artist, square jawed and handsomely tough, his dark hair curled above fearless eyes. This is the Whewell who was proud of a labourer's remark that he was too strong to be a clergyman. He represents the aspect of Romanticism that was mainly adventurous and assertive, not the wilting or over-sensitive soul. It is worth remembering that Wordsworth, or rather this aspect of the older Wordsworth, appeared to harmonize with this representative feature of the age.

Turning from poets to geologists, a kind of order appears to emerge very satisfactorily from studies which summarize the unity of a particular age in a nutshell phrase, while the disparate and contradictory evidence is discarded. Phrases like 'The Victorian Truth Complex', or 'The Broad Church' encapsulate deceptive similarities across a number of disciplinary fields, but it is a mistake to neglect the range of opinions, attitudes, and interests amongst the early geologists, even in religious belief! Though not of much interest for our own generation, profoundly important varieties of belief divided them. As explained in chapter four, Sedgwick's 'churchmanship' was resolutely Evangelical while Whewell's and Buckland's position was firmly orthodox 'centre'. Greenough's Unitarianism must be positioned in the spectrum of faith in the period covered by this study. In any consideration of Anglicanism, for instance, a label such as 'Broad Church', often loosely applied to studies of religion and geology, tells us little of the range of belief and orthodoxy in the 1820s and 1830s: a range which was to expand considerably in the next two decades as the Tractarians began to preach, to write and, for some, to create a schism.

Corsi (1988) is particularly helpful in understanding the varieties of religious and scientific attitude within the Anglican community in Oxford and Cambridge. Whewell's changing position is also well documented in that text. A recent study of Wordsworth's later poems and of his family's ecclesiastical careers by A. G. Hill (1992) suggests that

Figure 7. The Portland portrait of William Whewell as a young man.

the poet was aware of the varieties of faith and had considerable influence in reconciling divisions within Anglicanism and between Anglicanism and other denominations. Similarly, the Trinity geologists, when they met their colleagues in the Geological Society, mixed with many Nonconformists, including Quakers and Unitarians.

There were internal forces which operated to mask the varieties of belief in the world of science. Indeed, as Morrell and Thackray (1981) have pointed out, there was an unspoken determination to play down differences amongst the early founders of the British Association for the Advancement of Science in order to present an optimistic image of science to the fascinated world of the educated. They describe the early founders of the Association as 'meliorist, centrist, reforming...temperamentally they were conservative, piece-meal reformers opposed to the political claims of the die-hard Tories and fierce democrats'.[4] Greenough, although a determined innovator, founder of the Geological Society and, with others, an initiator of University College London, sought the virtues of gradualness. In his political notebooks, he wrote a manifesto of which any Fabian would have approved:

Our legislature, our government, our military are to be subjected to a certain excellent and beneficial reform, only let us not be in too great a hurry, let us not outrun the course of nature, lest us act as befits the times for certainly the times are bad and above all let us not take men to be what they were and what some wish they may be, but as they are at the present moment and as they are likely to be.[5]

Sedgwick's attitudes to university reform were similarly reforming yet cautious; Whewell was highly sceptical of reforms of university government, but fascinated by curriculum reform.

To write even in this way of the geologists as a group who buried essential differences in order to improve their world but not to turn it on its head implies a concerted scheme with an explicit manifesto. No such explicit political coherence can be seen. The historian has to identify from the study of deeper values the areas where the active participants found unity, despite their passionately fought controversies about college government, Actualism, or the distinctions in the Precambrian era. Some of the values, which they shared with each other and with Wordsworth, have been identified in this book. One overriding impression, wherever they stood on geological or on theological controversies, is their unanimity in praising the qualities that Wordsworth provided for them and for fellow intellectuals. Their studies took them into the realms of theory and the recording of facts, but their agenda included the world of feeling and particularly the way feeling was expressed by Wordsworth.

In order to illustrate the attraction Wordsworth held for some of his contemporaries, we can turn to two intellectuals of the period for guidance, John Stuart Mill and Charles Darwin. Mill's *Autobiography* identified the moments in his youth when Wordsworth opened a door to a richer, more colourful way of life after years of barren erudition. The account is worth repeating here because it demonstrates how one contemporary unconsciously imbibed Wordsworth's own language, a phenomenon which in this study has been most closely parallelled in the autobiographical writing of Adam Sedgwick and William Whewell. Whereas Whewell echoes 'Ode: Intimations of Immortality', Mill's language is from the 'Preface' to *Lyrical Ballads* of 1802. Mill says that Wordsworth's poem in the two-volume edition of 1815 expressed 'states of feeling, and of thought coloured by feeling, under the excitement of beauty'. Wordsworth's language had seeped into the philosopher's language and, without precisely knowing how it had happened, Mill gives an explanation which tells us much about the way geologists and other scientists felt able to approach this poet. He is not, says Mill, one of the 'greater poets', but instead he is 'the poet of unpoetical natures, possessed of quiet and contemplative tastes'.[6] Mill continues to say that those natures belong to those who seek poetic cultivation. By contrast he had found in Byron only a mirror of his own rejection of life and a consequent depression. Charles Darwin in his autobiography, claimed to have read *The Excursion* twice at a crucial period of his enquiries, finding there, not escape from his labour, but an infusion of feeling and of joy. Manier's study (1978) of Darwin's notebooks from 1837 to 1844 examines the fulfilment that Darwin found there: 'the young Darwin sought no theology beyond that of Wordsworth's poetic account of the excursive quest for the meaning of life within nature itself. His metaphors, read in the cultural context, indicate that his emotional relation to the world of his theory was not one of alienation, but one of self-reflective acceptance.'[7]

We should not assume that Sedgwick, Whewell, Buckland, and Lyell found exactly the same emotional response as that confessed to by Mill or by Darwin. Whether the beneficiaries of Wordsworth's poetic messages were, to use Mill's self-revealing phrase, 'men of quiet and contemplative tastes', or energetic, synthesizing young men like Darwin, or more extrovert spirits like Greenough, Sedgwick, and Whewell, they all relied in different ways upon the poet. He was vital to them not only because of his portrayal of the earth, their natural 'laboratory' or text, but also because he wrote about how the human heart as well as the human mind can be moved by its contact with Nature.

Susan Gliserman, in her study of Tennyson and the scientists who turned to him, used the powerful image of 'cultural interactions or cultural exchanges'. Her metaphor of a stock market commodity transference, an 'exchange of affective meaning',[8] is useful in helping us to understand the Victorian phenomenon of the great seer poet whom the scientists needed in order to interpret the new world which they were creating by their enquiries. In the period before Victoria's reign and then in its early years, Wordsworth's gift to the geologists was at one level complementary to their own values, at another level it provided something they felt they lacked. The geologists considered here already shared with Wordsworth intellectual presuppositions – the active human mind, the lessons that lay ready to be revealed in Nature, the belief that Nature's hidden laws would confirm their heartfelt intuitions of the essential rightness of a Divinely created world – but they were acutely aware that they needed help in opposing philosophical systems which were inimical to their own values. Utilitarianism and gross materialistic atheism were two of those threatening forces. Destructive powers had been released on the Continent in 1789 and seemed never far off in Britain. Wordsworth's prophetic message was necessary to his followers as a reassurance of the inherent goodwill of the human and natural system. After 1850 younger scientists presented their own threats of an intellectual revolution ultimately more corrosive of a unity of faith than the French, atheistical, rationalist variety. Different seers were required to sustain the scientists who continued to hold to traditional values, but, for decades after Wordsworth's death, he was quoted by geologists in their texts with talismanic confidence.

The geologists of Wordsworth's own lifetime, despite their different scientific, political, and religious orientations, shared one value which led them to revere Rydal Mount and its genius – the reverence for poetry. The prominence of poetry, and thence the poet, for all the geologists is undoubtedly a striking feature of the period. There are many explanations for the respect and even awe in which poetry was held. One is the common grounding of a classical literary education with poets accorded higher prestige than either Greek dramatists or the Latin political and philosophical thinkers. A more immediate explanation for the pre-eminence of poetry in the geologists' scale of worth was the mysterious elevation of the sensibility of certain human beings as 'poetic', a development out of the previous century's campaign for the 'improvement' of the human mind and feelings, boosted by the output of the vigorous poetic years that followed *Lyrical Ballads*. The redefinitions of the poet's task prominently set out by Wordsworth in the 'Preface' to *Lyrical Ballads*, somewhat obscurely incorporated into and generalized in Coleridge's broader mission for a 'clerisy', and politically defined in Shelley's vision of the poetic spirit, confirmed to intellectuals that poetry was at the highest point on a scale of sensitivity to nature and to human behaviour. Gradually the term 'romantic' took on board much of this burden of meaning and collected under one phrase all the diverse feelings, aesthetic, sentimental, and interpersonal.

The respectful place given to poetry in the private correspondence and journals of Greenough, Sedgwick, and Whewell can be further illustrated. Poets, and Wordsworth in particular, became the standard-bearers before the march of scientific advance. As Allen (1976) comments, in the period after 1820 it became 'all but obligatory to work into every book or article on Natural History a quota of lines from Wordsworth'. To redress any suggestion that Wordsworth stood alone, a glance at, for instance, Whewell's chapters and sections of *The History of the Inductive Sciences* reveals poetic 'tags' from the Psalms to Milton, with Wordsworth (clearly a member of this pantheon) noted as a guardian at the gates, as it were, of volume iii. Rupke notes Buckland's classical learning, but observes that from the 1820s onwards geologists also selected passages from English literature of the seventeenth and eighteenth centuries.[9]

Charles Lyell is interesting to consider as a geologist with a contemporary's interest in poetry, although, as his fame and seniority grew, he appears gradually to distance himself from an attitude of mind which Whewell and Sedgwick, his older colleagues, never abandoned. The letters of the young Lyell preparing for Oxford or travelling soon after graduating, reveal the Romantic young intellectual, indeed the word 'romantic' appears often in correspondence with his father. In 1817 on a visit to Scotland he composed (just as Wordsworth and Keats were to do) a poem to Staffa decorated with conventional Fancy:

> And at her voice, a thousand pillars tell
> She bade uprising lift the massy pile,
> And far within she carved a stately hall.[10]

In 1818 on his European travels, he noted in the Jura there 'formed a Romantic scene' and the Dent du Midi had 'extraordinary and picturesque forms'. Le Brison was 'a very picturesque mountain' and his 'ride was truly romantic the whole way'.[11] Like many travellers he found Schaffhausen Falls and the valley both sublime and 'very romantic'. Lyell read widely. Byron is appropriately quoted when the travellers pause at Chillon. In a very telling remark made to his fiancée, Miss Horner, about Madame de Stael, Lyell illustrates the premier position of poetry: 'Had she written first-rate poetry she would have shown that the very best power of mind which can be developed in man may belong to her sex.'[12] My reading of the sequence of letters in the biography by Mrs Lyell (1881) is of a decreasing use of aesthetic terms and a reduction in the language of literary feeling as Lyell gained international success as a geologist. Perhaps too the context in which he worked as a scientist changed as he grew older.

To return to men who were more closely associated with Wordsworth, one is struck by the power of poetry to turn their lives in a new direction. Initially, there may have been some doubt in Whewell's mind about the wisdom of balancing scientific judgement and the sensational judgement of poetry. He remonstrated in correspondence with Julius Hare in 1819, who had stoutly put forward the Wordsworthian doctrine of the fixing of character by early associations with nature: 'your principles of poetry are incompatible with the mental habits of men existing in a state of society like ours'. Science, he continued, is a 'much more satisfactory study'. However the same letter admits that 'there is much in the spiritual nature of man, that his reasoning powers are but a small portion of his existence'. The limitations of reason led him to conclude that he 'could almost find in my heart to forswear speculating about it, and to be content to feel and love the beautiful, or what seems to be so to me, without knowing why or caring wherefore'.[13] Hare was typical of the age's spiritual seriousness. Poetry for men like him was always more than an adornment. It was the voice of morality, coloured by feeling. This was Wordsworth's special quality for the geologists. Nature and Wordsworth combined produced a double benefit. Whewell, writing to Hare from Coniston in 1841, said that the Lakes have 'done something, I think, to tranquillize and strengthen me, and prepare me for active life, to which I may add repeated intercourse with our friend, that good old poet'.[14]

Wordsworth's poetry gave, at one level, reassurance to a broad range of contemporary intellectuals. Studies by Hassler (1984) and

Proffitt (1982) instance the support given by Wordsworth's verse to those oppressed by Lyellian geology and then by Darwinian biology. I hope I have given evidence of Wordsworth's poetry being used as an anchor for faith, a source of security, and, to use Mill's phrase again, for 'unpoetical natures possessed of quiet and contemplative tastes'. The filaments along which spiritual and emotional support was carried were never of one type. Some reassuring messages were moral, some were of spiritual hope, bulwarks against the depressing signals from materialism or from Utilitarianism. Others were a kind of licence or permit, a sanction to admit feeling and emotion, powerful but reassuringly controlled, into the realms where the geologists carried out their life's work in intercourse with Nature. Not so obvious to us, because time has obscured the evidence, was the influence of personal friendship between Wordsworth, Sedgwick, and Whewell which matured in mutual respect as the friends grew older. The detailed analysis of individual networks of association is vital to underpin generalizations about the interconnection between science and literature and I hope this text has added something to that necessary body of knowledge about science and the community in which it flourished. One area of connection which has not been fully explored is less individual and more difficult to relate specifically to matters of faith, but of undoubted significance in Wordsworth's later poems and in tracing the connections with the geologists. This dimension is visible where history and locality coexist – a sense of place.

A VISION OF A 'LAND'

Hartman, in a perplexed passage about Wordsworth's later poems, writes: 'There are, nevertheless, strange happenings in the later poetry which has a precarious quality of its own.'[15] Two of the strangest poetic happenings, which have had only a precarious hold on twentieth-century interest, are 'The Vernal Ode' and the 'Ode: Composed upon an Evening of Extraordinary Splendour and Beauty' referred to at length in chapter six with special reference to the theme of immortality. These odes also depict an essentially English locale for the sublime visitations of sunset, of visiting angel, of the eternal bee. Trickett has noted: 'Here in "The Vernal Ode" the creatures are singled out with an extraordinatory sense of the history of the kind.'[16] Jonathan Wordsworth expresses the same feeling of the contact between spirit and reality, when he writes, 'the clinging to the palpable of which Coleridge complained is often a saving grace of this later Christian poetry'.[17] This connection between the spiritually continuous, the history of a people, and the present actuality, which may be extinguished in one form but returns in another, forms one element in the assurance that Wordsworth conveyed to the intellectuals of his age from his increasingly Parnassian prominence. The two strands that twined together to create an increasingly firm hawser for the scientist's intellectual barque were geography and history. The term 'A Land', with its biblical tones of a particular place and a particular story, is the only equivalent I can find to summarize Wordsworth's vision of the fragile, but ultimately secure fulfilment of humanity and of the mission of a particular place for the location of that hope.[18]

In series of sonnets or collections of short poems and odes Wordsworth aimed to celebrate the long journey of Christianity which peaked at one level in European civilization at its greatest moments, but more securely achieved its culmination in England and in a particular English geographical setting, the traditional rural homeland. The European Wordsworth, the older traveller, not the voyager of 1790 or even the reminiscent poet of *The Prelude* of 1805, but the restless traveller of 1820, of the European visit of 1828 with Coleridge, and of the Italian journey of 1837 is rarely read, but deserves attention in the history of Wordsworth's ideas. The poems of these later years record historical excursions and, although they have a didactic purpose, carefully refer to actual geographical tours. The three considerable sequences, *Memorials of a Tour on the Continent, 1820, The Itinerary Poems of 1833*, and *Memorials of a Tour of Italy, 1837*, are contemporary journeys of the mind, and also intellectual statements about the origins of civilization. In the *Ecclesiastical Sonnets of 1822*, the tour is into the past, the history of the Christian Church in Europe, but the places are as Wordsworth saw them on his travels. These locations are identified in detail – the Jungfrau, the Falls of the Rhine near Schaffhausen, and the widening Rhine below the Falls, but this is not travel writing as a geographer, rather the writing of a missionary: a missionary of an ideal. That ideal was inherited from Milton. It was a vision of a world, saved by a dedicated nation. Wordsworth had taken on the mantle of the great poetic prophet with its commissioning of the English people for a lofty destiny.

It is important to make in parallel a note of the geologists' interests in Europe. If is often assumed that English geology between 1795 and 1835 developed its peculiar strength in isolation, supported by its peculiar, inward-looking Church, in disdain of European science.

Nothing could be further from the truth.[19] The French in general may have been regarded with suspicion, but individual French scientists were highly regarded. Cuvier was respected by British geologists. He was elected to the Geological Society as an ordinary member in June 1815 before the sound of gunfire had died away. The Minute books of the Geological Society record a collection of minerals 'arranged according to Brougniart' in May 1813. Although his name was not spelt correctly, his geological system was well known as was the research of his distinguished contemporaries. Cuvier and Werner were sent copies of the Society's *Transactions* in November 1814. Cuvier had visited England by 1818, as Lyell noted on his own visit to Paris and the Jardin des Plantes in that year. Two years later Wordsworth enjoyed the Natural History exhibits in the Jardin des Plantes.[20] Later (1823) Lyell was introduced by Cuvier to Professor van Breda of Holland whom he identified already as a friend of Greenough. German geology and (decreasingly) mineralogy, was an attraction for geologist travellers, such as Sedgwick, Whewell, Murchison, and Buckland. Sedgwick met Blumenbach and Alexander von Humboldt in Germany in 1829. Whewell travelled with his geological hammer to Germany and to Switzerland, typically noting architecture, customs, and dialects. Whewell makes a most European statement in his *The History of the Inductive Sciences*, identifying Werner, Cuvier, and Smith as the three main authors of geological classification.[21]

How far the geologists absorbed Wordsworth's increasing identification of Britain as the chosen home of angels and the ultimate in European civilization is not easy to say. Greenough, one conjectures, may have been more constitutionally sceptical about irrational patriotism, but he is politically a gradualist who sees no better state than the one in which he lives.[22] Whewell writing to James Marshall in 1842 makes a patriotic definition of truth quite remarkable for the man who in 1819 had remonstrated with Julius Hare on the superiority of scientific truth:

I have my answer ready, and you must not start at it. I believe in our National Constitution, and in our National Religion. I believe that these embody more of the truth, are better approaches to the true form of Church and State, than have ever yet been established. I am ready to act on this belief. I love them because I believe this, this is what I call believing, and this is my notion of the truth in which I believe...But I believe in the National Church and the National Constitution, not as mere formulae, but as living things, as the most essential part of the social and spiritual life of the nation.[23]

The language of geology itself was influenced in two ways, by classical tradition and by what was regarded as the typically English nature of geology. Greenough commends plain English terminology in geographical description. Whewell, the most active and influential of his generation in regulating nomenclature, was scrupulous about anchoring new conceptualizations in Greek or Latin terminology, but he advised Lyell in 1831 on the use of 'good looking English words' such as 'ridgeway', for the summit-line between the 'daleways' of two parallel valleys.[24] Perhaps one of the most vivid illustrations of the commanding position of British geology by the 1840s is the nomenclature applied in Europe to the major divisions of the geological time-scale. Wernerian terminology, which dominated stratigraphy in the first decade of the century, was replaced by new terms to describe the recently differentiated, more elaborate sequences. For the most part these strata had been explored and finely categorized by Sedgwick, Murchison, and, in the case of the Cretaceous, by Mantell. Whewell also added his contribution with the terms for the Tertiary beds.[25] The point to note is that the sequence from 'base' upwards in what we now call the Palaeozoic is a labelling of stratigraphy with the terminology of the prehistory of the English people as described by the Roman names (Silurian, Ordovician) or of the place-names of English geography (Devonian and Cambrian).

Whewell's statements about the National Church and the Constitution as 'living things' and his conflation of belief and truth set the tone for my concluding remarks on the nature of the geologists' feeling for landscape. Geology, and specifically geological exploration which had escaped from the drawing room and the cabinet, was a profoundly Romantic science for all kinds of reasons. We have seen its practitioners ranging wide over miles of difficult terrain and deep into thousands of years of time. Their enquiries led to the rich borders of knowledge in two senses, back into the possibilities of First Causes and forwards into the possibilities of a new earth. The demanding nature of such comprehensively large studies was part of the excitement and, the modern reader suspects, a component of the moral weight that dignified the geologists' tasks. Indeed the seriousness of the study of the rocks, despite the light-hearted geological dinners and the wit and mockery of some of the correspondence, is a hallmark of the age of British achievement. Again, where geology's frontiers touched other subjects, particularly history and philosophy, an entry was effected into the imponderable domains of morality and belief. In short, those whose business was with mountains, rivers, valleys, rocks, and the underlying strata were dealing not with dead, sterile material but with the very foundation of life where matter and mind met and commingled.

In Wordsworth the geologists found their emblem and the source of energy to fuel their intense commitment. He became for more than one generation a figure of such assurance that to be 'a Wordsworthian' was to say as much as needed to be said. One element of his attraction may have been the propriety and moral earnestness that we find in his later poems. The 'Parnassian' voice rather than the lyrical (to use Gerard Manley Hopkins's distinction) may have been his chief appeal particularly when allied to his expression of support for the conventional wisdom of the English Church and State. I believe that Wordsworth's message to the geologists about the qualities of their 'Land' was more than an intellectual reassurance, it included a powerful emotional component. Wordsworth's intense dedication to the reality of place and to one particular English location chimed with the geologists' commitment to their study in depth and to the reality of the localities they studied. They appreciated, sometimes explicitly, that the poet understood the land as they understood it, because they and he had worked in that location. Mapping, measuring, collecting, recording for them, and seeing, listening, and writing for him, were ways of celebrating a very special place. Wordsworth's vision of the mountains, lakes, and valleys placed their own subject, the study of the inanimate and of the long extinct forms of life, on the level of studies of conscious Nature. He was the poet above all others who infused mute stones with an active language.

A passage from *The Prelude* provides an instance of the power of the poet's mind to change the material world into something vibrant and alive. It will serve as an emblem for what the geologists found in him:

> Twas doubtless nothing more
> Than a black rock, which, wet with constant springs,
> Glistered far seen from out its lurking-place
> As soon as ever the declining sun
> Had smitten it. Beside our cottage hearth
> Sitting, with open door, a hundred times
> Upon this lustre have I gazed, that seemed
> To have some meaning which I could not find;
> And now it was a burnished shield, I fancied,
> Suspended over a knight's tomb, who lay
> Inglorious, buried in the dusky wood;
> An entrance now into some magic cave,
> Or palace for a fairy of the rock.[26]

Notes

I INTRODUCTION

1. J. W. Goethe, 1970, p. 114.
2. *DWJ* II, p. 192.
3. *WL* IV, p. 533.
4. Ibid., p. 574
5. Ibid., p. 540. Thomas de Quincey also uses 'ologies': 'He [M. Simond] had a smattering of mechanics, of physiology, geology, mineralogy, and all other *ologies* whatsoever' (T. De Quincey, 'Society of the Lakes' in *Recollections of the Lakes and the Lake Poets*, Penguin, 1970).
6. *WP* V, iii, 178–182.
7. *DW* II, p. 192.
8. N. Maxwell, 1984, p. 265.
9. A. O. Lovejoy, 1960 (1936) and H. W. Piper, 1962.
10. M. Butler, 1981, p. 2.
11. P. de Man, 1993, p. 4.
12. G. Durrant, 1970, argued powerfully for the pervasive influence of mathematics and Newtonian physics on Wordsworth's thought. More recently J. M. P. Fitzgerald, 1984, pp. 309–310 has produced extensive evidence of Wordsworth's (and Coleridge's) awareness of Priestley's chemical studies and of the theories of the last decade of the century about phlogiston and physiology. Returning to Newton, see also W. K. Thomas and W. V. Ober, 1989.
13. R. Sharrock, 1962. See also N. Roe, 1988, J. Barrell, 1988, and S. Gill, 1989.
14. M. Levinson, 1986, for instance, sees the institutions of 'Church and State under the aspect of traditional forms as a solution to [Wordsworth's] dilemma on the one hand destroying subjectivity and on the other of an alien outer objectivity,' p. 134.
15. H.C. Robinson, 1872, II, p. 188.
16. *WL* II, p. 91.
17. *Prelude*, 1805, II, 215–220.
18. Whewell, 1834, p. 59.
19. Whewell, 1840, p. cxiii.
20. *Prose* I, p. 135.

21. Ibid., p. 139.
22. Moorman's major biography uses the term 'the Later Years' for the period after 1803. Mark Reed, the 'registrar' of Wordsworth's chronology applies 'The Middle Years' to 1800–1815. The Oxford editions of Wordsworth's letters applies 'Middle Years' to 1806 onwards, then 'Later Years' to after 1821. Recent studies of aspects of the middle and later years are to be found in Butler, 1981, Hartman, 1987, Manning, 1990, Trickett, 1990, Gill, 1989 and 1994, and Hill, 1992.
23. Dora Wordsworth kept the Rydal Mount Visitors' Book from 1830 to 1847 and recorded visits by 'Mr Buckland' in 1833 and 1842.
24. M. Foucault, 1974, p. 38.
25. E. Griggs, 1956, 1, p. 538.
26. R. Harré (1983a), 1990, p. 5.
27. See F. Hodson, 1967, a geologist translating Addison. D. M. Hassler, 1984, connects Erasmus Darwin with Wordsworth, particularly focusing on the topic of evolution; Darwin's own *Zoonomia*, though largely devoted to animal life, acknowledges contemporary discoveries in chemistry and geology, 'enlarging and amplifying the power of the Great Cause' (p. 537). D. R. Dean, 1973, notes twelve references in *The Botanic Garden* to James Hutton.
28. E. Darwin, 1791, p. v.
29. M. Foucault, 1972, p. 38.
30. M. Allaby 1985, p. 166.
31. R. Porter, 1977, pp. 6, 236.
32. J. Secord, 1986, proposed that research should consider the way networks of researchers, individual careers, and institutional structures have shaped the addition of 'new' knowledge. T. W. Heyck, 1982, makes an interesting distinction between three 'classes' of intellectuals in Victorian England: the men of letters, the scientists, and the university teachers. My own study is about the 'classes' before these three categories could be identified as precisely as this. See also J. Golinski, 1992 for an analysis of 'the community of practitioners' in the development of chemistry in Britain from 1760–1820.
33. M. Butler, 1981, p. 10.
34. Roy Porter's article 'Gentlemen and Geology' (1978) is an invaluable guide to the emergence of scientific careers in the pre-professional period of geology. J. Secord, 1991 should be read to develop fully the idea of a scientific career later in the first half of the nineteenth century. Secord studies the development of Charles Darwin's geological identity.

2 WORDSWORTH'S GEOLOGY: REFERENCES AND ALLUSIONS

1. Cunningham and Jardine, 1990, present an important collection of essays on European Romanticism and the sciences. Geology appears in a new light in their analyses.

2. D. R. Dean, 1963, p. 3.
3. *Prose* II, pp. 175–176.
4. J. Playfair, 1802, II, pp. 97–98.
5. *Prose* II, p. 175.
6. J. Hutton, 1795, p. 408. The modern editor of Playfair's *Illustrations* (1802) in facsimile edition comments: 'the term "schistus" is used with various meanings, although "gneiss" is sometimes meant' (p. ix).
7. H. Davy, 1811, pp. 12, 20.
8. A. Sedgwick, 1831a, p. 247.
9. *WP* I, p. 74.
10. Ibid., pp. 64, 65.
11. *DWJ* II, 1941, pp. 196, 268, 285.
12. Coxe was obviously interested in a range of different aspects of geology, for instance, he described the Rigi as composed of a mixture of gravel and pudding stone leading by a sandstone ridge towards Schweis (W. Coxe, 1789, p. 260).
13. *Prose* II, p. 175.
14. *WP* III, p. 573. Modern guidebooks confirm Wordsworth's hunch. 'Rosa' does not refer to the redness of the rocks, but is described from the patois for 'ice' or 'glacier' (L. R. Muirhead, 1948, p. 164).
15. *WP* IV, p. 407. 'Basalt' also occurs in a letter of 1834 (*WL* v letter 855a) from Wordsworth to John Marshall, describing the Giants' Causeway as a 'basalt barrier'.
16. *WP* II, p. 364. Wordsworth commented on Mr Westall's preliminary notes to the poems mentioned in this paragraph (see *WP* III, p. 37).
17. W. Whewell, 1832, p. 183.
18. *WP* IV, p. 43. The source of Wordsworth's knowledge of Iona's geology appears to be a travel account, Martin's *Description of the Western Isles of Scotland*, not a contemporary work.
19. S. Gill, 1989, p. 285.
20. W. Gilpin, 1786, p. 107.
21. *Prose* II, p. 175.
22. Ibid., p. 353.
23. J. Hutton, 1795, pp. 408–409.
24. *Prose* II, p. 178.
25. Ibid., p. 184.
26. *WP* II, p. 237.
27. In the years before the publication of the sonnet sequence, there were family visits to the Duddon Valley. These visits were serious in purpose. Before metalled road systems were widely laid down, the Duddon Valley was not a genteel stroll through nature. Its terrain was rugged, so an excursion required forethought and preparation. Mark Reed, 1967 and 1975, lists three journeys between 1804 and 1811.
28. Twentieth-century geomorphology has continued to attend to the phenomena of rivers like the Duddon. Superimposition and antecedence are

terms used in this discipline to explain 'a drainage system which does not conform to the structural pattern of the region, although it may show local small adjustments to it' (D. Whitten, and J. Brooks, 1972, pp. 236–237). The first concept, superimposition, is where a drainage system has eroded younger rocks which lie uncomfortably upon an older series. In the course of time, the younger series will be removed, but, because the river system is well established, it will carry on eroding the older structures but will not be determined by them. The Victorian geologist, Mawe (1832–1912), was the first to use the term 'superimposition' in 1866. Antecedence is a theory to explain how a river system maintains itself across a geological structure which runs across its routes. One theory is that during a prolonged period of uplift the river maintained its course, thus cutting deep into the slowly rising rocks. Classical instances usually cited are the Brahmaputra Gorge, the Rhine, and the rivers of the Nashville Dome in Tennessee. Both concepts, superimposition and antecedence, could apply to the much smaller and perhaps less dominant Duddon. What matters in the landscape is that there are stretches of rock across which a river finds its way, against all the expected 'rules' of seeking structurally easy routes to travel. A river flowing in an open valley, like the Duddon above Seathwaite, within a few miles will reassume the features of a mountain stream – fast flow, deep water with boulders and pot-holes, and a narrow valley between precipices. Some river valleys in this phase also show evidence of earlier phases of erosion, with steeper cliffs set further back from the existing river's track. Wallowbarrow Crag and the Pen are such cliffs in relation to the Duddon, giving an indication of an earlier period of valley erosion, perhaps associated with glacial systems.

The geomorphological features just described were accepted, as the dating of Mawe's work indicates, at a much later period than the writing of the Duddon sonnets sequence. However, Chorley suggests that Hutton had given an early indication of features of superimposition in 1795, without, of course, using that term (R. Chorley, et al. 1964, p. 52). Dorothy Wordsworth's comment referred to in this chapter may not be a brilliant instance of innocent geologzsing, but may have been a partly-forgotten reference to something read in an encyclopaedia or a travel account, perhaps even a version of Hutton's theories. See also W. H. Pearsall and W. Pennington, 1973, p. 41.

29. *DWJ* II, pp. 130–131.
30. *WP* III, p. 510.
31. Mary Wordsworth, writing to her sister, Sara, in December 1818 said the poet was sleeping from 'sheer exhaustion' after writing twenty-one sonnets on the River Duddon. She added, 'they all together compose one poem'. The poet described them as a sequence (*WP* III, p. 508 and M. Moorman, 1965 II, p. 373).
32. *Prose* II, p. 251.

33. Ibid., p. 252.
34. The publications devoted to reconciling geological discovery and expla- nation with Biblical theory were considerable. Gillispie, 1951, Porter, 1977, Rupke, 1983, and Corsi, 1988 give detailed examples of the ingenious assimilations of traditional belief and geological theory. Such accommodations to faith are very different from out-and-out fundament- alism that affirmed that the biblical account of Creation was literally and exactly true. Brooke (1979 and 1991a) is the most recent and thorough source for studies of the relationship between science and religion in the period.
35. *WP* I, p. 82.
36. Ibid., p. 88.
37. See A. Bewell, 1989, p. 248.
38. *Prelude*, 1805, p. 218.
39. Ibid., pp. vi, 556–564, 568–572.
40. N. Rupke, 1983 stresses the distinctively English attitude to stratigraphy, particularly promulgated by Buckland, as a determinedly historical geology associated philosophically with progressivism.
41. N. Rupke, 1983a, p. 115.
42. *WP* IV, p. 97.
43. J. Butler, p. 404.
44. *WP* III, p. 252.
45. Ibid., p. 191.
46. Ibid., p. 485.
47. Ibid., p. 199.
48. *WP* IV, p. 36. Keats also wrote on the subject of Ailsa Craig. He is even more explicit about the geological theory explaining Ailsa Craig's position rising out of the sea, producing an orthodox Wernerian statement of the rocks' formation below the sea (J. Keats, 1958, p. 491).
49. T. Kelley, 1988, p. 215.
50. *WP* III, pp. 36–37.
51. C. J. Ketcham, pp. 277–278.
52. *WL* v, letter 819.
53. *Prose* II, p. 182.
54. Ibid., p. 181.
55. Ibid., p. 178.
56. Ibid., p. 181.
57. Ibid., p. 231.
58. *D.W.J.* II, p. 163.
59. *Prose* II, p. 188.
60. The major literary allusion to Burnet is J. Livingston Lowes (1927), for geological references see R. S. Porter, 1977 and S. J. Gould, 1983.
61. S. J. Gould, 1988, p. 22.
62. T. Burnet, 1684, pp. 142, 240.
63. See C. L. Shaver and A. C. Shaver, 1979 for a list of Wordsworth's books

including those of Coleridge which the Wordsworths kept for him at Rydal Mount. The Pinney family owned the house, Racedown Lodge, which William and Dorothy rented in 1795 (see S. Gill, 1989, chapter 4). The correspondence between William and the Pinneys is of value because of the links with radicalism in Wordsworth's early years. The library was checked during Wordsworth's tenancy. It contained about four hundred and seventy books, including works of geography and travel from the seventeenth and early eighteenth centuries. Amongst these were Ray's *Wisdom of God* (1691 and 1714 editions), Wells's *Geographical Grammar* (1714), and Burnet's *The Theory of the Earth* in English (1697).

64. *WP* v, ii, 359–364.
65. J. Otley, 1823, p. 94.
66. J. Hutton, 1797, I, ch.4.
67. S. J. Griggs, 1956, II, p. 977.
68. K.Coburn, 1957, I, 1656.
69. *Prose* II, p. 251.
70. T. Kelley, 1988, p. 10. See also M. Gaull, 1979 and 1988 and C. Gillispie, 1985. Gillispie's text on Genesis and its place in geological theory has now been superseded by more recent works on the history of geology.
71. J. Bate, 1991, p. 44.
72. Ibid., 1991, p. 45.

3 'PRONOUNCE THEIR BENEDICTION; SPEAK OF THEM AS POWERS': THE WIDER CONTEXT OF GEOLOGICAL INFORMATION

1. *Prelude*, 1805, 219–220.
2. A. Sheridan, 1980, p. 94.
3. *WL* IV, pp. 682–683.
4. Some controversy continues to surround the point whether Carbonnière's version of Coxe was actually used by Wordsworth in his journey of 1790 to France and Switzerland. Gill, 1990, is cautious about agreeing wholeheartedly with Sheats's view that Carbonnière was the direct influence on *Descriptive Sketches*. Wordsworth's own notes are quite clear. He gives full credit to Carbonnière (*WP* I, p. 64).
5. P. D. Sheats, 1973, pp. 64, 65.
6. J. W. Goethe, 1989, p. 66.
7. I. Kant, 1952, pp. 115–116, 130.
8. M. Abrams, 1973, p. 334.
9. *WP* II, iii, 93–100.
10. *WL* IV, p. 674.
11. Butler, *The Ruined Cottage*, p. 351.
12. *Prose* II, p. 316.
13. *Encyclopaedia Britannica*, 1797, VI, p. 262.
14. B. Darlington, 1982, p. 88.
15. R. Porter, 1977, ch. 5.

16. J. Beer, 1977, p. 44.
17. *WL* III, part 2, p. 216.
18. M. Foucault, 1970, p. 208.
19. W. Wordsworth, 1820. The advertisement also included Bakewell's text on mineralogy. Playfair's text advertised in the publisher's list was his *Outlines of Natural Philosophy*.
20. *WP* v, v, 58.
21. GBG UCL 7/12.
22. H. Davy, 1839, III, pp. 449, 460 and H. Davy, 1811, pp. 43, 44.
23. *WL* II, p. 188.
24. *WL* v, part 2, p. 415.
25. Cunningham and Jardine, 1990, p. 297.
26. T. Levere, 1981, p. 159.
27. *WL* II, p. 185.
28. R. Laudan, 1987, pp. 111, 112.
29. T. Levere, 1981, p. 171.
30. Ibid., 1981, p. 159.

4 TRINITY MEN

1. See P. Foster, 1988 for a detailed analysis of Gilbert White's range of scientific contacts. D. E. Allen, 1978 (1976), surveys natural history societies and local activities of scientists in early Victorian England, of course only part of the period of this study.
2. 1807 Minute book of the Geological Society.
3. M. Garland, 1980, p. 28.
4. J. A. Secord, 1986, p. 63.
5. See W./S.F. Cannon, 1964, 1978 and L. Merrill, 1989.
6. J. W. Clark and T. M. Hughes, 1890 II, p. 122.
7. CUL AS Add, 7652, pp. 15–19.
8. Adam Sedgwick's sister, Ann, married William Westall, whose drawings of limestone caverns stimulated Wordsworth's verse of 1818. See reference in J. C. Ward, 1877, p. 154, to the possibility of competition in sales between Wordsworth's *A Guide* and Mr Westall's *Panoramic Views*. See also M. Moorman, 1965, II, p. 373. William Westall's collection of drawings (see W. Westall, 1818) is preceded by brief notes on the features in the drawings. The notes contain geological references to 'horizontal strata', to 'calcareous rock', to 'petrifactions of animals no longer known to exist'. The author of the notes (presumably Westall) knew something of Wernerian stratigraphy, referring to the rocks as 'transition or mountain limestone' (p. 3).
9. A. Sedgwick, 1842, p. 54.
10. J. W. Clark and T. M. Hughes, 1890, I.
11. Ibid., II. p. 427.
12. A. Sedgwick, 1842, p. fol. 3.

13. *WP* v, iii, pp. 173, 189.
14. S. F. Cannon, 1978, p. 8.
15. J. W. Clark and T. M. Hughes, 1890, I, p. 249.
16. Sedgwick's field notebooks are bound notebooks designed for field-work. There are two kinds: the majority orderly and neatly entered, probably at the resting place of the night; and a few are field sketch books grubby from rain and soil. All appear to have been entered up at regular intervals. Some pages contain sketches of landforms and attempts at cross-sections of landscapes, with conjectures on the angle of the dip. As well as geological information there are notes on social engagements, architecture, and even two laundry lists.
17. J. C. Ward, 1877, p. 154.
18. C. Carlyon, 1836, I pp. 116–117; 1858, IV, index.
19. J. W. Clark and T. M. Hughes, 1890, II, p. 248.
20. A. Sedgwick, 1842, p. 54.
21. *WL* v, pp. 354–355.
22. Ibid., p. 398.
23. Ibid., p. 710.
24. Ibid., p. 708.
25. See letter from Sedgwick to Murchison in 1832, CULAS Add. 7652.
26. J. W. Clark and T. M. Hughes, 1890, I, p. 488. Also see a poem by Hartley Coleridge about Sedgwick in C. Speakman, 1982, p. 1.
27. See also Corsi, 1979 and 1988 for a discussion on the relation between geology and Anglicanism.
28. Whewell, 1967 (1847), p. iii.
29. I. Todhunter, 1876, I, p. 1.
30. M. Fisch, 1991 and M. Fisch and S. Shaffer, 1991.
31. R. P. Graves, 1832, II, p. 209.
32. *WL* v, ii, p. 546.
33. W. Cannon, 1964, N. Annan, 1985, and S. Gliserman, 1975.
34. *WP* v, viii, 482–536.
35. I. Todhunter, 1876, II, p. 37.
36. S. Douglas, 1881.
37. Ibid., 1881, p. 189.
38. M. Gaull, 1979, M. J. S. Rudwick, 1976, R. S. Porter, 1977.
39. *WL* I, p. 300. The scientific connections of the Marshall family were numerous and extended over generations. Jeremiah Marshall, the father of John, attended the Unitarian Chapel in Leeds where Priestley preached. James Watt junior refers to John Marshall in correspondence. Sir John Herschel's daughter married a nephew of the next generation of Marshalls. John Marshall was a supporter with Greenough of the establishment of University College London.
40. G. H. Healey, 1942.
41. R. P. Graves, 1882, II, p. 209. 'Spit and smokejack' is an odd expression. The *NED* helps – a smoke jack is a device for turning meat on a grill.

42. W. G. Rimmer, 1960, p. 223.
43. I. Todhunter, 1876, II, p. 319.
44. S. Douglas, 1881, pp. 28–29.
45. Ibid., 1881, p. 32.
46. Ibid., 1881, p. 77.
47. *WL* IV, p. 681.
48. S. Douglas, 1881, p. 32.
49. I. Todhunter, 1876, II, p. 43. The most likely source for 'tumbled the names together' is Wordsworth's poem 'To Joanna' of 1800 (*WP* II, pp. 112–114). J. Beer (1979, ch. 5) has a sensitive analysis of this poem.
50. *OED* gives this definition. G. Beer, 1983, pp. 14–15, has an interesting section on 'evolution'. Wordsworth uses the word, in Whewell's sense, when writing to Lady Beaumont in 1810 about his favourite image of a cloud-born 'station' later to be absorbed in *A Guide*: 'by evolving truly and distinctly the appearance from another' (*WL* II, p. 404).
51. S. Douglas, 1881, pp. 267–268.
52. Ibid., 1881, p. 273.
53. Ibid., 1881, p. 115.
54. I. Todhunter, 1876, I, p. 45.
55. G. Beer, 1990, p. 83.
56. I. Todhunter, 1876, I, p. 126.
57. S. Douglas, 1881, p. 581.
58. Ibid., 1881, p. 583.
59. Mrs Lyell, 1881, II, p. 34.
60. G. Beer, 1990, p. 83.
61. I. Todhunter, 1876, II, p. 233.
62. S. Prickett, 1976, p. 259.
63. I. Todhunter, 1876, II, p. 112.
64. S. Douglas, 1881, pp. 69, 72–73.
65. Whewell, 1967 (1847), p. 642.
66. J. Secord, 1986, p. 63.

5 ORDER, CLARITY, DISTINCTNESS

1. J. Hutton, 1795, I, p. 3.
2. Ibid., pp. 15–16.
3. Ibid., p. 216.
4. Ibid., p. 200.
5. Ibid., p. 281.
6. A. Chitnis, 1976, p. 171.
7. J. Hutton, 1794, II, pp. 88, 116.
8. Ibid., p. 286.
9. J. A. Secord, 1986, p. 57.
10. G. B. Greenough, UCL 29/3, p. 6.
11. A. Sedgwick, 1831, p. 247.

12. R.S. Porter, 1977, p. 142.
13. DCL, Whewell, Letter A/1.
14. In the seventeenth and eighteenth centuries mineralogical specimens and fossils were kept in an orderly fashion in specially designed cabinets, consisting usually of shallow drawers in which small items could be displayed. A magnificent example, with its specimens in the same positions as they occupied in the eighteenth century, can be seen at the University of Cambridge's Sedgwick Museum. To the 'new' geologists of the nineteenth century these cabinets appeared limited in their potential, particularly for handling large fossil specimens or for displaying the results of traverses made by energetic field-workers such as Buckland, Sedgwick, and Murchison. Contemporary mineralogists or chemists interested in mineralogy (such as Davy) were more concerned to conduct experiments on minerals, sometimes with portable apparatus in the field. (See Golinski, J. 1992, pp. 269–288.) Furthermore a 'cabinet' seems to have implied an out-dated 'cabinet mentality', related to collecting stones and gems and to theorizing rather than to empirical studies. To Words- worth, 'cabinets' stand for something boring and confusing (*The Excursion*, VII, 22–28). Wordsworth also uses 'cabinet' in a mildly pejorative sense in *The Prelude*.

> To thee, unblinded by these outward shows,
> The unity of all has been revealed;
> And thou wilt doubt with me, less aptly skilled
> Than many are to class the cabinet
> Of their sensations, and in voluble phrase
> Run through the history and birth of each
> As of a single independent thing.
> (*Prelude* 1805, II, 225–231)

This passage follows lines condemning false distinctions in science (knowl- edge) to which the last paragraphs of this chapter refer. In book II of *The Prelude* there is another reference to 'cabinet'. The poet takes a symbol of his young life in Cambridge: 'Carelessly / I gazed, roving as through a cabinet / Or wide museum' until 'a barren sense / Of gay confusion' is left, although something may remain in the memory (*Prelude* 1805, III, 652–669).

15. G. Cantor, 1991, p. 85.
16. J. W. Goethe, 1970, p. 38.
17. Whewell, 1834, p. 278.
18. Ibid., 1834, p. 288.
19. *WP* v, iv, 13–15.
20. Ibid., 332–335.
21. M. Nicolson, 1963, introduction.
22. *WP* v, iv, 1235–1242.
23. *WP* v, vii, 1004–1005.
24. *Prelude*, 1805, xi, 96–100.

25. Ibid., vii, 700–705.
26. G. Beer, 1983, p. 66. See also Herz, 1993.
27. G. Durrant, 1970, sees Wordsworth's interest in Newtonian astronomy and physics as an opposing strand to the principle of joy, offering 'no consolatory or merely encouraging account of life' (p. 16).
28. *WP* v, iv, 34–36.
29. *Prelude*, 1805, ii, 220–222.
30. *WP* v, iv, 958–963.
31. Ibid., 332–337.
32. *WL* v, p. 708.
33. G. B. Greenough UCL, 29/3, p. 93.
34. *Prose* ii, p. 185.
35. Ibid., p. 238.
36. Ibid., p. 238.
37. *WP* iii, pp. 382–383.
38. Ibid., p. 407.
39. *WP* iv, p. 32.
40. Ibid., p. 33.
41. J. W. Goethe, 1970, p. 23.
42. J. Hutton, 1794, ii, p. 48.
43. Whewell, 1841, p. 44.
44. Ibid., 1967 (1847), p. 646.
45. *WP* v, iv, 1251–1259.
46. The *Oxford English Dictionary* distinguishes as Dr Johnson did between 'distinctness' as separateness and 'distinctness' as clarity in perception or thought. It is interesting that William Whewell is one of the sources in *OED* for the word. I cannot trace 'distinctness' in poetry before Wordsworth. A modern instance of its use is: 'As a child grows, life is found to be more than bodily comfort. There comes self-knowledge, distinctness, individuality' (O. Chadwick, 1983, p. 27).
47. J. Ray, 1750, pp. 207–208.
48. *Prelude*, 1805, viii, 509–513.
49. *WP* v, iv, 944–947.
50. Ibid., 828–833.
51. To try to justify an influence of one writer on another, and to separate that influence from others which are contemporary is notoriously difficult, particularly where the writer is exceptionally widely read. John Ray's work was certainly read by Wordsworth, but it is not possible to claim that he is Wordsworth's main source of images for the powers of perception. Ray's work is itself an inheritance from Newton's theories, particularly from *The Optics*, which remained an important text for Cambridge undergraduates in Wordsworth's day and beyond (B. R. Schneider, 1957). We should also bear in mind, despite the general belief to the contrary, that Wordsworth may have had, through Coleridge, some knowledge of Kant. Kant proposes a 'continuous development and

progressive diversification' in nature (A. O. Lovejoy, 1960, p. 268), which accounts for nature's fruitfulness. The mind seeks out this diversity, distinguishing the parts (seeking distinctness), but not seeking to destroy the whole of which they are the interrelated components. To the educated person, identity and unity are both retained or, to use Wordsworth's own phrase, 'the exactness of a comprehensive mind' (*Prelude*, 1805, x, p. 844).

52. E. L. Griggs, ii, p. 864.
53. B. Darlington, 1977, 1006–1011.
54. *Prelude*, 1805, iii, 156–159.
55. *WP* v, iv, 332–337.
56. Minute book of the Geological Society, 1810.
57. CULAS, Add.7652, p. iii.
58. R. Laudan, 1977, p. 537.
59. A. Sedgwick, 1842, p. 52.
60. M. Abrams, 1973 (1971), p. 185.

6 'THE UNIVERSALITY OF NATURE'S KINGDOM'

1. A. Sedgwick, 1843, p. fol. 3.
2. T. Levere, 1990, p. 297.
3. J. W. Clark and T. M. Hughes, 1890, 1, p. 302.
4. A. Sedgwick, 1969, p. 13.
5. Ibid., 1842, p. 54.
6. Ibid., 1842, p. fol. 3. Sedgwick's preface to the *Catalogue of Fossils* was quoted at his funeral (R. Burns, 1873, p. 10).
7. Ibid., 1969, p. 13.
8. W/S. F. Cannon, 1978, p. 3.
9. A. Sedgwick, 1842, pp. 20, 21.
10. G. Beer, 1988, p. 66. Gillian Beer's study of Darwin also traces a reliance on 'permanently discoverable laws'. Sedgwick was, as it were, a member of the same 'intellectual collective'. An earlier example of a scientist's interest in universality is found in James Hutton's geology. James Hutton's sense of the unity of phenomena is often conveyed by human metaphors (for example of the circulation of the blood). Another of his figures of unity is of a woven picture as in: 'We perceive a fabric erected in Wisdom' (J. Hutton, 1795, p. 3).
11. G. B. Greenough, 1819, p. 113.
12. S. Gliserman, 1975, p. 295.
13. Whewell, 1857 (1840), pp. 485–486.
14. *WP* v, iv, 427–432.
15. Ibid., 445–448.
16. Ibid., 1251–1259.
17. *WP* v, ix, 1–15.
18. A. O. Lovejoy, 1960.

19. *WP* v, ix, 6, 9–10, 13–15, 25, 33–34, 37–38, 42, 46–48.
20. Ibid., 85–90.
21. A. S. Byatt, 1970, has engaged with the issue of unity in Coleridge's and in Wordsworth's poetry and she attends to the processes of perception of the sublime, its diversity and yet its strange unity holding differences in tension:

> Wordsworth's living sense of the unity of matter beneath the changing and shifting forms of natural objects, man rolled round in earth's diurnal course with rocks and stones and trees and his further sense of the unity of these in the way an imaginative vision sees one in the other, one form as an image of another form'. (A. S. Byatt, 1970, p. 272).

22. *WP* III, p. 245.
23. Ibid., p. 247.
24. Ibid., p. 254.
25. C. and M. Lamb, 1978, III, p. 95.
26. *Prose* II, pp. 194–195.
27. *WP* III, pp. 246–247.
28. W. Knight, 1896, p. 232.
29. *WP* III, p. 261.
30. Ketcham, p. 259.
31. Ibid., p. 544.
32. Ibid., p. 238.
33. Ibid., p. 240.
34. *WP* III, p. 267.
35. J. M. P. Fitzgerald, 1984, p. 18.
36. *WP* II, p. 330.
37. Ibid., p. 523.
38. DCL, AS.
39. *WP* II, p. 303.
40. T. H. Levere, 1981, p. 163.
41. *WP* v, iv, 460–465.
42. Ibid., 1035–1037.
43. Whewell, 1967 (1847), p. 3.
44. Ibid., p. 708.
45. I. Todhunter, 1876, II, p. 338.
46. *Prelude*, 1805, XIII, 445–452.

7 DURATION AND DECAY: THE ABYSS OF TIME

1. J. Playfair, 1803, p. 73.
2. *Prose* II, pp. 317–318.
3. S. Gill, 1989, p. 324.
4. *Prose* II, p. 51.
5. R. Laudan, 1987, p. 1.

6. R. S. Porter, 1977.
7. C. C. Gillispie, 1951, p. 151.
8. Whewell, 1967 (1847), pp. 670, 671.
9. Whewell, 1832.
10. Hutton was clearly not a believer in stability: 'rest exists not anywhere, nor is found in any other way except among the parts of space' (J. Hutton, 1795, p. 222).
11. Hutton's influence on geologists' working before Lyell's major work is traceable. In summary form in reference books such as the *Encyclopaedia Britannica* of 1797 and in travellers' handbooks such as Richard Sulivan's *A View of Nature* of 1794, Hutton's geology was available for any aspiring geologist. See D. R. Dean, 1992, for the reception of Hutton's work in the early nineteenth century.
12. Hutton's status in geological methodology still occasions controversy. Porter says that what was important about Hutton was 'the distinctive intellectual framework within which his fieldwork was undertaken' (R. S. Porter, 1977, p. 185), rather than strict application of observed phenomena to produce theoretical constructs. Gould, 1988 (1987), regards Playfair then Lyell as the source of the view that Hutton was first a field worker then a theorist, whereas Hutton, Gould continues, never misrepresented his own position as a speculative thinker who followed up theories with observation, rather than the other way round. Despite this ambiguity about Hutton's status as a field worker, his name is undeniably attached to specific sites which have become famous in the history of geology, such as the Jedburgh unconformity, the Glen Tilt intrusions, and sections he studied in Salisbury Crags, Edinburgh (see W. Wimbledon, 1991, pp. 23–24).
13. For the most recent discussion of Hutton and his range of studies, see D. R. Dean, 1992.
14. G. B. Greenough, UCL, 29/3. p. 25.
15. Whewell, 1858, p. 228.
16. T. McFarland, 1969, writing about Coleridge notes that ruin and incompleteness are part of Romantic ideology.
17. J. W. Goethe, 1989, pp. 65–66.
18. *DWJ* ii, p. 286.
19. Ibid., p. 163.
20. *Prelude*, 1805, vi, 556–563, 568–572.
21. J. Wordsworth, 1982, p. 193.
22. *Prose* ii, pp. 194–195.
23. Ibid., pp. 187.
24. A. S. Byatt, 1970, p. 274.
25. *Prose* ii, pp. 251, 252.
26. *WP* v, ii, 359–364.
27. 'Cirque' used in this passage, or 'cwm' or 'corrie' originate in local dialect names in Wales, the Lake District, and Scotland for the hollows in

glaciated mountain country. The image of 'armchair-like hollow' persists and reasonably describes the steep back and side walls of a cirque with a flatter lip often ending in a low moraine and a waterfall.

Glacial theories of large-scale erosion by ice-sheets gained acceptance during Wordsworth's lifetime, but not until the 1830s through the persistent campaigning by Louis Agassiz did they gain British support. The 'semi-cirque' used by Wordsworth is an expression used to mean a circle, or in this case a half circle, but usually in the sense of an edifice such as an ampitheatre. *OED* quotes William Shenston from the eighteenth century as the earliest recorded source of 'cirque', with a quotation from Keats in the nineteenth century.

28. *WP* v, iii, 50–55.
29. Ibid., 71–73.
30. Ibid., 89–90.
31. *WP* iv, p. 42.
32. Ibid., pp. 40–41.
33. P. De Man, 1993, p. 92.
34. Lord Shaftesbury, 1773, p. 214.
35. J. Hutton, 1795, p. 281.
36. H. Davy, 1811, pp. 43–44.
37. Lord Shaftesbury, 1773, p. 290.

8 GEOLOGY, THE POETIC DISCIPLINE

1. A. Sedgwick, 1842, p. 4.
2. D. R. Oldroyd, 1990, p. 1.
3. Rupke, 1983a, gives a very sympathetic description of the larger-than-life character of Buckland. Mrs Lyell, 1881, ii, in her biography of Sir Charles Lyell records Sedgwick lecturing on the seashore at the BAAS meeting based at Newcastle to 3,000 people. He 'made a great impression'. Some of the stirrings of discontent arose from scientists who noted how many ladies attended geological meetings compared with the attendance at other branches of science.
4. Such as D. E. Allen, 1978, R. S. Porter, 1977, M. J. S. Rudwick, 1963 and 1976.
5. A. Sedgwick, 1831, pp. 306, 312.
6. H. Miller, 1869, p. 196. L. Merrill, 1989, chapter ten is titled 'Hugh Miller and Evocative Geology'.
7. I. Todhunter, ii, p. 43.
8. G. B. Greenough, UCL, 7/10. Posillipo, about 12 kilometres from Naples' is a ridge between the Bay of Naples and the Bay of Pozzuoli where Virgil's tomb could be visited.
9. J. Playfair, 1802, p. 91.
10. *Prelude*, 1805, XIII, 445–452.
11. J. Hutton, 1794, ii, p. 419.

12. G. B. Greenough, 1819, p. 95.
13. Ibid., UCL, 7/5.
14. J. W. Clark and T. M. Hughes, 1890, II, pp. 23, 24.
15. There would be an interesting extension of Sykes Davies's work (1989) on Wordsworth's frequently used words if a study were to be made of his references to the human eye. One aspect of that study would be the use of the eye as an organ for linking the inner and outer life and the change from *The Prelude* of 1805 to *The Excursion* in the attribution of power to the eye in the development of the poet's mind. There is a parallel between John Ray's *Wisdom of God Manifested in the Works of Creation* and elements of *The Prelude* and *The Excursion*. Indeed, a number of passages describing the Wanderer's youth relate to the eye as a passage to the soul. The young Wanderer is pictured in book I solitary in a cave or on the 'naked crags' seeing with 'the power of a peculiar eye' in their 'fixed and steady lineaments...an ebbing and a flowing mind' (*WP* v, i, 155–162). In youth, the Wanderer's eye is an overriding faculty ('nor did he believe, – he *saw*' *WP* v, i, 232). Age may not have 'tamed the eye', but it depended for its power on the experience of childhood: 'under brows / Shaggy and grey, had meanings which it brought / From years of youth' (*WP* v, i, 428–430). In a later reference to his own declining physical powers in book IV, the Wanderer contemplates the possibilities of blindness. He will be sustained by the memory of the 'visionary powers of eye and soul'. (*WP* v, iv, 111). More significant for my purpose, however, is the relationship of the eye to the topic of clarity or 'distinctness', because, as I have attempted to explain in chapter five, this is a concept of importance for contemporary geologists.
16. Whewell, 1841, p. 36.
17. J. Hutton, 1794, III, p. 119.
18. A. Donovan and I. Prentiss, 1980, p. 29.
19. C. Lyell, 1872, I, p. 87.
20. Mrs Lyell, 1881, II, p. 181. L. Merrill, 1989, p. 70, writes about Lyell's poetic descriptions and his comparison between the geologist's 'free mind' and 'the spirit which the poet described as animating the Universe' in the 1830 introduction to *Principles of Geology*.
21. R. S. Porter, 1977, p. 141.
22. E. Manier, 1978, p. 94.
23. S. Douglas, 1881, pp. 267–268.
24. A. Sedgwick, 1865, p. 121.
25. Ibid., 1831, p. 306.
26. *WP* v, ii, 875–877.
27. D. Dean, 1968, p. 11.
28. H. Davy, 1811, p. 9.
29. A. Sedgwick, 1831, p. 97.
30. Whewell, 1857 (1840), p. 429. Buckland judged that geology was 'nobler' than mineralogy (see R. Porter, 1978, p. 820). To redress any false

impression that mineralogy was not pursued in any serious sense see Golinski, J., 1992, where the various developments linking the subject to chemistry are enunciated.

31. G. B. Greenough, UCL, 29/3.
32. M. J. S. Rudwick, 1963, p. 334.
33. A. Sedgwick, 1842, fol. 3.
34. *Prose* I, p. 141.
35. J. W. Clark and T. M. Hughes, I, p. 207.
36. A. Sedgwick, 1969, p. 28.
37. G. B. Greenough, UCL, 29/3, p. 68.
38. Ibid., p. 17.
39. H. J. Jackson, 1985, p. 204.
40. *WP* v, ix, 769 and *The Prelude* 1805, viii, 584.
41. A. Sedgwick, 1969, p. 17.
42. Ibid., 1969, p. 54.
43. Ibid., 1931b, p. 300.
44. As early as 1798 Wordsworth began to write an 'Essay on Morals' of which only a fragment survives (M. Reed, 1967, p. 34 and *Prose* I, pp. 101–104). The remnant of the essay is clearly a criticism of moral systems based purely on reason. Both Godwin's writing and Paley's *Principles of Moral and Political Philosophy* of 1785 are inadequate to teach good living: 'Now, I know no book or system of moral philosophy written with sufficient power to melt into our affections, to incorporate itself with the blood and vital juices of our minds...' (*Prose* I, p. 103). Many years later, Wordsworth responded to the section in Adam Sedgwick's *A Discourse on the Studies of the University* which had criticized Paley's work to agree with his friend's strictures and, incidentally, revealed that they had discussed that author together (*WP* v, p. 708).
45. *WP* v, p. 5.
46. A. Sedgwick, 1969, pp. 18, 42–43.
47. It is quite feasible to consider that Wordsworth may have been clear where to trace one important literary inspiration for the hierarchy of the activities of the human mind. James Thomson's closing lines of 'Summer' from *The Seasons* would be familiar to the poet and perhaps also to Sedgwick. Certainly Greenough (and we may make a bold guess at philosopher–geologist Hutton's knowledge of the poems) would be aware of Thomson's lines which are related to Locke's *Essay Concerning Human Understanding* (see J. Thomson, 1987 (1972), p. 227). Philosophy 'directs the ruling helm' and from her lofty position:

> With inward view
> Thence on the ideal kingdom swift she turns,
> Her eyes and instant, at her powerful glance,
> The obedient phantoms vanish or appear;
> Compound, divide, and into order shift,
> Each to his rank, from plain perception up

To the fair forms of fancy's fleeting train;
To reason then, deducing truth from truth
And notion quite abstract; where first begins
The world of spirits, action all, and life
Unfettered and unmixed:

(J. Thomson, 1987 (1972), p. 86: 1788–1798)

To Thomson, there is, however, a limit to how far the accumulating power of human thinking can go in proving 'the final issue of the words of God'.

48. A. Sedgwick, 1831a, p. 212.
49. R. R. Yeo, 1986, p. 270.
50. Ibid., 1979, p. 511.
51. Whewell, 1857 (1840), p. 3.
52. Ibid., p. 8.
53. M. Fisch, 1991, p. 137.
54. Whewell, 1967 (1847), p. 2.
55. Ibid., p. 26.
56. Ibid., p. 26. Whewell's quotation from Wordsworth is not accurate. He quotes, 'All the world / Of eye and ear etc...', Wordsworth's lines were '...of all the mighty world'. The main point, however, is Whewell's elaboration of the lines 'both of what they half create / And what perceive'. Whewell says, 'But, it is clear that though they half create, they do not wholly create. There must be an external world of colour and sound to give impressions to the eye and ear, as well as internal powers by which we perceive what is offered to our organs. The mind is in some way passive as well as active' (Whewell, 1967 (1847), p. 26). Wordsworth's thoughts are in essence not contradicted.
57. Whewell, 1967 (1847), p. 29.
58. Ibid., 1834, p. 252.
59. Ibid., 1841, p. 44.
60. S. T. Coleridge, 1818, pp. 520–521.
61. *Prelude*, 1805, 292–293.
62. N. P. Stallknecht, 1958, p. 209 and M. Fisch, 1991a.
63. R. Laudan, 1977, p. 537.
64. *WP* v, iv, 1259–1263.
65. *WP* III, p. 211.
66. Ibid., p. 212.
67. *WP* v, iii, 173–189.
68. R. P. Graves, 1882, p. 313, see also E. C. Batho, 1933, p. 30.

9 GEOLOGISTS AND HUMANITY

1. A. Cunningham and W. Jardine, 1990, is a recent valuable collection of essays on this. M. Abrams, 1956 and 1971, still remain key texts. See also P. Thorsley, 1993, for a discussion of European philosophy and its interests for a variety of intellectuals. P. Corsi, 1988, pp. 155, 156, gives a

detailed account of Whewell's growing interest in Kant. According to P. Corsi it was 1827 before Whewell read Kant in the original.

2. A. Cunningham and W. Jardine, 1990, p. 3.
3. Greenough's Unitarianism has yet to be thoroughly explored and such an enquiry may reveal further resonances with Coleridge's early affiliations. Greenough is at his most cooly rational about doctrinal issues: on the Trinity he writes, 'If a man sees double, he is thought drunk, if treble, orthodox' (G. B. Greenough, UCL 29/3, p. 57). A similar remark from the same source (p. 56) is 'Christianity is a religion without priests, sacrifices or ceremonies.'
4. G. B. Greenough, UCL 29/3, pp. 9, 13.
5. Ibid., pp. 46, 52.
6. Ibid., p. 39.
7. *Prelude* 1805, II, 334–341.
8. M. Abrams, 1973 (1971), p. 184.
9. J. Butler, 1979, p. 394.
10. Whewell, 1845, p. i.
11. DCL W. 14 October 1841.
12. For Cuvier's use of the analogy of antiquarian studies see D. Outram, 1984, p. 151.
13. Whewell, 1857 (1840), p. 398.
14. Ibid., p. 399.
15. *WP* v, iii, 131–136.
16. N. Rupke, 1983a, p. 201.
17. Ibid., 1983, p. 202.
18. Whewell, 1847, p. 638. Fisch, 1991, and Hodge, 1991, make an interesting play with the word 'Palaetiology' in order to demonstrate Whewell's understanding of the place of geology in the scientific spectrum.
19. Whewell, 1857 (1840), p. 496.
20. G. B. Greenough, UCL, Box 16.
21. Whewell, 1855, p. 211.
22. *Prelude*, 1805, viii, 48–63.
23. M. Butler, 1981, p. 68.
24. *WP* v, p. 5: 70. The complex alterations of the lines that we now can read in *Home at Grasmere* or in the 'Preface' of 1814 are examined in J. Wordsworth, 1982.
25. *WP* v, pp. 4–5: 52–58.
26. R. Burn, 1873, p. 23.
27. J. Hudson, 1853, p. 257.
28. G. B. Greenough, UCL 29/3, p. 56.
29. Ibid., UCL 29/3, p. 60.
30. Ibid., 1840, pp. x/viii–x/viv.
31. The reader of Wordsworth then and now might put the character of the Happy Warrior alongside the image created of Major Robinson by Greenough:

Who, with a natural instinct to discern
What knowledge can perform, is diligent to learn;
Abides by this resolve, and stops not there,
But makes his moral being his prime care;
Who, doomed to go in company with Pain,
And Fear, and Bloodshed, miserable train!
Turns his necessity to glorious gain;
In face of these doth exercise a power
Which is our human nature's highest dower
(WP IV, p. 86: 8–16)

32. Greenough's collection of letters includes many expressions of support for his action in resigning from a commission in the Light Horse Volunteers and in making a widely circulated public statement of protest following the Peterloo Massacre. There are passages in his journals of an earlier period (1805), where he stoutly attacked the Utilitarian arguments of those who employed child labour.
33. D. E. Allen, 1978 (1976), p. 76.
34. *WP* V, p. 3: 14–18.
35. S. F. Cannon, 1978, p. 8.
36. A. Sedgwick, 1842, fol. 3.
37. J. W. Clark and T. M. Hughes, 1890, II, pp. 357–358.
38. Ibid., p. 191.
39. A. Sedgwick, 1869, p. 46.
40. DCL, 10 August 1847.
41. G. B. Greenough, UCL, 16/1.
42. See also W. Spiegelmann, 1985, *Wordsworth's Heroes*.
43. *WP* III, p. 116.
44. F. Copleston, 1968, p. 216.
45. *Prose* I, p. 139.

10 CONCLUSION

1. P. B. Shelley, 1975, II, pp. 77–78: 69–74.
2. Wordsworth asked for a copy of Montgomery's epic on the Deluge together with Humboldt's account of his explorations in a letter (see *WL* III, p. 216).
3. P. B. Shelley, 1975, II, p. 10.
4. J. Morrell and A. Thackray, 1981, p. 25.
5. G. B. Greenough, UCL 26/2, p. 10. In the literary sphere also, there is evidence of scepticism about the pace of reform, causing Marilyn Butler to ask: 'Is the literature of the Age of Revolution a literature, at the profoundest level, in reaction?' (M. Butler, 1981, p. 5). See also P. Corsi, 1988, p. 198 for the varieties of attitude to reform in the Church within Cambridge.
6. J. S. Mill, 1873 (1824), pp. 125, 126. G. Hartman, 1993, p. 44, examines in depth the 'conversion process' and Wordsworth's influence.

7. E. Manier, 1978, p. 186.
8. S. Gliserman, 1975, p. 278.
9. N. Rupke, 1983a, pp. 57, 62–63.
10. Mrs Lyell, 1881, pp. 55–56.
11. Ibid., pp. 67–68.
12. Ibid., p. 324.
13. I. Todhunter, 1970 (1876), p. 32.
14. S. Douglas, 1881, p. 235.
15. G. Hartman, 1971 (1964), p. 331.
16. R. Trickett, 1990, p. 48.
17. J. Wordsworth, 1982, p. 35.
18. J. H. Houston, 1978, considers the ideas of 'place' and 'land' and their origins in the Judaeo-Christian tradition. For a detailed study of the growth of nationalism in the early nineteenth century see Colley, 1992. My argument is that Wordsworth's concept of 'Englishness' is of an older formation, indebted to Milton.
19. N. Rupke, 1983a, p. 5 argues that 'the English schools remained shielded from the increasingly secular philosophy of history propagated by Kant, Hegel and others'. My own view is that this is to accept too uncritically the views of the two older men, Buckland and Whewell. A younger generation, men like Julius Hare for instance, was quickly seized by the insights granted by German historicism, particularly from Niebuhr's work.
20 Mrs Lyell, 1881. Lyell read Cuvier's new book on the chalk scenery around Paris in the Bibliotheque du Roi. The reference to Cuvier's membership of the Geological Society is from the minute books of the Society. Werner was admitted on the same occasion. Wordsworth, visited the Jardin des Plantes and in a letter to Lord Lonsdale in 1820 explained that the animals and the Natural History moved him more than the exhibition of paintings (*WL* III, p. 42).
21. Whewell, 1857 (1840), pp. 423–425.
22. Greenough's philosophical doctrine of a gradual improvement of the human race when myth is replaced by rational understanding is a further example of the line of influence on him from the European Enlightenment. Abrams, 1973, p. 202 illustrates the origins of this strand of thought from Lessing's *The Education of the Human Race* of 1780. Greenough's education in Göttingen was a significant and lasting component of his intellectual progress.
23. S. Douglas, 1881, p. 282. Whether Whewell was using the term, 'National Church' in the sense Coleridge used it is doubtful. Although they met, not least at the British Association meeting where Coleridge opined on 'philosophers' of science, there does not seem to have been an exchange of ideas on philosophy.
24. I. Todhunter, 1970 (1876).
25. Ibid.
26. *Prelude*, 1805, VIII, 565–577.

Bibliography

ORIGINAL SOURCES

Buckland, W. 1823 *Reliquiae Diluvianae* London, Murray J.
   1836 *Geology and Mineralogy Considered with Reference to Natural Theology* 2 volumes London, Pickering, W.
Burn, R. 1873 *God Our Refuge: A Sermon Preached in the Chapel of Trinity College, Cambridge* Cambridge, Deighton and Bell.
Burnet, T. 1684 *The Theory of the Earth* London, Norton, R.
Carlyon, C. 1836, 1843, 1856, and 1858 *Early Years and Late Reflections* 4 volumes London, Whittaker.
Coburn K. ed. 1957, 1962, and 1973 *The Notebooks of Samuel Taylor Coleridge* London, Routledge & Kegan Paul.
Coleridge, S. T. 1969 *The Friend* volume 1 ed. Rooke, B. E. Princeton and London, Princeton University Press and Routledge & Kegan Paul.
   1983 *Biographia Literaria* volume 2 eds. Engell, J. and Bate, W. J. Princeton, Princeton University Press.
Conybeare, W. D. and Phillips, W. 1822 *Outlines of the Geology of England and Wales* London, William Phillips.
Cottle, J. 1970 (1848) *Reminiscences of Samuel Taylor Coleridge and Robert Southey* 2nd edition London, Houltson and Stoneman.
Coxe, W. 1789 *Travels in Switzerland in a Series of Letters* 3 volumes London, Cadell.
   1802 *Travels in Switzerland, with Notes and Observations by Mr Ramond* 3 volumes Basle, Decker, J.
Curry, K. ed. 1965 *New Letters of Robert Southey* 2 volumes New York, Columbia University Press.
Darwin, E. 1791 *The Botanic Garden*, London, Johnson, J.
   1796 *Zoonomia or the Laws of Organic Life* 2 volumes 2nd edition London, Johnson, J.
Davy, H. 1811 *Sketch of Mr Davy's Lectures on Geology* Edinburgh, Allen, T.
   1839 *The Collected Works of Sir Humphry Davy, Bart. Vol III Early Miscellaneous Papers* London, Smith, Elder and Co.
   1851 *Consolations in Travel or the Last Days of a Philosopher* London, Murray, J.
Davy, J. ed. 1858 *Fragmentary Remains Literary and Scientific of Sir Humphry Davy, Bart.* London, Churchill.

251

Encyclopaedia Britannica or a Dictionary of Arts, Sciences and Miscellaneous Literature 1797 third edition Edinburgh, Bell, A. and MacFarquhar, C.

Gilpin, W. 1786 *Observations on the Mountains and Lakes of Cumberland and Westmoreland* Facsimile edition 1973 Richmond, Richmond Publishing Co.

Gordon, E. O. 1894 *The Life and Correspondence of William Buckland, D.D., F.R.S.* London, John Murray.

Gray, T. 1968 (1769) 'Journal in the Lakes' in the *Works of Thomas Gray in Prose* ed. Gosse, E. New York, A. M. S. Press.

Greenough, G. B. 1819 *A Critical Examination of the First Principles of Geology*, London, Longman, Hurst, Rees, Orme, Brown.

　CUL, UCL, and GS papers (see abbreviations).

Griggs, E. L. ed. 1956, 1956, 1959, and 1971 *The Collected Letters of Samuel Taylor Coleridge* 6 volumes Oxford, Oxford University Press.

Healey, G. H. ed. 1942 *Wordsworth's Pocket Notebook* Ithaca, Cornell University Press.

Housman, J. 1800 *A Topographical Description of Cumberland, Westmoreland, Lancashire and a Part of the West Riding of Yorkshire* Carlisle, Jollif, F.

Hudson, J. ed. 1853 *A Complete Guide to the Lakes* 4th edition Kendal, Hudson.

Hutton J. 1785 'Concerning the system of the Earth, its duration and decay' (Abstract of papers read to the Royal Society of Edinburgh) Facsimile edition 1970 Connecticut, Hafner. (See also Eyles, V. A. 1950.)

　1790 'Observations on granite' (Paper read to the Royal Society of Edinburgh). Facsimile edition 1970 Connecticut, Hafner.

　1792 *Dissertations on Different Subjects in Natural Philosophy* Edinburgh, Strachan, A. and Cadell, J.

　1794 *An Investigation of the Principles of Knowledge and of the Progress of Reason from Sense to Science and Philosophy* 3 volumes Edinburgh, Strachan, A. and Cadell, J.

　1795 *Theory of the Earth with Proofs and Illustrations* Edinburgh, Cadell, Jr and Davies. Facsimile edition 1959 Caldicote, Herts, Engelmann, Wheldon and Wesley.

Lamb, C. and M. A. 1978 *The Letters of Charles and Mary Anne Lamb Volume III* ed. Marrs, E. W. Ithaca, Cornell University Press.

Lyell, C. 1872 *Principles of Geology* 11th edition 2 volumes London, Murray, J.

Otley, J. 1819 'Account of the Floating Island in Derwent Lake, Keswick, 1814' *Manchester Philosophical Society Memoirs* III 64–69.

　1823 *A Concise Description of the English Lakes, the Mountains in their Vicinity and the Roads by which they may be Visited* Keswick, Richardson, J. and Foster, A.

Playfair, J. 1802 *Illustrations of the Huttonian Theory of the Earth* Edinburgh, Cadell and Davies.

　1803 *Biographical Account of the Late Doctor James Hutton* Facsimile edition 1970 Connecticut, Hafner.

Price, U. 1796 and 1798 *Essays on the Picturesque* 2 volumes Hereford, Walker.

Ray, J. 1750 *The Wisdom of God Manifested in the Works of Creation* 12th edition Glasgow, Duncan, W.

Robinson, H. C. 1872 *The Diaries of Henry Crabb Robinson* 2 volumes ed. Sadler, T. London, Macmillan.

Rydal Mount *1830–1847 Visitors' Book* Grasmere, Dove Cottage Library.

    1859 *Catalogue of the Varied and Valuable Historical, Poetical, Theological and Miscellaneous Library of the late Venerated Poet – Laureate William Wordsworth Esquire DCL Sold by Auction* 19, 21, and 22 of July 1859.

Sedgwick, A. 1830 'Address as President of the Geological Society of London' *Proceedings of the Geological Society of London* 1 15.

    1831a 'The general structure of the Lake Mountains of the North of England and in the great dislocations by which they have been separated from the neighbouring chains' *Proceedings of the Geological Society* 1 19.

    1831b 'Second Presidential address' *Proceedings of the Geological Society of London* 8 281ff.

    1842 'Three letters upon the geology of the Lake District' Hudson and Nicholson eds. *A Complete Guide to the Lakes* London, Longman. (For 4th edition, 1853, see Hudson, J. 1853.)

    1969 *A Discourse on the Studies of the University* introduction Ashby, E. and Anderson, M. Leicester and New York, Humanities Press.

    Field Journals Cambridge University Sedgwick Geological Museum.

    CUL, DCL, TCL papers (see abbreviations).

Shaftesbury, Lord 1773 *Characteristicks Volume II: An Enquiry Concerning Virtue and Merit, the Moralists, A Philosophical Rhapsody* Birmingham, Baskerville, J.

Sotheby, W. 1832 *Lines Suggested by the Third Meeting of the British Association for the Advancement of Science at Cambridge in June 1832* London, Nicol, G. and W.

Southey, R. ed. 1799 *The Annual Anthology* 2 volumes Bristol.

Sulivan, R. J. 1794 *A View of Nature in Letters to a Traveller among the Alps* 6 volumes London, Becket, T.

Todhunter, I. 1876 *William Whewell D.D. Master of Trinity College, Cambridge, an Account of his Writings* 2 volumes reprint 1970 Sources of Science Series 92 New York and London, Johnson Reprint.

West, T. 1780 *A Guide to the Lakes in Cumberland, Westmoreland and Lancashire* London, Richardson and Urquhart.

Westall, W. 1818 *Views of the Caves near Ingleton, Gordale Scar and Malham Cove in Yorkshire* London, John Murray.

Whewell, W. 1832 'Review of Charles Lyell's *Principles of Geology*' *British Critic* 9 180–206.

    1834a 'On the connexion of the physical sciences by Mrs Somerville' *Quarterly Review* 51 54–68.

    1834b *The Bridgewater Treatise III: Astronomy and General Physics considered with Reference to Natural Theology* London, Pickering, W.

    1838 'Presidential address to the Geological Society' *Proceedings of the Geological Society of London* 1838 649.

1840 *The Philosophy of the Inductive Sciences* ed. Parker J. W. Sedgwick's personal copy in University of Cambridge, Sedgwick Museum of Geology.

1841 *Two Introductory Lectures to Two Courses of Lectures on Moral Philosophy* Cambridge, Pitt Press.

1845 *The Elements of Morality Including Polity Volume 1* London, Parker, J. W.

1847 *The Philosophy of the Inductive Sciences* facsimile edition 1967 London, Cass, F.

1855 *Of the Plurality of Worlds* London, Parker, J. W.

1857 (1840) *The History of the Inductive Sciences* 3 volumes London, Parker, J. W.

1858 *The Novum Organon Renovatum* 3rd edition London, Parker, J. W.

TCL papers (see abbreviations).

Wilkinson, J. 1810 *Select Views in Cumberland Westmoreland and Lancashire* London, Ackermann.

Wordsworth, M. 1958 *The Letters of Mary Wordsworth* ed. Burton, M. E. Oxford, Clarendon Press.

Wordsworth, W. 1820a *The River Duddon, Vandracour and Julia and other Poems and a Topographical Description etc.* London, Longman, Hurst, Rees, Orme, Brown.

1820b *Poems including River Duddon, Vaudracour and Julia, Peter Bell, The Waggoner, A Thanksgiving Ode and Miscellaneous Pieces, Volume IV* London, Longman, Hurst, Rees, Orme, Brown.

Wordsworth, W. and D. other texts: see list of abbreviations.

Wordsworth, W. and M. 1982 *The Love Letters of William and Mary Wordsworth* ed. Darlington, B. London, Chatto and Windus.

SECONDARY SOURCES

Abrams, M. H. 1973 (1971) *Natural Supernaturalism, Tradition and Revolution in Romantic Literature* New York, Norton.

Abrams, M. H. ed. 1972 *Wordsworth: a Collection of Critical Essays* New Jersey, Prentice Hall.

Allaby, M. ed. 1985 *The Oxford Dictionary of Natural History* Oxford, Oxford University Press.

Allen, D. E. 1978 (1976) *The Naturalist in Britain* Harmondsworth, Penguin.

Annan, G. 1955 'Intellectual aristocracy' in Plumb, J. H. 1955.

Aubin, R. A. 1936 *Topographical Poetry in XVIII-Century England* New York, The Modern Language Association of America.

Bailey, E. B. 1967 *James Hutton – the Founder of Modern Geology* Amsterdam, Elsevier.

Barnes, B. 1974 *Scientific Knowledge and Sociological Theory* London, Routledge.

Barnes, B. and Shapin, S. eds. 1979 *Natural Order: Historical Studies of Scientific Culture* Beverly Hills and London, Sage Publications.

Barrell, J. 1988 *Poetry, Language and Politics*, Manchester, Manchester University Press.

Bate, J. 1991 *Romantic Ecology, Wordsworth and the Environmental Tradition*, London, Routledge.

Batho, E. C. 1933 *The Later Wordsworth* Cambridge, Cambridge University Press.

Baumgärtel, H. 1969 'Alexander von Humboldt's remarks on the meaning of hypothesis in his geological researches' in Schneer, C. J. ed. pp. 19–35.

Becker, H. W. 1991 'William Whewell's odyssey: from mathematics to moral philosophy' in Fisch, M. and Schaffer, S. eds. pp. 1–29.

Beer, G. 1983 *Darwin's Plots: Evolutionary Narrative in Darwin, George Eliot and Nineteenth-Century Fiction* London, Routledge & Kegan Paul.

   1990 'Translation of transformation? The relations of literature and science' *Notes and Records of the Royal Society* 44 81–99.

Beer, J. 1977 *Coleridge's Poetic Intelligence*, London, Macmillan.

   1979 *Wordsworth in Time* London, Faber and Faber.

Bernhardt-Kabisch, E. 1979 'Wordsworth and the Simplon revisited' *The Wordsworth Circle* 10:4 381–385.

Bewell, A. 1989 *Wordsworth and the Enlightenment* New Haven and London, Yale University Press.

Brooke, J. H. 1979 'The natural theology of the geologists: some theological strata' in Jordanova, J. and Porter, R. S. eds. 1979 pp. 39–56.

   1991 'Indications of a creator: Whewell as an apologist and priest' in Fisch, M. and Schaffer, S. eds. 1991 pp. 149–173.

   1991a *Science and Religion: Some Historical Perspectives* Cambridge, Cambridge University Press.

Burt, E. J., Newmark, K., and Watminski, A., eds. 1993 *Romanticism and Contemporary Criticism* Baltimore, Johns Hopkins, University Press.

Butler, M. 1981 *Romantics, Rebels and Reactionaries* Oxford, Oxford University Press.

Butler, M. 1988 'Romanticism in England' in Porter, R. S. and Teich, M. eds. 1988.

   1993 'Culture's medium: the role of the review' in Curran, S. ed. 1993 pp. 120–147.

Butler, M. ed. 1984 *Burke, Paine, Godwin, and the Revolution Controversy* Cambridge, Cambridge University Press.

Byatt, A. S. 1970 *Wordsworth and Coleridge in Their Time* London, Nelson.

Cannon, S.F. 1964 'The normative role of science in early Victorian thought' *Journal of the History of Ideas* 25 487–502.

   1978 *Science in Culture: the Early Victorian Period* New York, Science History Publications.

Cannon, W. 1964 'Scientists and broad churchmen: an early Victorian intellectual network' *Journal of British Studies* 4 65–88.

Cantor, G. 1991 'Between rationalism and romanticism: Whewell's historiography of the inductive sciences' in Fisch, M. and Schaffer, S. eds. pp. 67–86.

Chadwick, O. 1983 *Newman* Oxford, Oxford University Press.

Chase, C. ed. 1993 *Romanticism*, London, Longmans.

Chitnis, A. C. 1970 'The University of Edinburgh's natural history museum and the Huttonian-Wernerian debate' *Annals of Science* 26:2 85–94.

1986a *The Scottish Enlightenment: a Social History* London, Croom Helm.

1986b *The Scottish Enlightenment and Early Victorian Society* London, Croom Helm.

Chorley, R. J., Dunn, A. J., and Beckinsale, R. P. 1964 *The History of the Study of Landforms or the Development of Geomorphology Volume 1* London, Methuen.

Clark, J. W. and Hughes, T. M. 1890 *The Life and Letters of the Reverend Adam Sedgwick* 2 volumes, Cambridge, Cambridge University Press.

Coe, C. N. 1953 *Wordsworth and the Literature of Travel* New York, Bookman Association.

Colley, L. 1992 *Britons: Forging the Nation, 1707–1837*, New Haven, Yale University Press.

Cooke, K. 1979 *Coleridge* London, Routledge & Kegan Paul.

Copleston, F. 1968 *A History of Philosophy Volume VI Wolff to Kant* London, Burns and Oates.

Corsi, P. 1979 'Sciences in culture' *Isis* 70 (1979) 593–595.

1988 *Science and Religion: Baden Powell and the Anglican Debate, 1800–1860* Cambridge, Cambridge University Press.

Crowe, M. J. 1986 *The Extra-terrestrial Life Debate* Cambridge, Cambridge University Press.

Cunningham, A. and Jardine, W. eds. 1990 *Romanticism and Natural Science* Cambridge, Cambridge University Press.

Curran, S. ed. 1993 *The Cambridge Companion to British Romanticism* Cambridge, Cambridge University Press.

Davies, H. Sykes 1989 *Wordsworth and the Worth of Words* Cambridge, Cambridge University Press.

Dean, D. R. 1968 *Geology and English Literature: Cross-currents, 1770–1830* Ph.D. dissertation reprint, University of Wisconsin.

1973 'James Hutton and his public: 1785–1802' *Annals of Science* 30:1 89–106.

1981 'Through science to despair: geology and the Victorians' in Paradis, J. and Posteurat, T. eds. 1981.

1992 *James Hutton and the History of Geology* Ithaca, Cornell University Press.

De Man, P. 1984 *The Rhetoric of Romanticism* New York, Columbia University Press.

1993 'Time and history in Wordsworth' in Burt, E. J. et al., 1993.

De Quincey, T. 1970 *Recollections of the Lakes and the Lake Poets* Harmondsworth, Penguin.

Distad, N. M. 1979 *Guessing at Truth: the Life of Julius Charles Hare* Shepherdstown, Patmos Press.

Donovan, A. L. and Prentiss, J. 1980 'James Hutton's medical dissertation' *Transactions of the Amercian Philosophical Society* 70:6 3–47.

Douglas, S. 1881 *The Life and Selections from the Correspondence of William Whewell D.D.* London, Kegan, Paul.

Durrant, G. 1970 *Wordsworth and the Great System* Cambridge, Cambridge University Press.

Edinburgh Review 1832 *General Index to the Edinburgh Review – First to Fifteenth Volumes inclusive 1813–1830* Edinburgh, Black, A.

Eichner, H. 1972 'The rise of modern science and the genesis of Romanticism' *PMLA* 8–30.

Eyles, W. A. 1950 'Notes on the original publication of Hutton's *Theory of the Earth* and on the subsequent forms in which it was issued' *Proceedings of the Royal Society of Edinburgh* Section B 63:4 377–386.

1979 'The extent of geological knowledge in the eighteenth century and the methods by which it was diffused' in Schneer, C.J. ed. 1979 pp. 159–183.

Fisch, M. 1991a *William Whewell: Philosopher of Science* Oxford, Oxford University Press.

1991b 'Antithetical knowledge' in Fisch, M. and Schaffer, S. eds. 1991 pp. 289–309.

Fisch, M. and Schaffer, S. eds. 1991 *William Whewell: a Composite Portrait* Oxford, Clarendon Press.

Fitzgerald, J. M. P. 1984 *Wordsworth's Natural Philosophy: Phlogiston and Physiology in Wordsworth's Poetry, 1798–1800* Unpublished Ph.D. dissertation, University of Cambridge.

Foster, P. G. M. 1988 *Gilbert White and his Records: A Scientific Biography*, London, Helm.

Foucault, M. 1974 (1972) *The Archeology of Knowledge* trans. Smith, A. M. S. London, Tavistock.

1981 (1970) 'The order of discourse' in Young, R. ed. 1981 pp. 48–78.

Gates, B. T. 1978 'Providential history and *The Excursion*' *The Wordsworth Circle* 9:2 178–181.

Gaull, M. 1979 'From Wordsworth to Darwin: on to fields of Praise' *The Wordsworth Circle* 10:1 33–48.

1988 *English Romanticism: The Human Context* New York, Norton, W.W.

1990 'Under Romantic skies: astronomy and the poets' *The Wordsworth Circle* 21:1 34–41.

Gill, S. 1983 'Wordsworth's poems: the question of text' *The Review of English Studies* new series, 34 172–190.

1989 *William Wordsworth: A Life* Oxford, Clarendon Press.

1994 'Wordsworth and "Catholic Truth": the role of Frederick William Faber' *The Review of English Studies* new series, 45:178 204–220.

Gillispie, C. C. 1951 *Genesis and Geology* Cambridge, Mass., Harvard University Press.

Gliserman, S. 1975 'Early Victorian science writers and Tennyson's "In Memoriam": a study in cultural exchange' *Victorian Studies* 18 227–308, 437–459.

Goethe, J. W. 1970 *Italian Journey, 1786–1788*, trans. Auden, W. H. and Mayer, E., London, Penguin.

1989 *The Sorrows of Young Werther*, trans. Hulse, M. London, Penguin.

Golden, J. 1981 *A List of Papers and Correspondence Held in University College Library: George Bellas Greenough* London, University College.

Golinski, J. 1992 *Science as Public Culture: Chemistry and Enlightenment in Britain, 1760–1820* Cambridge, Cambridge University Press.

Gould, S. J. 1982 'Hutton's purposeful view' *Natural History* 19:5 6–12.

1988 (1987) *Time's Arrow, Time's Cycle* Harmondsworth, Penguin.

Grainger, M. and Chandler, J. 1988 'From Helpston to Burghley' *The John Clare Society Journal* 7 26–40.

Graves, R. P. 1882 *The Life of Sir William Rowan Hamilton* 3 volumes Dublin, Hodge and Figgis.

Greene, M. F. 1982 *Geology in the Nineteenth Century* Ithaca and London, Cornell University Press.

Gutting, G. 1988 *Michel Foucault's Archeology of Scientific Reason* Cambridge, Cambridge University Press.

Hallam, A. 1989 *Great Geological Controversies* Oxford, Oxford University Press.

Harré, R. 1983a 'Davy and Coleridge' in Pollock, M. ed. 1983 pp. 53–63.

1983b 'What is the *Zeitgeist?*' in Pollock, M. ed. 1983 pp. 1–8.

Hartman, G. H. 1987 *The Unremarkable Wordsworth* London, Methuen.

1993 'Romanticism and anti-self-consciousness' in Chase, C. ed. 1993 pp. 43–54.

Hassler, D. M. 1984 'New diggings in old mines: Erasmus Darwin and Romantic views on evolution' *The Wordsworth Circle* 25:1 26–28.

Hayden, J. O. 1969 *The Romantic Reviewers, 1802–1824* London, R. K. P.

Hazen, R. M. 1982 *The Poetry of Geology* London, Allen and Unwin.

Hazlitt, W. 1906 *The Spirit of the Age* London, Bell, G.

Herz, N. 1993 'The notion of blockage in the literature of the sublime' in Chase, C. 1993, pp. 78–97.

Heyck, T. W. 1982 *The Transformation of Intellectual Life in Victorian England* London, Croom Helm.

Hill, A. G. 1992, 'Poetry and Ecumenism: the legacy of the Wordsworths' *Lambeth Palace Library, Annual Review*.

Hodge, M. J. S. 1991 'The history of the earth, life, and man: Whewell and Palaetiological Science' in Fisch, M. and Schaffer, S. eds. 1991 pp. 255–258.

Hodson, F. 1961 *Fossils: an Inaugural Lecture* Southampton, University of Southampton.

1967a trans. *Joseph Addison's Complimentary Verses to Thomas Burnet* Southampton, Camelot Press.

1967b 'Presidential address: some aspects of geological studies in the late seventeenth century' *Proceedings of the Geological Society* 1967.

Hope, V. ed. 1984 *Philosophers of the Scottish Enlightenment* Edinburgh, Edinburgh University Press.

Houston, J. M. 1978 'The concepts of "place" and "land" in Judaeo-Christian tradition' in Ley, D. and Samuels, M. S. eds. 1979 pp. 224–237.

Jackson, H. J. ed. 1985 *The Oxford Authors: Samuel Taylor Coleridge* Oxford, Oxford University Press.

Johnson, L. M. 1973 *Wordsworth and the Sonnet* Copenhagen, Rosenkilde and Bagger.

Johnston, K. R. 1978 'Wordsworth's reckless recluse, the Solitary' *The Wordsworth Circle* 9:2 131–144.

Jones, P. 1984 'An outline of the philosophy of James Hutton' in Hope, V. ed. 1984 pp. 182–210.

Jordanova, L. J. and Porter, R. S. eds. 1979 *Images of the Earth: Essays in the History of the Environmental Sciences Monograph 1* Chalfont St Giles, British Society for the History of Science.

Kant, I. 1952 *The Critique of Judgement* trans. Meredith, J. C. Oxford, Clarendon Press.

Kelley, T. M. 1988 *Wordsworth's Revisionary Aesthetics* Cambridge, Cambridge University Press.

King-Hele, D. 1986 *Erasmus Darwin and the Romantic Poets* London, Macmillan.

Kipling, C. 1987 'A note on Wordsworth's mathematical education' *Charles Lamb Bulletin* new series 5A 96–102.

Knight, D. 1990 'Romanticism and the sciences' in Cunningham, A. and Jardine, W. 1990 pp. 13–24.

Knight, W. ed. 1889 *Wordsworthiana: a Selection of Papers Read to the Wordsworth Society* London, Macmillan.

Kuhn, T. S. 1970 *The Structure of Scientific Revolutions* Chicago, University of Chicago Press.

Laudan, R. (Bush) 1974 *The Development of Geological Mapping In Britain 1790–1825* Unpublished Ph.D thesis, University of London.

1977 'Ideas and organizations in British geology' *Isis* 68:244 527–538.

1987 *From Mineralogy to Geology: the Foundations of a Science 1650–1830* Chicago, University of Chicago Press.

Lawrence, C. 1990 'The power and the glory: Humphry Davy and Romanticism' in Cunningham, A. and Jardine, W. 1990 pp. 213–227.

Leavis, F. R. 1967 *English Literature in Our Time and the University* (the Clark Lectures) Cambridge, Cambridge University Press.

Levere, T. H. 1981 *Poetry Realized in Nature: Samuel Taylor Coleridge and Early Nineteenth-Century Science* Cambridge, Cambridge University Press.

1990 'Coleridge and the Sciences' in Cunningham, A. and Jardine, W. 1990 pp. 295–306.

Levin, H. 1988 (1978) *The Earth through Time* Philadelphia, Holt, Rinehart, Winston.

Levinson, M. 1986 *Wordsworth's Great Period Poems: Four Essays* Cambridge, Cambridge University Press.

Levinson, M., Butler, M., McGann, J., and Hamilton, P. 1989 *Re-thinking Historicism* Oxford, Blackwell.

Ley, D. and Samuels, M. S. eds. 1978 *Humanistic Geography: Prospects and Problems* London, Croom Helm.

Lovejoy, A. O. 1948 *Essays in the History of Ideas* Baltimore, Johns Hopkins University Press.
  1960 (1936) *The Great Chain of Being: a Study of the History of an Idea* New York, Harper and Row.
Lowes, J. L. 1927 *The Road to Xanadu: a Study in the Ways of Imagination* London, Constable.
Lyell, Mrs ed. 1881 *Life, Letters and Journals of Sir Charles Lyell, Bart.* 2 volumes London, Murray, J.
Lyon, J. S. 1970 *The Excursion: a Study* Yale, Anchor Books.
McCracken, D. 1985 (1984) *Wordsworth and the Lake District* Oxford, Oxford University Press.
McFarland, T. 1987 *Romantic Cruxes: the English Essayists and the Spirit of the Age* Oxford, Oxford University Press.
McGann, J. 1983 *The Romantic Ideology* Chicago, University of Chicago Press.
Manier, E. 1978 *The Young Darwin and his Cultural Circle* Dordrecht and Boston, Reidel, D.
Manning, P. J. 1990 *Reading Romantics, Texts and Contexts* Oxford, Oxford University Press.
Marston, V. P. 1984 *Science, Methodology and Religion in the Work of Adam Sedgwick* Unpublished Ph.D. thesis, The Open University.
Maxwell, N. 1984 *From Knowledge to Wisdom* Oxford, Blackwell.
Merrill, L. 1989 *The Romance of Victorian Natural History* Oxford, Oxford University Press.
Mill, J. S. 1971 *Autobiography* ed. Stillinger, J. Oxford, Oxford University Press.
Miller, H. 1869 *The Testimony of the Rocks* Edinburgh, Nimmo, W.
Miller, J. H. 1981 'The stone and the shell: the problem of poetic form in Wordsworth's dream of the Arab' in Young, R. ed. 1981 pp. 244–265.
Moorman, M. 1968 (1957 and 1965) *William Wordsworth: a Biography* 2 volumes Oxford, Oxford University Press.
Morrell, J. and Thackray, A. 1981 *Gentlemen of Science: Early Years of the British Association for the Advancement of Science* Oxford, Oxford University Press.
Morrell, J. and Thackray, A. eds. 1984 *Gentlemen of Science: Early Correspondence of the B.A.A.S.* London Royal Historical Society.
Muirhead, L. R. ed. 1948 *The Blue Guides: Switzerland* London, Benn.
Newby, P. T. 1981 'Literature and the fashioning of tourist taste' in Pocock, D. C. D. 1981 pp. 130–142.
Nicholson, N. 1944 *Five Rivers* London, Faber and Faber.
Nicolson, M. H. 1963 (1959) *Mountain Gloom and Mountain Glory: the Development of the Aesthetics of the Infinite* New York, Norton, W. W.
Noyes, R. 1973 'Why read *The Excursion?*' *The Wordsworth Circle* 4:2 139–157.
Oldroyd, D. R. 1990 *The Highlands Controversy: Constructing Geological Knowledge through Fieldwork in Nineteenth-Century Britain* Chicago, University of Chicago Press.
Ousby, I. 1990 *The Englishman's England* Cambridge, Cambridge University Press.

Outram, D. 1984 *Georges Cuvier: Vocation, Science and Authority in Post-revolutionary France* Manchester, Manchester University Press.

Page, L. E. 1969 'Diluvialism and its critics in Great Britain in the early nineteenth century' in Schneer, C. J. ed. 1969 pp. 257–271.

Paradis, J. and Posteurat, T. eds. 1981 *Victorian Science and Victorian Values: Literary Perspectives* Annals of the New York Academy of Sciences, 360.

Paris, J. A. 1831 *The Life of Sir Humphry Davy, Bart* London, Colburn, H. and Bentley, R.

Pearsall, W. H. and Pennington, W. 1973 *The Lake District* London, Collins.

Piper, H. W. 1962 *The Active Universe: Pantheism and the Concept of the Imagination in the English Romantic Poets* London, Athlone Press.

Pittman, C. L. 1950 'An introduction to Wordsworth's reading in science' *Furman Studies* 33:5 27–60.

Plumb, J. H. 1955 *Studies in Social History* London, Longmans.

Pocock, D. C. D. ed. 1981 *Humanistic Geography and Literature* London, Croom Helm.

Pointon, M. 1979 'Geology and landscape painting in nineteenth-century England' in Jordanova, L. and Porter, R. S. eds. 1979 pp. 84–108.

Pollock, M. ed. 1983 *Common Denominators in Art and Science* Aberdeen, Aberdeen University Press.

Porter, R. S. 1977 *The Making of Geology, Earth Science in Britain, 1660–1815* Cambridge, Cambridge University Press.

1978a 'Gentlemen and geology: the emergence of a scientific career, 1660–1920' *The Historical Journal* 21:4, pp. 809–83.

1978b 'Philosophy and politics of a geologist: G. H. Toulmin, (1754–1817)' *Journal of the History of Ideas* 39:3 435–450.

Porter, R. S. and Teich, M. eds 1988 *Romanticism in National Context* Cambridge, Cambridge University Press.

Prickett, S. 1976 *Romanticism and Religion: the Tradition of Coleridge and Wordsworth in the Victorian Church* Cambridge, Cambridge University Press.

1980 (1970) *Coleridge and Wordsworth, the Poetry of Growth* Cambridge, Cambridge University Press.

Profitt, H. E. 1982 'Though inland for we be '*The Wordsworth Circle*' 13:2, 88–90.

Rappaport, R. 1978, 'Geology and orthodoxy: the case of Noah's Flood' *British Journal for the History of Science* ii Part i: 37, 1–18.

Raub, C. Q. 1988 'Robert Chambers and William Whewell: a nineteenth-century debate over the origins of language' *Journal of the History of Ideas* 49:2 287–300.

Ravetz, J. 1971 *Scientific Knowledge and its Social Problems* Oxford, Oxford University Press.

Reed, M. L. 1967 *Wordsworth: The Chronology of the Early Years* Cambridge, Mass., Harvard University Press.

1975 *Wordsworth: the Chronology of the Middle Years* Cambridge, Mass., Harvard University Press.

Rimmer, W. G. 1960 *Marshalls of Leeds: Flax Spinners 1788–1886* Cambridge, Cambridge University Press.

Roe, N. 1988 *Wordsworth and Coleridge: the Radical Years* Oxford, Clarendon Press.

Roller, D. H. D. ed. 1971 *Perspectives in the History of Science and Technology* Norman, Oklahama University Press.

Rudwick, M. J. S. 1962 'Hutton and Werner compared' *British Journal for the History of Science* 1:2 117–135.

    1963 'The foundation of the Geological Society of London: its scheme for cooperative research and its struggle for independence' *British Journal for the History of Science* 1:4 325–355.

    1970 'The strategy of Lyell's *Principles of Geology*' *Isis* 60 5–33.

    1971 'Uniformity and progression' in Roller, D. H. D. ed. 1971 pp. 209–237.

    1976a *The Meaning of Fossils, Episodes in the History of Palaeontology* New York, Science History Publications.

    1976b 'The emergency of a visual language for geological science' *The British Journal for the History of Science* 10:4 149–195.

    1979 'Transposed concepts from the human sciences in the early work of Charles Lyell' in Jordanova L. and Porter, R.S. eds. 1979 pp. 64–83.

    1985 *The Great Devonian Controversy: the Shaping of Scientific Knowledge among Gentlemen Specialists* Chicago, University of Chicago.

Rupke, N. A. 1983a *The Great Chain of History: William Buckland and the English School of Geology 1814–1849* Oxford, Clarendon Press.

    1983b 'The apocalyptic denominator in English culture of the early 19th century' in Pollock, M. ed. 1983 pp. 30–41.

    1990 'Caves, fossils and the history of the earth' in Cunningham, A. and Jardine, W. eds. 1990 pp. 241–259.

Ruse, M. 1991 'William Whewell: omniscient' in Fisch, M. and Schaffer, S. eds. 1991 pp. 87–116.

Sarjeant, W. A. S. 1980 *Geologists and the History of Geology: an International Bibliography from the Origins to 1978* New York, Arno.

Schaffer, S. 1991 'The history and geography of the intellectual world: Whewell's politics of language' in Fisch, M. and Schaffer, S. eds. 1991 pp. 201–231.

Schneer, C. J. ed. 1969 *Toward a History of Geology* Cambridge, Mass., MIT Press.

Schneider, B. R. 1957 *Wordsworth's Cambridge Education* Cambridge, Cambridge University Press.

Schuster, J. A. and Yeo, R. R. eds. 1986 *The Politics and Rhetoric of Scientific Method: Historical Studies* Dordrecht, Reidel, D.

Secord, J. A. 1986 *Controversy in Victorian Geology: the Cambrian-Silurian Dispute* Princeton, University of Princeton Press.

    1991 'The discovery of a vocation: Darwin's early geology' *British Journal for the History of Science*, 24 133–157.

Shaffer, E. 1974 'Coleridge and Natural Philosophy: a review of recent literary and historical research' *The History of Science* 12 284–298.

Shapin, S. 1982 'History of Science and its sociological reconstructions' *The History of Science* 20 157–211.

Sharrock, R. 1962 'Sir Humphry Davy and the "Preface" to *Lyrical Ballads*' *Notes and Records of the Royal Society of London* 27 57–76.

Shaver, C. L. and A. C. 1979 *Wordsworth's Library, a Catalogue* New York and London, Garland.

Sheats, P. D. 1973 *The Making of Wordsworth's Poetry, 1785–1799* Cambridge, Mass., Harvard University Press.

Sheets-Pyenson, S. 1982 'Geological communication in the nineteenth century' *Bulletin of the British Museum (Natural History)* 10:6.

Shelley, P. B. 1975 *The Complete Poetical Works of Percy Bysshe Shelley* ed. Rogers, N. Oxford, Oxford University Press.

Sheppard, T. 1917 'William Smith, his map and memoirs' *Proceedings of the Yorkshire Geological Society* 29:3 75–253.

Smith D. Q. 1978 'The Wanderer's silence: a strange reticence in Book IX of *The Excursion*' *The Wordsworth Circle* 9:2 162–172.

Snow, C. P. 1959 *The Two Cultures and the Scientific Revolution* Cambridge, Cambridge University Press.

Speakman, C. 1982 *Adam Sedgwick, Geologist and Dalesman* London, Broadoak Press.

Spiegelmann, W. 1985 *Wordsworth's Heroes* Los Angeles, California University Press.

Stafford, B. M. 1984 *Voyage into Substance Art, Science, Nature and the Illustrated Travel Account, 1760–1840* Cambridge Mass., MIT Press.

Stallknecht, N. P. 1958 (1945) *Strange Seas of Thought: Studies in Wordsworth's Philosophy of Man and Nature* Bloomington, Indiana University Press.

Sultana, D. 1969 *Samuel Taylor Coleridge in Malta and Italy* New York, Barnes and Noble.

Thomson, J. 1972 *The Seasons and the Castle of Indolence* ed. Sambrook, J. Oxford, Clarendon Press.

Thorsley, P. 1993 'German Idealism' in Curran, S., ed. 1993 pp. 74–94.

Tillyard, A. I. 1913 *A History of University Reform from 1800* Cambridge, Heffer.

Todhunter, I. 1876 *William Whewell, D. D. An Account of his Writings with Selections from his Literary and Scientific Correspondence* London, Macmillan.

Trickett, R. 1990 'The language of Wordsworth's later poems' *The Wordsworth Circle* 21:1 46–51.

Trott, N. 1990 'Wordsworth making amends' *The Wordsworth Circle* 21:1 27–33.

Ulrich, D. W. 1984 'Distinctions in poetic and intellectual influence' *The Wordsworth Circle* 15:2 74–80.

Ward, J. C. 1877 'Jonathan Otley, the geologist and guide' *Cumberland Association for the Advancement of Literature and Science* 2 125–169.

Watson, J. R. 1970 *Picturesque Landscape and English Romantic Poetry* London, Hutchinson.

Watson, R. S. 1889 'Wordsworth's relations to science' in Knight, W. ed. 1889 pp. 199–218.

Wesling, D. 1970 *Wordsworth and the Adequacy of Landscape* London, Routledge & Kegan Paul.

Whitten, D. and Brooks, J. 1972 *The Penguin Dictionary of Geology* Harmondsworth, Penguin.

Wilcox, S. C. 1954 'Wordsworth's River Duddon sonnets' *Proceedings of the Modern Language Association* 69 136–138.

Williams, P. 1991 'Passing on the torch: Whewell's philosophy and the principles of English university education' in Fisch, M. and Schaffer, S. eds. 1991 pp. 117–147.

Wimbledon, W. 1991 'Historical sites for the geological conservation review' *Geoscientist* 1:2 23–24.

Wolfson, S. 1988 'Individual in community, Dorothy Wordsworth in conversation with William' in Mellor A. K., ed. 1988, pp. 139–145.

Woodward, H. B. 1907 *The History of the Geological Society* London, Geological Society.

Wordsworth, J. 1982 *William Wordsworth: the Borders of Vision* Oxford, Clarendon Press.

Yeo, R. R. 1979 'William Whewell, natural theology and the philosophy of science in mid-nineteenth-century Britain' *Annals of Science* 36 493–516.

 1986 'Method and the rhetoric of science' in Schuster, J. A. and Yeo, R. R. eds. 1986 pp. 270ff.

Index

(excluding single references to secondary sources)

CAMBRIDGE STUDIES IN ROMANTICISM

TITLES PUBLISHED